REFORMING AMERICAN EDUCATION

Books by Alvin C. Eurich

Reforming American Education

The Reading Abilities of College Students

Educational Psychology (*with Herbert A. Carroll*)

An Evaluation of Modern Education (*with J. Paul Leonard*)
In 1936 (*with Elmo C. Wilson*)
In 1937 (*with Elmo C. Wilson*)

Editor:

Campus 1980: The Shape of the Future in American Higher Education

The Changing Educational World

Reforming
American Education

THE INNOVATIVE APPROACH TO

IMPROVING OUR SCHOOLS AND COLLEGES

BY Alvin C. Eurich

1817

HARPER & ROW, PUBLISHERS

NEW YORK, EVANSTON, AND LONDON

FIRST EDITION

LIBRARY OF CONGRESS CATALOG CARD NUMBER: 68–28194

B-T

Contents

Acknowledgments

This book has evolved out of a lifetime of most fortunate professional and personal associations. I am especially grateful to my colleagues of thirteen years in the Fund for the Advancement of Education and the Ford Foundation. Indeed, I have drawn heavily from "Decade of Experiment," a report of the first ten years of the Fund's operations.

For critically reading the manuscript and making valuable suggestions, I am indebted to Lucien B. Kinney and Paul Woodring. I also acknowledge with deep appreciation the special help from my associates in the Academy for Educational Development: Joan Braucher, Carol Florio, Judith Murphy, and most especially, Ronald Gross, who through daily associations in all stages of the preparation and writing has made this book far better than it otherwise would have been. And finally my thanks to Nancy Sills, of Harper & Row, who edited the book with extraordinary skill and intelligence.

Acknowledgments

We are all born as originals but die as copies.

—Henning Neerland
Drammen, Norway

Introduction: The Innovative Spirit in Education

The innovative spirit seeks improvement in every aspect of teaching and learning. It questions accepted ideas and is open to new ones.

It recognizes that the educator's job is not merely to sustain and maintain the educational enterprise—whether it is a classroom, a school or college, or an entire educational system—but to change it for the better.

The innovative educator recognizes the awesome responsibility assumed by anyone who tries to shape young minds. But move ahead he must, since standing still in a time of headlong change is to fall behind. Therefore he combines humility with boldness, confident that with the constant feedback and flexibility of a democratic system, mistakes can be corrected.

The innovative educator is not merely open to change: he *plans* for change. And he builds the process of change and self-renewal into the system, making it a continuing responsibility for himself and his staff.

The innovative educator strives to maintain an open system— open classrooms, open schools, an open administration—open to new ideas, to public and professional scrutiny, to correction of inevitable flaws and abuses.

He realizes that, while he cannot *produce* creativity and initiative in others, he can find and foster these qualities. Rather than relying on rules and precedents, therefore, he is open to new ideas from every source, including his students, fellow educators, and the world outside the schools.

He knows that each student must learn for himself, at his own rate, in his own style. No one can learn for anybody else. But the educator can create environments that encourage learning and enhance its power and delight.

The innovative educator is interested primarily in results—in the *real* progress students make in knowledge and understanding.

He appraises new ideas for their proved or potential effectiveness toward this end, not because of their authoritative backing or popularity. He recognizes the folly of change *qua* change, just as he discriminates between old ideas that have merit and those that don't.

He knows, too, that forces outside of the classroom affect his students' lives more than what goes on in school. Therefore he takes an active part in shaping the quality of life in the community and the nation. He actively collaborates with outside organizations and individuals to share community resources.

The innovative spirit transcends the labels and abstractions that often obscure the reality of problems. It distinguishes between one student and another, one teacher and another, one classroom or school and another, one point in time and another. And it encourages the procedures that take account of these significant differences.

Knowing how little he knows, the innovative educator listens more than he talks. He knows that no teacher, no school, no educational system can do everything. Therefore he sets priorities among the infinite tasks the school *might* perform in order to determine those it must or can best perform.

*　　*　　*

This book aims to describe and define this spirit in American education today: the *innovative* approach to improving our schools and colleges. My thesis is that education must be vastly improved to meet the challenges of the present and future; that the innovative approach is the most promising strategy for bringing about such improvement; and that, therefore, everyone concerned with education, at whatever level and in whatever capacity, should affirm and act upon a commitment to bold, imaginative, purposeful innovation in policies, programs, and practices.

I want to take a wide-angle view of the innovative approach to improving our schools and colleges. Specifically I shall discuss

- rigid dogmas, still believed by most educators, which block progress toward better schooling;

- bold public policies—local, state, and national—needed to encourage the innovative approach to educational challenges;

- the dramatic struggle to revamp our blackboard-and-eraser educational system to meet the nation's needs in an automated age;

- provocative new developments which are already revolutionizing American education, including programed instruction, television, team teaching, new curricula, etc.;

- promising new patterns for reform from kindergarten through post-graduate training, based not on abstract theory, but on specific innovations which have emerged in the past decade in the schools and colleges themselves;

- basic principles upon which any teacher or administrator can build innovation and experimentation into his classroom or school;

- mechanisms by which an innovative spirit—and the money to support it—can be generated throughout our educational system; and

- the shape and thrust of American education as the central institution of an "educative society."

The greatest gap in education has always been that between theory and practice, between what we claim to be doing for young people and what we actually are doing. This gap, unlike the missile gap, has not been closed. Educators tend to be bold in thought but timid in action. All too often educators have built grand theories while the schools and colleges stayed in their comfortable ruts.

I hope that this book will help to bridge that gap. There is a new and hopeful outlook in American education today, a dynamic new approach to the improvement of teaching and learning. It is mostly pragmatic, much concerned with concrete techniques and measurable results. It does stem from a broad and vital concept of learning but avoids the old ideological battles between progressives and traditionalists.

This new spirit has been building momentum throughout our educational system for more than a decade. Some of the milestones in its evolution have been:

• the development of teaching machines and programed learning started by Harvard Professor B. F. Skinner, in 1954. (Although Sidney Pressey of Ohio State built the first machine twenty years earlier, teaching machines did not become known or used until Professor Skinner's experiments were publicized.)

• the creation of the first of the "new curricula," in high school physics, by the Physical Science Study Committee in 1956.

• the reforms throughout the 1950's designed to bring teacher education back into the liberal arts tradition.

• the development and application of the nongraded school principle by educators like B. Frank Brown and John Goodlad in the late 1950's.

• the widespread experimentation with television, language laboratories, computers, and other forms of instructional technology in the 1950's and early 1960's.

• the publication, in 1960, of Jerome Bruner's classic *The Process of Education.*

- the massive infusion of federal government aid into education, with strong emphasis on the innovative approach, in the early 1960's.

- the publication, in the late fifties and the sixties, of James B. Conant's sweeping and perceptive recommendations for the improvement of secondary education, teacher education, and public policy on education.

- the 1965 White House Conference on Education, which sidestepped the traditional ideological themes and focused squarely on the actual problems facing the nation's schools.

- the federal appointments which put the national educational authority in the hands of leaders of education's "new guard": John W. Gardner, whose two and a half years as Secretary of Health, Education, and Welfare revitalized that unwieldy department; Francis Keppel, an active and imaginative U.S. Commissioner of Education and later Assistant Secretary of HEW, until he left the government to become chairman of General Learning Corporation; and Harold Howe II, the courageous recent Commissioner.

- above all, the unprecedented realization, by the American people, of the critical importance a vital and improved educational system will have to future generations living in a democratic technological society that will be an example to nations all over the world.

The men and women who are taking this innovative approach—teachers, administrators, psychologists, sociologists, government officials, laymen of various sorts—have perforce overcome their vested interest in any established educational philosophy or way of doing things. They have their eyes firmly focused on particular problems and the development of individual students. They are willing to disrupt the status quo in search for better ways to encourage learning.

In attempting to distinguish the worthwhile from the ephemeral in this movement, I will try to answer questions like the following: What is the real significance for the individual student of the new procedures in education? How do these procedures work in concert? How can their use be promoted in particular classrooms, schools, school systems, colleges, or universities? Are schools and colleges pursuing novelty for the sake of novelty in education? Are new methods overturning tried and proved conventional procedures? Is mechanization and dehumanization a danger? Will television and teaching machines replace the classroom teacher? Do these techniques intensify—or can they be used to offset—the impersonal vastness of today's educational enterprises? *And above all—where are we going in education? And why? Where should we be going? And why?*

I hope to convey some of the excitement of this new spirit. But I shall hold no brief for any specific innovation, theory, or practice. I believe that the "innovative approach" is wholly independent of any particular device such as teaching machines, television, team teaching, or new math. I support these innovations for the simple reason that they really do help to solve urgent educational problems. As the problems change, I would change my prescription. Rather than fixing on any one new technique, I think the innovative approach can and must inform everything the teacher does in the classroom, every decision the administrator makes, every item of planning in the school or college budget, every program established by state departments of education and boards of trustees, every federal bill introduced in the field of education.

The innovative approach is broad enough and potent enough to include both the teacher who, discovering that a music box works on the same principle as the genetic code, uses the analogy to motivate students to learn about genetic structure, and the federal official searching for a way to break the cycle of poverty and deprivation which blocks slum youngsters' quest for a better life. The new approach is being used by textbook publishers, curriculum planners, college administrators, guidance counselors, and hundreds of other educational professionals. But it is most valuable at the cutting edge of learning: in the encounter between teacher and student in the classroom.

The innovative approach can be found in the Aspen high school's "total exposure" program as well as in the Harvard Graduate School of Education. It can thrive in small private colleges and in gigantic school systems. It can be sparked by a single enterprising teacher or curious amateur pedagogue, just as it can be greased by an enormous foundation grant. On modest scale or major, however, innovation is to me the heart of the adventure of education.

1 Old Dogmas versus New Ideas

The greatest tyrants over men are their own unexamined ideas. Such ideas shape our behavior more than we usually realize. Anthropologists have shown that everything, from our preference for a specific form of government to the distance we maintain when speaking with someone face to face, is in part a function of the culture from which we have absorbed our notions of what is right and proper. On the other hand, nothing can be so effective in liberating men than the right new idea at the right time.

Education, too, shares what John Kenneth Galbraith calls "the conventional wisdom"—unexamined and therefore constricting ideas. The very language of education embodies and perpetuates certain fixed assumptions.

For example, psychologist Jerome Bruner, among others, helped to start a revolution in early schooling when he scrutinized the educational concept of "readiness," and found that this ubiquitous term, with all that it implies, often had no valid referent in children's actual behavior. The result was to break through the standard assumptions regarding the learning capacities of young children.[1]

[1] Jerome S. Bruner, *The Process of Education* (Cambridge, Mass.: Harvard University Press, 1960).

At the other end of the educational spectrum, Clark Kerr examined higher education with a fresh eye and found that America had created a species of institution for which there was no name. This he called the "multiversity," and by analyzing this new concept added to our understanding of the distinctive mid-twentieth century form of higher education.[2]

A dramatic experiment by Robert Bush and Dwight Allen of Stanford University revealed not long ago in what very specific ways unexamined ideas balk the imagination and creativity of school administrators and teachers:

It is useful—and interesting—to identify some of the curricular assumptions which are made to accommodate current schedule rigidity. When one group of curriculum experts was consulted and asked the question, "How would you schedule your subject, or courses in your subject, if you had complete freedom to schedule them in any way you wish?", over 80 per cent of the answers mentioned some variation of thirty students meeting for a class hour. In some instances, double periods were suggested; it was also suggested that two or more classes be combined for certain purposes. It was certainly quite clear, however, that the traditional base of thirty students meeting for one hour was accepted with little question. Later, after a curriculum module of fifteen students meeting for one-half hour had been suggested, and after several of the structures indicated above were discussed with this same group, the experts were again asked to develop ideal instructional patterns for each of their subjects. This time less than 5 per cent of the suggested classes called for thirty students meeting for one hour, or variations of this standard pattern. Experts, answering in this fashion, suggest that we may unwittingly limit the number of alternatives from which we select the course structures which will be implemented in school curriculums.[3]

The first step in developing an innovative approach to improving our schools and colleges, then, is a critical one. We must examine some of the "unalterable truths"—the generally accepted

[2] Clark Kerr, *The Uses of the University* (Cambridge, Mass.: Harvard University Press, 1964).
[3] Robert N. Bush and Dwight W. Allen, *A New Design for High School Education* (New York: McGraw-Hill, 1964), pp. 33–34.

but unexamined premises—on which we are still operating our educational system today. Until we make these assumptions conscious and submit them to scrutiny they will hinder us in being truly creative.

Because so much in education depends upon it, *the first shibboleth that requires critical examination is the fixed teacher-student ratio.* State budgets for education are usually based on the number of pupils in school, and this in turn automatically fixes the number of teachers needed. This teacher-student ratio also determines the number of classrooms required and forms the basis for school construction. It is usually assumed that the all-important radio must be maintained at any cost and lowered if possible: 1 to 30 at the elementary level, 1 to 25 for high schools, and 1 to 13 for colleges. Yet the results of a half century of experimental work do not support this fixation. Students do as well on examinations, and in many cases better, if taught in larger classes *by superior teachers.* A comprehensive summary in the *Encyclopedia of Educational Research* of fifty years of investigation on class size states: "Is there an optimum class size? . . . There is nothing in the evidence to suggest that large classes materially affected attainment in subject matter under teaching techniques considered typical at that time. Subsequent studies of the relation of class size to student attention, discipline, self-reliance, attitudes, and work habits failed to establish a research basis for decisions on class size."[4]

In practice, however, and in any general consideration of the class size issue, teachers, administrators, and others tend to place the burden of proof upon those suggesting that large classes might be most effective to achieve certain objectives. While it should be self-evident that the *quality* of the instruction is the paramount consideration, the educational numbers game tends to bypass the obvious. It is hard to imagine anything more stultifying than a bad

[4] John I. Goodlad, "Classroom Organization," in *Encyclopedia of Educational Research,* 3rd ed., ed. by Charles W. Harris (New York: The Macmillan Co., 1960).

teacher in a small class. The American ideal of education has long been Mark Hopkins on one end of the log and a student on the other. But President James A. Garfield significantly added: "If I could be taken back into boyhood days and had all the libraries and apparatus of a university with ordinary routine professors offered me on the one hand and on the other a great, luminous, rich-souled man, such as Dr. Hopkins was twenty years ago, in a tent in the woods alone, I should say give me Dr. Hopkins for my college course rather than any university with only routine professors."

For many years I wondered where the idea of an ideal fixed teacher-student ratio came from. Finally, with the aid of a Talmudic scholar, I learned that in the Babylonian Talmud a rule was established by Rabbi Raba, an authoritative sage of the third century A.D.: "Twenty-five students are to be enrolled in one class. If there are from 25 to 40, an assistant must be obtained. Above 40, two teachers are engaged." This rule, established long before the days of printed books, undoubtedly reflected even earlier practices. Rigidly to accept today such a fixed ratio is like adhering to Ptolemy's theory of the universe after Einstein has introduced his theory of relativity.

There is a tacit assumption that the European universities, particularly the German institutions after which America fashioned its own, are of the highest quality; but these paradigms make no effort to adhere to any specific teacher-student ratio. On the contrary, these universities operate on quite the opposite assumption. Regardless of the number of students, each German university appoints only one major professor to each field. Indeed, the built-in incentives are to make it attractive for a professor to teach more and more students, for the professor, I am told, earns three to four times his basic guaranteed salary from his share of tuition fees.

Under this system the Free University of Berlin has become a distinguished university in the very short interval of twenty-odd years. Approximately 16,000 students are now registered, and another 1,000 students are expected to enroll within the next two or three years. The faculty is outstanding, on a par with professors at other leading German universities. The Free University has only one faculty member for about every fifty students. To achieve the ratio American institutions consider mandatory would have required a faculty four times the size of the university's present faculty. Obviously distinction would have suffered proportionately.

Similarly, the Sorbonne with 123,000 or more students follows the German pattern of one major professor for each field, as do other major European universities. I am not saying that we should follow this same pattern, which, in some respects, applies assumptions just as rigid as our own. The lesson of the European pattern for us lies in the fact that, based on opposite assumptions, it has achieved some enviable success. The example of institutions of very high quality functioning well under completely different assumptions, particularly with respect to the teacher-student ratio, should give us pause. Perhaps we could better attain our own educational goals by re-examining our assumptions.

Like everybody else, teachers differ. It has been repeatedly demonstrated that when the teacher has the opportunity to use his special talents beyond the confines of the conventional classroom the result is better instruction for more students. Efforts to utilize teachers more effectively have led to greater flexibility in class size and to the use of teachers' assistants, team teaching, of television, motion pictures, and even teaching machines.

In citing examples, I want it clearly understood that I am not advocating that television or any other device replace the teacher. Nothing could be further from my intention. A basic principle is involved, which is simply this: any device or arrangement that improves communication with the student should be used. *Used—* not merely tacked onto the existing system—in order to exploit the unique capacities of the new medium. As Marshall McLuhan delights in pointing out, the usual way of dealing with new media is to consider them mere additions to the old way of doing things. But any new medium of instruction, to be effective, means structural changes in the system and new and different ways of using individual talents.

The invention of printing changed all teaching; the development of laboratory methods brought about a revolution in the teaching of science. These changes were not easy to incorporate into the schools and colleges. It took several generations to learn how to use the printed book. The Dartmouth library, for example, was open for only one hour every two weeks in its early days and only five students were admitted at a time. Freshmen were allowed to have one book, sophomores and juniors two, and seniors three.

Similarly, it was many years after the laboratory had proved its value to the men of science that it was permitted within the hallowed walls of educational institutions. Laboratory work was first confined to the professor's demonstration of experiments to his class, and even this was considered revolutionary at Yale in the beginning of the nineteenth century. Professor Benjamin Silliman, about 1803, performed many such experiments outside the regular curriculum, and it was a student of his who went to Rensselaer and inaugurated one of the first laboratories in which students themselves performed experiments as part of the learning process. And yet books, libraries, and laboratories—which in their day were considered revolutionary—are today commonly accepted and regarded as indispensable to our process of instruction.

Similarly, new instructional techniques should change ideas about the teacher-student ratio. The learning process is greatly improved by placing more responsibility on the student. After all, regardless of the teaching techniques, everything a student learns he must learn for himself; no teacher can learn for him. Successful demonstrations of independent study and honors courses have been carried out extensively throughout the country. And yet we are reluctant to give students the responsibilities implied by such courses. Students have also learned much by serving as teachers' aides, by teaching others, and by using various new self-instructional devices. Strange as it may seem, one of the major untapped resources for learning is the student himself!

A second "unalterable truth" of education is that the number of years in school determines the student's educational attainment. We all know how fallacious this is from our own day-to-day experience, even though we don't all number Eric Hoffers among our acquaintances. This "truth" has been disproved officially as well, over and over. Tests have shown that sheer time spent in school is no measure of a student's academic attainment, which depends in part on the student himself, in part on the schools he has attended. The honors students in a poor college may be no better than the worst students in a very rigorous college. In fact, seniors in some outstanding secondary schools, such as the Bronx High School of Science, are better educated than some college graduates. I may add that holding a bachelor's degree from a so-called accredited college gets some students into the graduate schools of universities that would not have admitted them as freshmen. To say a person is a college graduate is, under these conditions, quite meaningless. A degree, as we all know, confers no special competence.

In like fashion we cling to the assumption that the required years spent in school plus a few professional courses are all that is required to prepare a teacher for the public schools. Such a record may satisfy the state's certification standards, but it is ridiculous to assume that it in any way guarantees high quality of teaching. Almost uniformly across the country, students complain of the elaboration of the obvious in education courses. That is natural. Teaching is unlike any other profession in that everyone who goes into it has spent approximately seventeen years in close contact with the profession. Assume, for instance, that a child from the age of five had the opportunity to observe doctors' behavior as he does that of teachers. We would consider it utterly absurd to think he had learned nothing of the practice of medicine. Would it not be less wasteful of human energy to determine first what it is that a teacher has to know and then find out whether he already knows it before insisting that he study it over again? We have followed this simple procedure in other professions. A short time ago, for example, a woman passed the New York State bar examinations without having gone to a law school at all. Doubtless some people could do equally well when it comes to qualifying for teaching.

The whole educational process, moreover, would become more meaningful if each state would establish a system of comprehensive examinations to determine the actual achievement of students. On other occasions, when confronted with a really critical situation, we have resorted to the wholesale use of examinations to determine the most effective use of our human resources, so why not now? During World War II and even earlier we used examinations to great advantage in the armed forces to place trainees in schools, colleges, and jobs. Furthermore, we are not in the least reluctant to give comprehensive examinations for admission to college. The College Entrance Board examinations are now administered at between 3,000 and 4,000 centers each year and are required by over 700 colleges and universities. Even some of our state universities have found it expedient to use these examinations as a basis for admission; the University of California some years ago instituted such a system. If examinations are important and worthwhile as a basis for admission to college, could they not also be effective for college graduation and at other points in the school system?

Of course, not all desirable human characteristics can be tested, and other types of judgments must be made. But tests are available and can be constructed for most academic skills and subjects; examinations have been improved considerably in recent years, even to the point of requiring written exercises instead of simply depending on yes and no or multiple choice answers.

Similarly, our present method of certifying teachers could be replaced by a system of examinations. Instead of depending upon accumulated academic credits, would it not be reasonable to expect that a person going out to teach others history, mathematics, English, or any other subject should be able to pass a comprehensive examination in that subject before he undertakes his duties as a teacher? In this way it would, perhaps, be possible for a truly educated person to become a teacher even though the ledger of his academic credits does not balance with an arbitrarily fixed requirement. For that matter, knowledge of education as such, as well as of subject matter, could easily be tested. A college teacher might conceivably teach in high school now and then if he were not required to go back to school to accumulate "education" credits. Is there such a sharp dividing line between teaching 17-year-olds in high school and 18-year-olds in college that it justifies completely different systems of preparation and certification? This is certainly a matter for reappraisal in the interests of improving our educational program, and I will discuss it in more detail in Chapter 4.

Moreover, the increased use of achievement and placement tests makes it essential to sharpen our concept of what an education should add up to. *And this brings us to a third shibboleth, concerning the curriculum: that subject matter or courses fit neatly into specific grade or age levels.* In attempting to adapt the curriculum to everybody, either by aiming for the average student at each grade level and stifling the exceptional or by offering such a wide diversity of courses that anyone may select an array of disjointed segments, we have fabricated a mosaic without pattern, a program which is indefinable.

Many reforms in this area were prompted by a special concern for the gifted or talented child. Portland, Oregon, achieved the unusual distinction of devoting as much time and attention to the education of the talented child as it devotes to the education of the handicapped. This concern has caused a general reorganization of the Portland school curriculum. In Texas the San Angelo schools have experimented with a "three-rail" curriculum, and Ossining and Long Beach, New York, have tried a "dual-progress" plan—both are attempts to give each pupil the opportunity to progress in each subject at his own rate.

At the higher education level two major adjustments have been made to eliminate duplication of learning and make it possible for the bright student to advance more quickly. One is early admission to college. This innovation began in 1951 in twelve colleges and has now been extended to many more on the basis of satisfactory results. The other is admission with advanced standing, and it, too, has proved effective and spread rapidly. Both of these methods tend to reduce boredom and wasteful human activity and, concurrently, to establish more economical and efficient procedures.

B. Frank Brown, of Melbourne High School, describes an excellent example of how such programs can profoundly affect the individual student's experience:

The Advanced Placement Program in mathematics at Melbourne begins with calculus. The basic text for this course is *Elements of Analytical Geometry and Calculus* by Professor G. B. Thomas of the Massachusetts Institute of Technology; it is used for the first three semesters of mathematics at that institution. Talented high school students master the principles of calculus easily, and for those who are ready to go beyond calculus, Melbourne High offers a course in differential equations. . . .

The high school begins preparing students for this depth program in mathematics upon their entry from the ninth grade of junior high school. Students who are able and ambitious in mathematics are encouraged, upon entering Melbourne High, to pursue two courses in mathematics instead of one. This overturns conventionality and upsets traditional inconsistencies in scope and sequence. For instance, about half of the schools in the United States rigidly sandwich plane geometry between Algebra 1 and Algebra 2. The other half, with equal inflexibility, place plane geometry after Algebra 2. At Melbourne the talented mathematics student is encouraged to take both plane geometry and one of the algebra courses simultaneously. This becomes possible in gradeless schools where study halls have been eliminated and all students are required to schedule six subjects. Trigonometry can also be taken concurrently with Algebra 2.

When students with a special aptitude for mathematics are allowed to move deeply and broadly from the beginning, they acquire considerable depth and breadth of knowledge. While still in high school they go extensively into what has been customarily regarded as college mathematics. Students graduating from Melbourne High School who have pursued the mathematics offerings in depth are receiving up to fifteen semester hours credit upon entry into college.[5]

Such an approach needs to be extended to the entire spectrum of the grades and the entire range of subjects. A number of enterprising school administrators are already thinking in these terms. In Seattle, for example, Superintendent Forbes Bottomly has mapped plans for a system of ungraded educational centers likely to include pupils from Grade 5 through the first two years of community college. Except for Grades 1 through 3 or 4, traditional neighborhood schools would become things of the past. Late in 1967 the Seattle School Board disclosed that it would adopt the continuous-progress concept "as an educational goal" in all schools, and would decide after further study about building an educational center. The Seattle plan calls for tailoring course work to the needs, abilities, and individual achievements of pupils, with nongraded classes in which pupils would advance according to achievement and not move automatically into the next grade after the end of each school year.

The curriculum further needs to be scrutinized to reduce the alarming multiplication of courses and to make sure students' programs aren't spread too thin. This requires clearer and more precise goals for schools and colleges. Over the years some institutions have taken on functions that had better be left with such agencies as the Girl and Boy Scouts, the home, and the church. There are colleges, indeed, that offer courses for credit in Practice in Home-making; Pleasure-Horse Appreciation and Use; Walking, Standing, Sitting, and Lying; and some even offer postgraduate credit for Clothing Construction and Healthful Living for Teachers. One university offers about sixty courses in school administration. I am sure that the job of governor is more complex than that of the school principal or the superintendent, but even so, can you imagine devising sixty courses on how to be a state governor? If we

[5] B. Frank Brown, *The Nongraded High School* (Englewood Cliffs, N.J.: Prentice-Hall, 1963), p. 85.

are really serious about better education the least we can do is to eliminate the more obvious absurdities.

It is no longer necessary for every school to try to offer everything. Instead, the very best can be given to a far greater number of students than ever before. Our great natural resources in museums of science, history, and art can serve as rich educative laboratories for all children. With television these resources could be made available to school children throughout the country and not, as previously, only to the lucky few who can visit them in person.

Now that we have looked hard at several basic assumptions which block progress in education, let us consider some new axioms, suggested for the most part by recent successful experiments with teachers and students. These axioms are equally basic, but they commend themselves as more accurate, more fruitful, and more flexible than those we examined above. Perhaps they can form the basis for a forward-looking pedagogy.

We need new assumptions which can guide us toward the intelligent utilization of our teachers and of any new means of communication that may stimulate and facilitate learning. We have ample resources—human, natural, and financial—to effect vast improvement in our educational program and to make its progress commensurate with other aspects of our society. We have the means to adapt mass education to the individual. We have the techniques and devices which can be used to adjust our instruction to different achievement levels and learning rates. We need the determination and the imagination to seize these opportunities.

Among the most promising of the new tools are television, teaching teams (ranging from the master-teacher to the aide), programed learning, language laboratories, high-quality motion pictures, and flexible arrangements of instructional resources, personnel, and curricula. In the years ahead the computer will become more readily available and more versatile.

Even up to now the use of these instruments and arrangements has reinforced some basic psychological principles of efficient teaching and learning. In the light of new developments, we must now reconsider our basic educational assumptions and formulate new assumptions which can replace the old dogmas and can stimulate rather than obstruct creative change.

First, everything a student learns he must learn for himself; no teacher can learn for him. It would be hard to find an educator who does not accept this view of the learning process. Teachers realize that a child learns only from his own effort. Learning does not flow from the teacher to the pupil like water through a pipe or, as the saying goes, from the notebook of one to the notebook of the other without passing through the mind of either. The teacher's words are interpreted by the student according to his own experience, knowledge, and capacities. And since no two students are alike, they do not learn exactly the same things even though they are exposed to identical instruction. Every teacher has been disillusioned in finding on test after test the vast differences in what his pupils have learned from the same instruction. What more dramatic proof is needed that the teacher cannot learn for the student? He can only stimulate and guide.

Until recently, however, we have relied almost wholly on only two instructional resources: teachers and books. Thus the stimulation the student gets in a conventional classroom is limited by the narrow range of his teacher's insight and the confines of the printed word. If the teacher is weak in one respect—and no teacher can be omnicompetent—the student who learns exclusively from him is circumscribed in his learning. If the material to be learned cannot be treated adequately in printed form, as in learning to pronounce correctly a foreign language, the student cannot learn on his own solely from the book. Even the two together—book and teacher—are not always enough to stretch the ablest student's mind.

Fortunately, a variety of innovations in learning are at hand which can motivate the student—who is the only real resource in education—to greater effort. Through team teaching students can be exposed to the total competencies of a group, which go beyond those of any single teacher regardless of how capable he may be. Through television and films, the leading authorities in various fields and demonstrations using expensive equipment not available to a single school can be brought into the classroom. Through language laboratories students can learn to pronounce foreign languages by continual and closely supervised imitation of the best possible models. Thus the student is provided with richer resources for learning than any teacher alone can possibly offer.

With our present knowledge of individual differences, the teacher can no longer dismiss his own inadequacies by saying that a student is too dull to learn. Such a statement merely means that the teacher is unprepared to adapt his instruction or develop the necessary instructional materials for each student to learn all that he is capable of learning.

Second, regardless of how a teacher paces the instruction, each student will learn at his own rate.

We have long recognized this principle throughout the range of grades in the educational system. For example, we have expected college students to go faster than high school pupils in mastering a language. In general our rule of thumb has been: two years of high school instruction in French equals one year at the college level.

We have not been as perceptive in recognizing different rates of learning within a single class or in admitting pupils to school. Our teaching and admission practices have been adjusted to the average. This is just as fallacious as trying to adapt instruction in French to the average rate of learning for pupils from the third grade to graduate students at a university.

With programed materials, for example, instruction in every subject can be adapted to the learning rate of each student. This method of teaching permits a learner to proceed at his own pace, in contrast to the sacrosanct lecture method which frequently bores the upper third of the class and mystifies the lower third. Those who learn quickly know what the teacher is going to say before he has finished saying it, while the slower students have not fully grasped a point before the teacher is into the next one. The faster students thus become bored and uninterested and the slower accumulate deficits in learning which become so great that further learning is impossible. When students move at their own rates, the whole class—with its slow pupils as well as its fast ones—is likely to learn much more.

Even if we could attain our ideal of having a teacher on one end of the log and a student on the other we would find very few teachers with the patience required to adjust to the wide range of learning rates. Yet this is exactly what programed material accomplishes. The student sets his pace precisely as he would in running the hundred-yard dash. In the latter we would not think of having everyone run at an average speed. We now know enough in psychology to realize that it is just as absurd to expect an "average" rate of learning in any subject.

Various other means of adapting instruction to the individual have long been used, some quite generally, others only in special situations. Reading assignments, arithmetic drills, and laboratory work have commonly served this purpose. Independent study and honors courses have also been offered but less widely. Today the range of possibilities for a student to learn at his maximum pace is much greater. Because of its demonstrated capacity in this regard the IPI system (Individually Prescribed Instruction), which was developed by the Learning Research and Development Center of the University of Pittsburgh and spread to many schools with support from the U.S. Office of Education, is one of the most highly regarded innovations in the elementary school today.

Third, students learn more when each step learned is immediately reinforced. Every good teacher uses this principle when he turns from the blackboard after having written a point and asks questions about it. Language laboratories provide for such reinforcement in a systematic, consistent way. Instead of waiting until the end of the day, the week, or the month, the student learns right away if he has mastered all of the material; he is tested at once and finds out.

Clearly, immediate questioning and reinforcement can make even testing the educational experience it should be. Dr. Clarence F. Willey of Norwich University has, in fact, invented an inexpensive IBM-card "punchboard" which can turn any test into a type of programed learning lesson. While the student's responses are indelibly recorded for appraisal, he also discovers whether his answer is right or wrong, and if wrong, what is right. Thus as we measure achievement we can prod the student to correct his errors and see where he has made his mistakes. Learning becomes not a boring chore but the fascinating game it should be.

Fourth, full rather than partial mastery of each step makes total learning more meaningful. Conventional classroom teaching proceeds on the basis of partial learning rather than mastery. A striking example of this is in the study of languages, where students frequently are able to earn satisfactory grades by cramming for each test, but fail to acquire a real command of the language. By using audiotapes, language laboratories provide each student with an opportunity to practice, to listen to accurate pronunciation, and to correct his mistakes. Programed learning also requires the student to give the right answer to each item before he goes on. As has been repeatedly shown, this method results in greater retention than does the partial learning which is characteristic of traditional teaching.

Fifth, virtually anything can be taught to any student at any age in an intellectually honest form, a principle emphasized by Jerome Bruner.

We now have some outstanding examples of this principle, notably in the pioneering "new math" curricula such as the School Mathematics Study Group's efforts. The Physical Science Study Committee physics program includes many concepts formerly taught in college. This course is being offered successfully in secondary schools from coast to coast. And on the elementary level Robert Karplus, chairman of the Department of Physics at the University of California at Berkeley, has had phenomenal success teaching such things as Newton's laws of motion to elementary school children.

Similarly, the use of television and motion pictures now enables educators to offer instruction in languages, such as French and Spanish, to elementary school children, and they are finding many advantages in doing so. No longer can we say with confidence that a certain subject cannot be taught to fourth- or fifth-grade pupils. Such an admission can only mean that we have not yet tried to prepare the necessary instructional materials. We now have at hand, as never before, the means for reconstructing the whole school and college curriculum in order to challenge students to work at full capacity.

Every student's opportunities for learning will be greatly enhanced when the learning situation is designed so as to permit him to learn for himself, go at his own rate, reinforce immediately everything he learns, master each step completely, and have both instructor and materials adapted to his level of development. With these principles in mind we will search for every available means to aid each student.

2 Public Policy for Educational Innovation

The key to reforming American education is new ideas: new ideas to challenge educational dogmas; new ideas to stimulate change; new ideas to suggest lines of research and development. And back of these new ideas a total *innovative approach* which asks constantly: Why? *Why* are we doing things this way rather than another, possibly better, way? *Why* do we assume that students learn in such and such a fashion? *Why* do we limit our learning resources to such a slim sliver of the available technology and materials? *Why* do we organize our schools and colleges into self-contained classrooms and uniform-size classes each taught by a single teacher? *Why*, in fact, do we build schools, staff them with teachers, and attempt to educate at all?

New ideas are the key to educational reform. But public policy for education in the United States has not developed in such a way as to support innovation and change. We have simply not organized our educational enterprise to encourage rapid progress. This failure must be examined if we are to present an honest picture of the obstacles to reform.

John Gardner has pointed out that we must pay attention to the ways in which we *organize* an enterprise like education (and its all-important public policies) because if we don't pay attention our organization and policies will come to dominate our philosophy. This is precisely what has happened in the field of education. Only an unflinching scrutiny of current public policies and organization will enable us to take an innovative approach to improvement. Only by knowing these sobering facts can we take the steps neccssary to change them radically.

To foreigners the most puzzling aspect of American education is that no public policy is apparent and that local control and responsibility are considered essential. Strong opposition toward centralized control, whether it be federal, state, or even regional, is persistently voiced. Federal aid is often resisted in principle—and accepted in fact.

These confusing characteristics are, however, understandable in the light of the society in which our educational system developed. In the late eighteenth century it took three days to get from New York to Philadelphia and back by horse; we can now fly completely around the world in less time than that. For a long time the economy was predominantly agricultural and consisted for the most part of small, self-sufficient communities surrounded by large sparsely populated areas. As early schools grew up in these isolated communities, local control simply occurred naturally as an outgrowth of cultural, geographic, and economic conditions. It was neither a matter of plan nor of policy.

Now we live in the world's most highly industrialized country, with modes of communication and transportation that were unimagined even fifty years ago. Economic growth has been accompanied by greater productivity and more centralized control. Gradually, in all fields except education, we have acknowledged that when growth is so great that it affects the general welfare governmental involvement and guidance are in the public interest. This is seen in business, agriculture, transportation, utilities, radio and television, and in many other areas.

The transition in education from the belief that the children's education is a private matter to the recognition that the national government has real responsibility for it was never made. We are just now beginning to take the initial steps. Although the educational system also expanded greatly during this same period of economic growth, it has consistently lagged behind advances in industry and agriculture. Given such changed conditions, can we seriously maintain that public policies suitable to the eighteenth century are appropriate for the twentieth or twenty-first?

In a democracy the scattered forces operating in many directions at all levels from local to federal make it very difficult to formulate clear-cut procedures for developing public policies. These difficulties do not, however, absolve us from making the effort to find out what we are doing now in education, why we are doing it, and how we can do it better. For these policies, however derived, have a profound effect upon every part of our educational system. They affect the financing, construction, and staffing of our schools. They influence what is taught and how it is taught in regulations about curriculum, textbooks, and teacher certification. Logically they must be integrated with the major goals of schools and colleges.

Thus the basic difficulties in formulating public policies for education arise from the fact that we do not know who controls education nor even what the major issues are to which such policies should be directed. At the same time an examination of our system shows a disconcerting series of contradictions between noble ideals only partly realized and observable events. From the many discrepancies existing between facts and commonly held assumptions, I shall discuss the most significant.

Assumption Number 1
   Education is primarily a local responsibility.

Because we have sanctified the historical accident of local control, this issue is one around which there is great confusion with unfortunate consequences. When the public schools were largely financed by local funds, regulated by local ordinances, and fully governed by the local school board and administrators this assumption had a basis in reality. But neither financing nor regulation of the schools is any longer *predominantly* local. The inadequacy of local resources to build schools and pay teachers, and the consequent limits on true local control, became vividly clear to nearly everybody after the Second World War. Today the plight of big-city schools is dramatizing the issue even more forcefully. Just recently the Detroit School Board sued the state of Michigan in an unprecedented effort to force adequate state aid for inner-city schools.

The American public school system consists of about 104,000 schools in 23,400 local school districts in fifty states, administered by more than 124,000 school board members. Yet the regulations which these school board members are responsible for administering include a conflicting maze derived from local, state, and federal statutes.

State law determines the age limits of compulsory education, which in turn determines the educational facilities which must be provided in a local community. The state also defines the codes and specifications for building schools, the basic school curriculum, the training and certification of teachers, and even, in certain states, which textbooks should be used. While these regulations vary greatly from one state to the next, their total effect has been to take much of the initiative away from the community. The controlling authority vested in local school districts is now history.

Who pays for the public schools? At one time this was wholly the responsibility of the local community. Over the past three and a half decades, however, the pattern has changed. At present the money comes from a combination of local taxes, state appropriations, and, increasingly, from federal funds. For the elementary and secondary public school system, local support dropped from 83 percent in 1929–30 to 41 percent in 1966–67; state support in the same period increased from 17 percent to 38 percent; and federal funds rose from 0.4 percent to 11 percent. Federal money supports not merely school lunch programs, rural libraries, construction, and vocational education, but also the instructional program of the schools through the provisions of the National Defense Education

Act and the Elementary and Secondary Education Act. At the college and university level federal support has become increasingly complex and extensive. In no sense am I deploring this shift in financing or direction of the educational system. It has been an essential part of our dynamic society with its greater ease and speed of transportation and communication and logically follows the shift in our methods of taxation from predominantly local to predominantly federal.

Technological change also has heightened the conflict between the old ideal of local autonomy in education and the facts of contemporary life. For such change is bound to mean a redefinition of education in efficient, productive units: a redefinition of the spaces in which to conduct education; of the number of students and ways they can be grouped in these spaces; of the number and kinds of teachers needed to instruct these groups in these spaces; and of the "machinery" of education, the inventions through which communication is now irrevocably changed, qualitatively and quantitatively. If education is to keep pace with rapidly changing society, we must begin to distinguish between a valid end—educational policies democratically formulated—and a historically outmoded means—the assumption of full local support and control.[1]

Where local authority prevents an objective analysis or obstructs improvement, it is clearly in conflict with the directions of modern society. To oversimplify, by analogy: a school district was once defined on the basis of how far a child would walk. Would we now refuse to let children come to school on newfangled buses because such change would involve changing district administrative patterns or the use of some radical new invention? And, if so,

[1] By the same token, however, we must be willing to recognize those situations in which local control can be the most effective means toward democratically formulated and executed educational policies. In the big city ghettos, for example, Negro parents have been demanding community control over the schools which serve their children. Considering the record of the schools' failure to reach these children and the undoubted overcentralization of some urban school systems, such demands deserve respectful consideration.

would local control be serving community interests? Such a question leads directly to other common assumptions concerning public policy for education.

Assumption Number 2

Local control encourages diversity, takes account of differences among individuals and differences between communities, and gives local boards the power to experiment and thereby exert leadership.

Unfortunately the available evidence does not support this commonly held belief. First of all, the local unit generally tends to be conservative and poorly informed about experimentation and research in education.

Even more important, perhaps: in those cases where local policy makers and administrators *are* venturesome, their initiative is often stifled. To clarify this point I should like to mention two recent examples in the fields of instructional media and utilization of manpower which show how the state can prevent local communities from adopting new procedures. In each case the local school system has been hindered from improving itself by obsolete patterns of control.

Televised instruction, although obviously not a substitute for the full teaching job, can reach many more children than a single teacher can handle in the usual classroom. It has the potential advantage of offering the ablest teachers to the largest number of students, thereby upgrading all instruction and at the same time helping to alleviate the shortage of really able teachers. This increased efficiency could logically mean saving personnel and money. The funds saved could be used to raise teachers' salaries, among other things, thereby making it possible to attract and hold more of the ablest men and women who are so desperately needed in the teaching profession today. Let us see, however, how the state can prevent or handicap local experiment.

In Washington County, Maryland, one of the most extensive and successful experiments in television teaching was begun in 1956. By 1961 it became clear that the money saved through this new procedure could pay the entire capital costs of a closed-circuit TV system which now reached approximately 22,000 pupils in Grades 1 through 12. However, if the county found that using television could provide superior instruction with, say, three quarters of the teachers the schools would require without television, then by law it could receive only three quarters of its usual funds from the state, since these funds were allocated on a teacher-unit basis. There was no legal way in which the county could realize its savings by receiving state funds and redeploying them.

Since 1964 this particular situation has improved somewhat. New legislation in Maryland provides that part of the state school funds are distributed on the basis of the number of pupils enrolled. The number of teachers employed, however, is still a determining factor for part of the fund distribution. Thus a school system can actually find itself penalized for devising new ways to make its instructional program more efficient.

Efforts to make more efficient use of professional manpower, a critical problem at all grade levels, are also currently obstructed by confusion about controls and responsibilities for education. An extensive experimental program in the use of teacher aides was conducted in Michigan for more than six years. The result was a new pattern to make better use of the competencies of teachers. It was found that persons without professional training could, as aides, perform the nonprofessional chores which took from 21 to 69 percent of the teachers' time. By employing these aides at salary levels appropriate for nonprofessional work, funds could have been made available to increase professional salaries and, more importantly, trained teachers could use their energies and professional talents wholly for teaching rather than for routine clerical work.

But when the local school system wanted to employ teacher aides regularly on the basis of the experiment's demonstrated success, it was found that the school board could not legally spend public funds to employ nonprofessional personnel unless the jobs were already included in Civil Service categories. Such examples could be multiplied over and over again across the country. The point, however, is clear. Obsolete state regulations often inhibit local communities from making more efficient use of their resources to improve education through the exercise of ingenuity. In each of these instances we have school systems being penalized for experimentation and efficiency. Students, teachers, citizens, taxpayers, and ultimately society, all pay for this anachronism.

In higher education, too, our vaunted pluralism has not exactly given rise to a plethora of diverse experiments. In fact, as Harold Howe II, U.S. Commissioner of Education, has recently noted:

Despite our national pride in diversity, a surprising "sameness" permeates most of American higher education. . . . At a time when the public schools are realizing the importance of individual differences and are adopting individualized instruction, independent study, flexible scheduling, team teaching, nongraded classes, and similar practices, most colleges and universities still subscribe to a uniform four-year, 125-unit system.[2]

Howe went on to score college administrators for adhering to the sorts of shibboleths we examined in the preceding chapter:

. . . such old standards as the four-year baccalaureate (why four; why not two, or six, or ten?), the residence requirement (why not a couple of years with the Peace Corps in Ethiopia or with VISTA in Chicago?), the "A" to "F" grading system (why not more sophisticated evaluation with *real* validity?), the 50-minute lecture and the semester-long course (why not more flexible learning units varying from two minutes to two years?), the discipline-oriented curriculum (why not curricula which revolve around such problems as poverty, or peace, or urban planning?).

Even more recently Alan Pifer, president of the Carnegie Corporation (one of the nation's most influential foundations),

---

[2] Address to the National Student Association, University of Maryland, Aug. 22, 1967, reported in *Higher Education and National Affairs*, XVI, 29 (American Council on Education).

warned American colleges and universities of the disastrous consequences of continuing in their outmoded, laissez-faire, each-institution-for-itself approach to the future. "We can no longer afford the luxury of an unplanned, wasteful, chaotic approach to higher education," said Mr. Pifer.

Assumption Number 3

Public policies for education are determined primarily by laws and regulations which specifically govern education.

In thinking about public policies for education we generally tend to be concerned only with statutes that relate directly to the construction and operation of schools and colleges. Other laws, however, may be of equal or greater importance in shaping the character of our whole educational program. Most important among these are provisions for taxation. When taxes were primarily a local matter, local authorities decided how much money should go to the schools and the purposes for which funds would be spent. With the extension of taxing power to the state and finally to the federal government through the Sixteenth Amendment to the Constitution, a new public policy was formulated which has had a profound effect upon the entire educational system.

One measure of that effect can be seen in the money being spent today by business and industry for instructional programs entirely outside of the formal educational system. Since the end of World War II they have built up virtually a whole new educational system of their own, which includes subjects taught at high school, college, and postgraduate levels. According to estimates that have been made by the Center for the Study of Liberal Education for Business, the cost of these programs is currently running nearly $20 billion a year. Our tax laws have encouraged industry's new system of education since roughly half of their cost would otherwise be paid to the federal government in taxes. Thus the federal government indirectly supports the training programs of industry.

Another example: a number of university presidents have vigorously protested the way in which federal grants for research distort higher education by their emphasis on business and national defense. Some of them urged that universities turn down such "handouts" and work toward the advancement of the total educational program. These are just a few instances of how tax laws and the appropriation of funds not directly geared to the formal educational process have a strong bearing upon our instructional programs.

These three assumptions about the policies that mold the educational system are suggestive of many assumptions so widely accepted that the public hardly ever questions them. They illustrate the need for more realistic approaches to the development of public policies for education. To this end, we must consider:

1. *Clarification of our educational goals.* It is in this sphere that our nation is most seriously handicapped in competition with Russia, whose schools exist for the purpose of achieving the goals of Soviet society. These goals are clearly stated for five, seven, or ten years in advance.

In contrast, what are our hopes for the United States? Where do we want to be ten years from now? We know fairly well what our population will be at that time. We can predict our approximate gross national product. But what about our cultural and international aims? Without a clear notion of where we want to go as a nation it is virtually impossible to clarify the goals of our educational system. If the nation drifts, the school system will drift along with it and public policies for education will remain unformulated, conflicting, and haphazard.

2. *Greater flexibility in the area of public controls for education.* For some years we have gone through a period of consolidating school districts. Such consolidations have enlarged the scope of

effective authority and operation. New developments now confront us with a whole new set of problems. Television, for instance, crosses school district lines and even state lines. With airborne TV and transmission by satellite, separate local, district, and state jurisdictions break down further. What policies should be developed? What sorts of new agencies are needed in order to make maximum use of television as a major new educational resource? Another example, far more critical and portentous: how can *de facto* segregation in urban schools be effectively modified, if not eradicated, without some modifications in the political boundaries of overwhelmingly Negro school districts in the cities and overwhelmingly white suburban districts?

3. *Clarification in the relationship of the public schools to industrial training programs.* What is the bearing, if any, of this vast new educational enterprise in the United States upon our public school system and upon the financing of the schools?

4. *Clarification of the federal government's support of schools and colleges and its proper relationship to state and local support.* Currently we are attempting to settle the matter in debates on appropriations or bond issues. This is difficult because we have not clearly defined the issues or even attempted to set up criteria for making the decisions on appropriations.

5. *Finally, and most important, we must recognize that federal participation in education is a fact,* and a fact which must be dealt with intelligently, not ignored or denied. As television and other forms of communication, as well as new forms of transportation, make our nation, in effect, smaller and smaller, and as innovations in educational method and technology make the job of education more and more complex, the federal role will become increasingly important, indeed essential. But the federal role must be organized so that it is not haphazard, wasteful, authoritarian, or top-heavy with bureaucracy, in order that it may best serve the educational goals of the nation.

Representative Edith Green, who headed the Special House

Subcommittee on Education, put it well when she wrote in the *New York Times* in 1968:

Congress has started a reversal—small but real—in the tendency to centralize the power and the authority of Federal education programs in Washington.

Some parts of the 1967 Elementary and Secondary Education Act and the "war on poverty" legislation, as well as the Teacher Corps legislation, were amended to give state and local authorities more responsibility in planning programs, establishing priorities, selecting personnel and controlling funds.

This major change in direction rests on the assumption that all initiative and wisdom does not somehow automatically flow to, and collect upon, the banks of the Potomac. Problems and priorities are different in Tampa and Portland, Cedar Rapids and New York City; thus the Education Act specifically encourages state boards of education to plan for and carry out the tasks in their states that this society imposes upon American educators.

These, in brief, are some of the problems that need thorough study if the United States is to clarify its educational policies and see them carried out.

Some steps toward shaping better policies have already been taken. A promising one is the Compact for Education, which would *coordinate* the interests of state governments, thus providing a broader perspective.

Under the Compact the states agree to join together for the improvement of education. Its governing board is a nationwide Education Commission of the States, with governmental and educational representatives from each state, which has the power to authorize studies, suggest policy alternatives, collect data, disseminate information, and in general serve to stimulate state action for the advancement of education. The Education Commission does not have the authority nor is it expected to set policy.

The development of the Compact is worth reviewing in some detail as an example of how an innovation in educational policy making can be created by the imagination and initiative of private citizens. The idea originated in 1964 when James B. Conant, president emeritus of Harvard University, after analyzing the formation of educational policy in the United States, concluded:

It is my thesis that such a jumble of influential private and public bodies does not correspond to the needs of the nation in the 1960's. Some degree of order needs to be brought out of this chaos, primarily for the benefit of the oncoming generations, but also, to achieve a more effective use of public moneys. . . .

Let me be bold and make a suggestion for a possible way by which the road to the development of a nationwide educational policy might be opened up. Let the fifty states, or at least fifteen to twenty of the more populous states, enter into a compact for the creation of an "Interstate Commission for Planning a Nationwide Educational Policy." . . .[3]

In a speech to the National Governors' Conference the following year, he carried the idea further:

I am convinced Washington alone cannot do the job that must be done. The consequence of failure of the states to act together, and together with the Federal authorities, will be confusion doubly compounded. The vast increase in Federal funds for education, which I heartily welcome, is all too likely to result in a tangled mess that no one can straighten out unless the states take new and energetic action. And they can only plan together if they can obtain and share information. In short, without some such device as an Interstate Planning Commission, I do not see how a nationwide educational policy can be shaped and made effective. The times challenge educators and statesmen alike. What will be the response from the states?[4]

After considerable spadework and opinion polling by Terry Sanford, then Governor of North Carolina, the idea of an Interstate Compact for Education was submitted to the National Governors' Conference in July, 1965, by the Governors' Confer-

[3] James B. Conant, Shaping Educational Policy (New York: McGraw-Hill, 1964), pp. 109, 123.
[4] James B. Conant, Address to the National Governors' Conference, July 27, 1965, Minneapolis, Minn.

ence Committee on Human Relations. The committee said it believed that the "proposals are of such a lasting significance and far-reaching importance as to be the subject of a special report to this Conference." Believing that educational policy-making leadership must "remain with the states," the committee strongly recommended a mechanism to weld the states together, intensify communication among them, and mobilize "the vigorous leadership of the governors." The Governors' Conference unanimously adopted the committee's recommendation. A few months later a general planning conference approved the Compact for Education, took steps to put it into effect, and approved a schedule of fees, reflecting both population and per capita wealth of member states. Initial charges, plus income from foundation grants, were to carry the organization until the end of 1967, when an annual fee would be levied. It was estimated that the income from fees, also based on a sliding schedule, would net $626,000 if all eligible states and territories became partners to the Compact. The planning conference also completed plans for the Compact's functional arm, the Education Commission of the States.

In June, 1966, the first full meeting of the Education Commission was held in Chicago. It approved the first seven research studies for the Commission's staff to undertake, which it was expected would generate specific and significant recommendations for the improvement of education in member states.

The seven studies are as follows:

1. Methods of Financing Elementary and Secondary Education.
2. Community-centered Post High School Education.
3. Trends and Needs in Vocational and Technical Education; What is Being Done, What Can Be Done, for the General Education of Vocational Students.
4. Coordination of Higher Education.
5. Ways States Can Attack the Special Problems of Urban Schools.

6. Techniques Employed in the Various States to Secure Communication and Understanding Among All Groups and Individuals Involved in the Education Process.
7. The Size of School Districts.

The Education Compact of the States, with its integral Education Commission, strikes me as an excellent and important innovation which *could* do much to enliven state leadership in education and to enhance what one of the Compact's committees called "the invaluable diversity" of our federal system while at the same time exploiting the possibilities inherent in real, down-to-earth cooperation among the states on all educational fronts. To be truly effective, however, the Commission must recognize the interdependence in education of federal and local, as well as state, participation, recalling that Dr. Conant's warning of "confusion doubly compounded" concerned not only the failure of the states to act together but also their failure to work with Washington.

A proposal—but it is still only a proposal—that could greatly improve national policy making in *higher* education was put forward early in 1968. At the same time that he warned college leaders of the inevitable consequences of business-as-usual, as noted above, Alan Pifer of the Carnegie Corporation released an extensive and hard-hitting report on the future of higher education. It is Mr. Pifer's conviction that the federal government will have to assume the principal support of higher education, and he called for a strong policy-planning center "close to the summit of the federal government where it can influence all federal action that impinges on higher educational institutions." Recognizing that his plea for massive federal support would bring forth cries from many college and university leaders of "un-American, unconstitutional, and dangerous nonsense," Mr. Pifer nonetheless stuck to his guns. "It is extraordinary," he said, "when a government says it wants to hear the views of higher education but still does its planning in an aura of secrecy, and when all the sectors of higher education are busy framing essentially self-serving statements for delivery in Washington, we still lack a high-level, dispassionate, nonpolitical debate on the future of higher education."

The center proposed by Mr. Pifer would be presided over by the Secretary of Health, Education, and Welfare, although perhaps located outside the department. It would be responsible for long-range planning, cooperation with the states in framing national policy, and through its membership would be "as much of higher education itself as it is of government." Anticipating the "power-play" argument, he laid stress on the fact that the proposed policy-planning center would exert no centralized control over the faculty, student body, or academic offerings of any individual institution.

Meantime, just the month before the Carnegie Corporation proposal, the Educational Policies Commission was suddenly, quietly, and mysteriously put out of business by its sponsors, the National Education Association and the American Association of School Administrators. It was the nation's only body devoted to formulating and publishing broad, long-range national objectives and policies for public education. Many noted educators expressed shock and regret, including Dr. Conant, who had served on the commission for most of its 33-year history. The commission has had its critics down the years, including the present writer (among other things, it moved so slowly that it tended to echo rather than influence national policy on matters like school integration). But it was unique and valuable; its sudden demise leaves a vacuum.

What I should like to propose now is a wholly new body that, embracing some features of the old EPC and many features of Mr. Pifer's center, would go beyond them both to encompass the entire range of formal education. I suggest the appointment of a Presidential Commission on Public Policies for Education, with a life span of ten years. The members should compare in stature to the members of the University Grant Committee in England and be, much more than they, free from political involvement so that they could study the question of public policies for education objectively and with vision.

Essentially the task of this commission would be twofold: first, to present within two or three years after its creation a clear picture of public policies for education at all levels of the educational system and government. In other words, the American people should know how public policies at the present time are being established, and the effect of those policies on the schools and colleges and on the education of children. We should know, too, whether these policies help our institutions to improve and to meet the critical needs of our times, or the opposite.

The second responsibility of this commission would be to chart a course, within five years of its creation, for public policy at all levels of the educational system—federal, regional, state, and local. Here the central goal should be to establish conditions whereby the United States can maintain a strong educational system aimed at developing the capacities of *all* our citizens so that they can derive the greatest satisfaction from living and so that society can realize the maximum from our potential human resources. Such a commission should be informative and provocative. Perhaps out of the ensuing debate would emerge public policies for education appropriate to a nation in America's position of world leadership.

But I believe we must go further, and faster, than top-down policy planning can take us. Although the federal government is increasingly involved in education, the locus of educational power still rests with the state, the local school board, and the individual university. Therefore I suggest that each state and every large school system and university set up a Commission on Educational Development. It would be the task of each commission to look to the future constantly and to devote its entire attention to the improvement of education. Obviously, such commissions would follow no uniform pattern. But they should in every case create a climate for education like the climate in agriculture, industry, or medicine that fosters the will and ability to do the job better every year.

Consider for a moment what has been achieved in these fields through the deliberate application of trained intelligence. The United States began as an agricultural economy. But despite the natural fertility of land and almost limitless resources, Americans were not content to follow forever the old ways and sought constant improvement. The nation established land-grant colleges, with experimental stations and extension services, and the government went into agricultural research on a large scale. By 1900 only 37 percent of our gainfully employed people needed to be engaged in agriculture. Intensified research meant that by 1964 only 8 percent of our workers were needed to raise all our food. Crops improved, herds produced infinitely more milk and better meat. Even with this small fraction of the population engaged in agriculture, farm surplus products became a major national problem.

Meanwhile, America transformed itself into a highly industrialized nation. Mass production techniques and now the "second industrial revolution" of automation have lifted the standard of living to utopian levels. In industry, as in agriculture, the constant effort is to surpass last year's record. In dynamic industries such as oil, chemicals, drugs, electronics, automobiles, airplane manufacturing, and plastics, the successful companies *organize* for change. They stress research and development and strive to achieve results more effectively. The search is always for greater productivity of the worker, wider markets, and better methods.

Similarly, America's progress in health and medicine has been revolutionized through research and scientific discovery and prompt development. It is a startling fact that 90 percent of the drugs doctors prescribe today were unknown thirty years ago.

America's enormous scientific research effort is now attacking virtually every kind of problem—missiles and space ships, water supply, uses of atomic energy, and even the creation of life. We are continuously searching for the new and better.

But the effort doesn't come cheap. In 1968 industry allocated over $8.1 billion for research and development. The federal government now spends approximately $15 billion a year on scientific research and development. The total of these two figures comes to very roughly half the amount we devote to the *operation* of our *entire* educational system. Moreover, the federal government spends relatively nothing—less than 1 percent of its R & D total— on *educational* research and development. Is it any wonder that the country isn't making as much progress in education as it should be making?

Americans must apply to the schools and colleges the lessons learned in the dynamic development of our society. To be sure, we differ on the details of education and how to achieve our goals. But we are in substantial agreement that sweeping improvements must be made and we know that money alone is not the answer. Even if we were to double the total expenditure for education, all those extra billions would not, per se, make up the deficit of able teachers or transform the curriculum and procedures of our schools. As is true of most complex problems, there is no single solution or panacea.

At the outset the American creative genius must concentrate on making the best possible use of the most gifted teachers now at work or that can be recruited and trained. As *Fortune* magazine has said: "There never can be enough truly gifted teachers; the qualities that make for greatness in teaching—like those that make for greatness in any field—are rare. And given the current ratio of students to teachers, the supply even of ordinarily competent teachers is almost bound to fall short of the demand. . . . It is clear that the schools must learn to utilize their teachers, especially their gifted teachers, more effectively than they do now."

Something can be done about this. Something must be done. The way has already been pointed by those educators who have carried on experiments for the better use of people and facilities. Some results have been tremendously successful. Out of these experiments have come some comprehensive demonstrations which combine techniques in the better utilization of teaching resources.

What is needed in education, then, is a research-and-development approach like that in other fields. In industry, health and agriculture, agencies had to be set up to nurture this approach. Research-and-development divisions, health laboratories or institutes, and agricultural experiment stations have been most effective in serving this purpose. Where would we be if we had depended on the practicing farmers for research and development in agriculture, on our managers and operating personnel in industry, or on our general practitioners in medicine?

Some vehicle, then, is required for education. The federal government has recognized the need by providing funds, under the Elementary and Secondary Education Act, for experimentation and innovation. The Office of Education, for example, has begun to finance "policy research centers" that are designed to analyze future educational needs and resources, providing policy makers with requisite information, techniques, and alternatives. The private foundations have also helped through grants to organizations in this field such as Educational Services, Inc., which carried on the work of the Physical Science Study Committee and became a center of curriculum reform. ESI has now merged with the Institute for Educational Innovation, a federally sponsored laboratory, to form the Educational Development Center.

But it is necessary now to institutionalize this kind of innovative enterprise within the state systems of education. That is why I suggest Commissions on Educational Development. The membership of such commissions should be of high caliber, and they should work with highly qualified staffs. Each commission would have no administrative responsibilities. It would serve primarily three functions:

1. It would sponsor experiments designed to provide better education with due regard for efficiency and economy;

2. It would disseminate information about new developments not only within the state but throughout the country, issue an annual report, and recommend necessary legislation; and

3. It would promote the adoption of new developments that have been tried and found successful.

A State Commission for Educational Development should be financed through a fixed percentage of the state's budget for education—something of the magnitude of ½ of 1 percent, to start with—and it should be authorized to make grants to educational institutions for experiments designed to improve educational methods. I am confident that the educational return on such an investment would be rewarding beyond our wildest dreams.

At the outset each commission would identify areas to work in. It could well begin by re-examining the so-called "unalterable truths"—the implicit premises—on which the American educational system now operates. Obviously, a mechanism would have to be devised to prevent duplication of effort and enable the commission to find programs for adoption within its own state. To do this each commission would need to work closely with a nation-wide Research Committee, composed of eminent scholars and charged with the task of guidance.

Much can be done, too, locally. In the Cleveland area, for example, industrial leaders have joined the schools to finance an Educational Research Council, which provides local school systems, at reasonable cost, with research facilities none of them could afford individually. The first result was an improved mathematics program incorporating the newest concepts of mathematical theory and teaching. Since then the Council has initiated projects in social science, the humanities, science, reading, health and physical education, vocational education, and a pioneering total curriculum reorganization. The president, George Baird, has written in the Compact's 1967 prospectus:

The Council was started with one basic conviction: Elementary and secondary education is perennially in need of reforms which can be seriously analyzed, defined, and formulated only if the vast resources and refined procedures of modern research are brought to bear on educational research at that specific level. Since no such program existed in 1959, the Council's first task was to work out a model of modern research for elementary and secondary education.

It is well known that after the First and Second World Wars, the resources of research which had been mobilized and organized to ensure victory went into industry and commerce, where there was risk money to sustain research. None of these tremendous resources were used to serve elementary and secondary education. Why not? Because our elementary and secondary school system is fragmented into small local districts, and at the local level, no research money was available. In this respect, elementary and secondary education was (and for the most part, still is) a poor relative in the big family of education. Whatever research was done for elementary and secondary education was done in colleges, on a part-time basis. The research was mostly on administrative matters tangential to education; it was performed with all the detachment of amateurism and with the most archaic means, as though elementary and secondary education did not matter very much—as though it was not important enough to have a research apparatus of its own. Such attitudes were wrong, and the ensuing "de facto" situation was a bad one. In terms of money alone, elementary and secondary education is a business involving some 30 billion dollars a year—a big business any way you look at it.

There is another matter quite apart from those of finance and prestige: The problems of elementary and secondary education are so specific and so particular to their field that they must be handled by specially trained, full-time research personnel. These problems must be observed where they occur and they must be solved there also, for only there can they be properly analyzed and evaluated. Such research must be done in the elementary and secondary classroom and nowhere else—not even in the most illustrious college or university. When changes occur in aims and atmosphere, the preoccupation with elementary and secondary education cannot help but change. Inevitably it becomes incidental to problems of higher education. The Educational Research Council of Greater Cleveland was established with this in mind; therefore, its guiding purpose is both simple and profound. The Council does everything within its power to mobilize and organize the resources of modern research for the exclusive service of elementary and secondary education. For us, in summary, elementary and secondary education comes first. That is what makes us unique.

This illustrates the kind of action every large community across the nation could take if it is seriously interested in helping its citizens and developing better communities through better schools.

We all agree that it will take more money to provide for all our children the kind of education demanded by these critical times. We may differ on the sources from which the money should come, how much education should have, and how it should be spent, but we all agree that we want the best education that our ingenuity can devise. Most of us would agree that we want the most effective education at the lowest possible cost. Many of us agree that we need to pay much higher salaries to our most competent teachers if we are to attract able people into the teaching profession and that current salary scales, based on degrees earned, tenure, and years served, doom the profession to mediocrity. But to accomplish the things on which we agree we must break through our hard shell of encrusted tradition as we have in industry, agriculture, and health.

3   Risk Capital for Innovation:
The Role of the Private Foundation

The innovative approach to improving American education has been greatly encouraged by the private foundations: Ford, Carnegie, Sloan, Rockefeller, Kettering, and smaller ones like the New World and Stern foundations. Time and again they have warmly welcomed enterprising college presidents and schoolmen with ideas and the courage to put them into practice. Local (or state) tax funds are hard to get for experimental, high-risk, or even just new programs; state and federal programs are almost always heavily restricted to established ways of doing things.[1] An educational administrator with far-out and imaginative ideas may convince his teachers, inspire his colleagues, and even swing his board—but without some "risk capital" his idea may never get out of the talking stage.

Looking back, one can see that some of the major advances in American education have been sparked by private philanthropy. Undoubtedly the most far-reaching effect foundations have had upon education is in the field of medical education. In 1910 the Carnegie Foundation for the Advancement of Teaching had good

---

[1] The provision of funds specifically for "innovative" programs in the Elementary and Secondary Education Act of 1965 was a notable advance in this regard.

reason to suspect that the general state of the country's medical schools was "scandalous." They engaged Abraham Flexner to make a detailed study of all the schools—then numbering 155 and mostly proprietary. He visited every one of them. As the result of the Flexner report, which exposed almost incredible shoddiness and worse, John D. Rockefeller, Sr., and the General Education Board decided to put large sums of money into a few medical schools and raised standards to the point where the fly-by-night schools would have to close. As a result, a full half of the medical schools operating in 1910 closed their doors during the next quarter of a century, the remaining schools improved themselves, good new schools were founded, and medical education reached a standard unequaled anywhere else in the world. This was a revolution in medicine for which all of us can be grateful today because the higher health standards that have come as a result have benefited every one of us. The process of achieving this, however, met with strong resistance and even bitter hostility.

Talking with Abraham Flexner just a few years before his death at the age of ninety-two, I asked him whether a similar task could be undertaken in teacher education, a critical area for the entire educational system. In his characteristically forthright way he said that the field was too amorphous, too vast, too controlled, and that the fight to retain the status quo would be more intense and vicious than in medical education. Perhaps that is why no one has even attempted a Flexner study of teacher education. But more on this later.

It is, by the way, significant to note what had moved Andrew Carnegie in the first place to set up the foundation that sponsored the Flexner report with its considerable impact. When Andrew Carnegie was made a trustee of Cornell University he was shocked to discover that college teachers were paid only about as much as office clerks. He therefore decided to set up the Carnegie Foundation for the Advancement of Teaching and persuaded Henry Smith Pritchett, president of the Massachusetts Institute of Technology, to become its head. The fund's primary purpose was to provide pensions for retiring college professors. In order to build the program on a more permanent basis this fund, in turn, established the Teachers Insurance & Annuity Association of America, which now provides a forward-looking retirement plan for many colleges and universities throughout the country. The Carnegie Foundation and the Teachers Insurance & Annuity Association thus pioneered in a field of growing importance. Andrew Carnegie's "risk" capital provided the basis for many of our retirement programs today. In fact, group annuities, which are in general use today, were first established by life insurance companies in 1921, sixteen years after the Carnegie program. This is merely another example of how venture capital blazed the trail just as funds for research and experimentation in the scientific field have generated new discoveries.

It is against this backdrop that the Ford Foundation—the largest of the philanthropic foundations and the one I had the privilege of being associated with from 1951 to 1964—projected its education program. The funds were limited until 1948. With the settlement of the Henry and Edsel Ford estates larger resources became available. The trustees appointed a study committee with H. Rowan Gaither, Jr., as director, which worked for a period of two years reviewing the possible contributions of foundations to the critical problems facing civilization today. The committee then recommended to the trustees that the Ford Foundation concentrate its resources on five major areas and support activities of critical importance: (1) the promotion of international understanding and world peace, for without them the very basis of civilization is placed in jeopardy; (2) the strengthening of democratic institutions and processes, for these are fundamental to any meaningful concept of human welfare; (3) the advancement of economic well-being, for economic strength is essential to man's pursuit of his larger goals; (4) *the extension and improvement of education, for education is vital to a free society;* and (5) the enlargement of scientific knowledge or understanding of man and his behavior, for man himself is the basic element in a democratic society.

To accomplish these objectives the trustees of the Ford Foundation have, since 1936, made commitments of close to $3 billion, well over half the total going directly to the support of education. The story of the Ford Foundation's Fund for the Advancement of Education, from its inception in 1950 to its official termination in 1967, is central to the theme of this book. For the Fund constitutes the most notable recent example of what a private, experimental, philanthropic agency can and cannot accomplish when it consciously sets out to encourage educational reform through the innovative approach. The major activities of the Fund—in teacher training, curriculum reform, scholarship assistance, use of technology, new ways of organizing schools, etc.—have touched nearly every teacher and student in the country. If American educators are really turning to the innovative approach now, they have much to learn about the dynamics of educational change from the successes and failures of the Fund.

In 1950, when the Fund was conceived by Paul Hoffman (then director of the Ford Foundation) and his associate directors, the educational establishment was reeling under the impact of an unprecedented combination of forces: the postwar population boom, the explosive increase of knowledge, and the urgent demands for a vast new supply of highly trained manpower.

The population explosion alone would have been a severe burden on the schools. In 1945 demographers of the Census Bureau expected that the population might reach 165 million by the end of the century. The figure was reached, however, not in fifty-five years but in ten. In that single decade elementary school enrollments rose from 20 million to 28 million. The schools staggered under the load, and high schools and colleges waited apprehensively for the avalanche to reach them in a few more years.

To make matters still worse, American society was pushing toward the ideal of universal secondary education. At the turn of the century only 11 percent of the young people were going to high school as against close to 100 percent today; and only 4 percent of America's young people were going on to college—today about 40 percent do so. The ultimate effects of this change are all but incalculable, but a short visit to almost any campus reveals the immediate effects in the form of overcrowded classrooms, mushrooming new buildings, and a constant stream of visiting high school seniors wearing worried looks, revealing their intense desire to be accepted and their fear that there will be no room for them.

At all educational levels, indeed, the swelling enrollments produced the same physical problems: too few chairs per classroom, too few rooms per building, too few buildings per school, and too few supplies of all sorts. Although taxpayers groaned and protested, money could make up for these deficits in *quantity* in fairly short order. But money could not make up the growing threat to the *quality* of instruction, the major cause of which was a severe and increasing shortage of able teachers. Teacher salaries had failed to keep pace with industrial pay scales and some of the ablest teachers left the schools. Many students who might have thought of teaching as a career excluded it from their plans. The result was not merely undersupply but a threat to the quality of education.

Quality also suffered from the extension of secondary education. The American people encouraged this spread of an ideal without stopping to rethink the purpose of secondary education or the problems in trying to educate the bright and the dull, the scholarly and the worldly, the artist and the Philistine, the native born and the immigrant. In consequence, by mid-century the typical high school was a hodgepodge of heterogeneous persons and programs, and its curriculum was a potpourri of general education, college preparation, vocational training, and adjustment-to-life. It had been thrown together in the effort to satisfy everyone; not surprisingly, it satisfied very few.

The educational system has never been without its critics, but in the crisis of the 1950's the schools came under heavy fire from all quarters and for a variety of reasons, some bad, some irrelevant, some good but inconsistent. Many of the arguments clustered about an old issue. For some years a debate about teaching means and ends had been going on between the scholars and intellectuals, who clung to the traditional beliefs, and professional educators who favored the informal activity-centered programs known as "progressive education." (There was, to be sure, some crossing of party lines in both directions.)

The deepening educational crisis of the postwar years fanned this dispute into a blaze that excited and alarmed the public. A torrent of books and articles angrily charged quackery in education, protested that Johnny couldn't read, that the schools failed to equip youth for higher studies, for responsible jobs, or even for writing a grammatical letter. Among the new critics were generals and admirals, politicians, scientists, and industrialists; each with his own notions as to what the schools are for, what is wrong and what to do about it. But invective does not in itself point the way to constructive changes. A foundation, however, not embroiled in factional disputes, independent of the educational system, and not forced to yield to public pressure, might encourage new approaches and support experiments, demonstrations, and pilot programs too uncertain of success or too controversial to be paid for by public tax money. It could, in short, encourage institutions to try out many new ideas. With this avowed purpose the Fund for the Advancement of Education got under way in April, 1951. Those of us directly involved then embarked on some exciting and rewarding years.

Because the Fund for the Advancement of Education was pioneering and experimental, it excluded projects, however worthy, that belong within regular institutional budgets, making no grants, for example, for building or general operating expenses. The Fund used its resources not to sustain the sure thing but to try out those new, relatively untested things—television teaching, nonprofessional teacher aides, "fifth-year" teacher training for liberal arts graduates, team teaching, and others—that held some promise of helping the educational system meet the needs of modern society more effectively.

Yet a private foundation of this size could not expect either to create or to halt potent trends in education. It would have been futile, for instance, to invest grant money in the more efficient utilization of teachers in the thirties, when there were more teachers than jobs, and little reason for citizen support of such efforts. Such a foundation can, however, select promising areas and, with good timing, make a relatively small grant have ripple effects. It tries to study the power structure of the educational system, gauge the temper of the times, appraise the array of forces for and against any particular change, and then throw its weight at the right moment behind the most promising trends in the hope of converting them into dominant ones.

For this reason, as well as to avoid the "scatteration of funds" against which Abraham Flexner strongly argued at the time, the Fund concentrated on five major areas of American education: (1) the recruitment and training of teachers; (2) the better use of teachers' time and talent; (3) extension to all of full educational opportunity commensurate with ability; (4) improvements in curricula, and (5) improvements in school management and financing.

Of these, the first received about half the money granted by the Fund in its first decade of operation because of the conviction that attracting and keeping gifted teachers is one of the most basic of all the problems facing education. Second to this interest was the Fund's concern with the more efficient use of teachers' time and energy. The underlying aim of these so-called "utilization" programs was not to replace teachers but to multiply their effectiveness by new techniques and devices. Television, for instance, was thoroughly demonstrated not as an embellishment or teacher substitute but as an effective medium of communication, capable of bringing the best teachers into direct contact with a greatly increased number of students.

In striving to advance American education through these ventures the staff of the Fund evolved its concept of "advancement" from a number of fundamental convictions. Some of these—such as the belief that everyone should have an equal opportunity to as full an education as he can benefit by—were generally accepted, but others were controversial and may long continue to be so. One such was the Fund's conviction that a liberal education is the first essential in the education of every American, and particularly of every teacher. Another was that it is in no way undemocratic to seek out and nurture superior talent and that, in fact, the democratic way of life is bound to suffer if this is not done. A third was that American schools, if they are to produce any significant number of intellectually superior human beings, must re-establish the priority of the intellect. While the Fund had no ideological commitment to any *means* of educational advancement, it did have a commitment to these basic *ends* of education. Although these ends were (and still are) subject to debate, the Fund hoped that in future decades they would become the core of a public philosophy of education to which a majority of Americans would subscribe.

To implement this hope for a growing public consensus on educational goals, the Fund also supported projects designed to help clarify the question of what kinds of schools America needs, what they should do, and what the facts are in the important issues in education. Among such projects were conferences and workshops, grants to colleges for self-studies, fellowships for educational reporting, and publications dealing with a wide variety of specific educational problems. The Fund supported, for example, the National Citizens Commission for the Public Schools (later the National Citizens Council for Better Schools), which under the able chairmanship of Roy Larsen, then president of Time, Inc., activated several thousand citizen groups and was instrumental in distributing many thousands of pamphlets on the critical issues facing the schools, with practical suggestions on how to meet them. To create a new avenue for informing the public about educational matters the Fund sponsored a monthly supplement in the *Saturday Review*, entitled "Education in America" (the supplement continues, now sponsored by the Charles F. Kettering Foundation).

But the major thrust of the Fund's program, as already noted, was behind certain new approaches to the nation's pressing educational problems, to be discussed in subsequent chapters. The Appendix examines one such effort—instructional television—in some depth, as a case study in the innovative approach in action. The account is not a success story, but it is all the more instructive for that reason. It reveals the complexities which confront any large-scale attempt to attack with the spirit of innovation a major problem of our schools and colleges.

Like other institutions concerned broadly with human welfare, the foundations have an enormous task. Like all men, their officers and directors make mistakes. They cannot possibly know the final answers to society's most perplexing problems. They can only support promising ideas that may yield better answers. To carry out their task they need to depend upon wise counsel from people with a wide diversity of experience, as well as upon their own judgment. Exemplifying the "innovative spirit," their actions must reflect reserved assurance with a deep sense of the dignity of man. But because they are concerned with the wisest use of "risk" capital they must have courage. The accelerated governmental support of scientific research, education, and other worthwhile activities has, to be sure, somewhat changed the emphasis of foundation concern. But new challenges face these organizations on every side, and if they function as great foundations have functioned in the past—with vision, creativity, and courage—they have unending opportunity to advance human welfare by assisting able people in the search for better answers.

4   Innovative Teachers for Innovative Schools

Despite the urgency of innovations in the substance and mode of education—technical, organizational, curricular—which constitute much of this book's message, the core of good instruction is now as always the good teacher. And our schools *are* getting better teachers, though still too few of them, and they're paying them better, though still not enough.

It is worthwhile to look closely at the process by which training programs for teachers have improved over the past few decades. For these programs are the sources that nourish the entire educational system. The improving quality and vitality of teacher education will determine the health of our schools for the foreseeable future. If the training of teachers is weak or misguided, we will not get young people entering the schools who are capable of the innovative approach. But if the sources of our new teachers continue upgrading the quality of their programs, the schools can look forward to a self-renewing flow of talent. Nothing could augur better for the future of public education.

Teacher education in America is in a state of incipient revolution. The old forms are crumbling; new demands are sparking experimentation and an innovative approach. Looking back over the past twenty-five years one finds that a sharp break with tradition came during the decade of the fifties. Looking at the present situation, one can discern the seeds of what the future will bring. Looking into the future one can hope that the revolution will realize its promise for improving American education.

Controversy about teacher education continues, long after Sputnik, even longer since the publication of Arthur Bestor's *Educational Wastelands*. But the style of the controversy is different from what it was in previous decades. The public argument, for all its excesses, helped clear the air; and after the smoke of battle vanished and the casual troops drifted away the leading warriors proceeded to the slow, difficult task of working out a truce and, from this base, of building solid improvements in the education of teachers. The extremists on either side may still send off an occasional fusillade. But a rapprochement, with many concrete accomplishments already to its credit, has undeniably taken place.

The teachers college, *by that name*, is virtually extinct, like the normal school before it. The substance of the teachers colleges has changed, too, although not as much as some of us might desire. A growing number of teachers colleges have become general colleges, and many have become universities. Only a small fraction of new teachers is now graduated from teachers colleges per se; all the rest come from general colleges and universities, although some of these are but lately transformed from "teachers colleges" and are still some distance from making their programs and outlook match their new names.

The change in teacher education in America started less than two decades ago. In 1950 not only was the educational system in immediate need of thousands of teachers, but all predictions of enrollments indicated that the schools and colleges would have even greater needs for new teachers to deal with unprecedented expansion. By 1955 it was estimated that if one half of all young people graduating from college in the next ten years went into teaching, the shortage would be met, but the actual figure was only about 20 percent. Then, as now, moreover, most of them were women; they would drop out of the schools in a few years to raise their own families, and many would not return to work for years, if ever.

How could the rapidly increasing number of students be educated—and better educated—by an instructional force whose relative numerical position was getting worse and worse. Technology could help a great deal, but clearly there was need for a redoubled effort to recruit more new teachers and to train them to be better ones. There were many varied and divergent opinions as to how to accomplish this, but some things were apparent to all.

Recruitment and training, it was evident, are not separate entities, but two interacting aspects of a single problem. Many of the brightest and most able college students, for instance, were rejecting teaching as a career not only because of low salaries and diminishing status but because conventional teacher-training programs were heavily weighted with courses in professional education, the content of which frequently did not capture their imaginations.

For this reason many educators came to the Fund for the Advancement of Education, at that time the one agency willing to invest substantial amounts of money in unconventional approaches to this problem. The Fund's early efforts consisted of projects centered in twenty-four colleges and universities, from which they reached out to forty-three other institutions, plus many more school systems. Although there was considerable variation in the details, most of the programs were efforts to tap the largest reservoir of unused teaching talent—the liberal arts graduates who had not taken undergraduate courses in education.

Without such courses these people could not enter teaching because of prevailing teacher certification laws. The general pattern of training that led to certification for secondary school teaching in most of the United States had come to be a four-year program, the first two years of which were devoted largely to general and liberal arts education and the last two to subject specialization, professional education courses, and practice teaching. The tendency of teacher-training institutions to emphasize professional courses was reflected in rigid state certification requirements. Many of the better liberal arts colleges were unwilling to increase the time devoted to such courses, and consequently turned out fewer and fewer teachers. The barriers erected by the certifying agencies became increasingly costly and difficult for liberal arts graduates to surmount, and still more so for mature men and women who, years after graduation, might wish to enter teaching. This was especially unfortunate in view of the fact that a large pool of potential teachers consists of middle-aged college women whose children are old enough to be in school during much of the day and whose family duties are rapidly dwindling.

For these reasons the great majority of Fund for the Advancement of Education grants for teacher training went to explore and support "fifth-year programs," in which postgraduate training prepares college graduates who did no work in education. (Other programs tested the hypothesis that a sound liberal arts education plus adequate professional training, including practice teaching, can be combined in a four-year undergraduate program.) The underlying assumption was that bright candidates, after spending sixteen years in elementary, secondary, and college classrooms, have inevitably absorbed a good deal of knowledge about classroom management and techniques of teaching, and that with this backlog of experience a high level of professional skill could be rapidly reached through special courses, seminars, classroom experience, and discussions. The term "fifth-year program" need not denote a conventional academic year, but may mean concentrated postgraduate training, ranging from six weeks during the summer to two full graduate years, either full time or part time, and leading either to a graduate degree or only to a teaching certificate.

The earliest activity along these lines by the Fund for the Advancement of Education was in 1951 as a modest grant (later renewed and enlarged) to the University of Arkansas to assist in planning a statewide experiment in the university and fourteen colleges. The project strengthened the liberal arts and general education courses in the four-year colleges that trained teachers.

The graduates of the experimental programs then qualified for certification by taking a fifth year, either at the University of Arkansas or at Arkansas State Teachers College, consisting of professional study and a teaching internship. The Arkansas experiment became one of the Fund's most widely publicized efforts, receiving a great deal of hostile comment from professional educators (who even called it "The Arkansas Purchase"), approval from many scholars, and a little of each from the public.

Being a large-scale statewide effort and a striking departure from conventional teacher-training programs, the experiment was highly visible and produced a series of secondary effects elsewhere. It provoked widespread public discussion of teacher-training programs; it stimulated colleges in all parts of the country to re-examine their own programs; and, most important, it provided a model and demonstration for dozens of similar experiments.

Teacher-training institutions had, for many years prior to the start of the fifth-year programs, offered programs that extended for five years. Usually these traditional programs provided extra professional work and led to an advanced degree or a certificate in education. They were likely to be found in the larger state universities and colleges that turned out teachers in volume. While a few of them entailed innovations and improvements, for the most part the extended programs could be categorized as "more of the same." The experimental programs of the postwar years, however, represented a marked departure from conventional teacher training. While varying in many details, they were all built on a common core: strong liberal arts content; intensive subject matter specialization; concentrated professional courses, often in the form of seminars; and supervised teaching, usually and preferably in the form of a paid internship.

One of the serious obstacles to the recruitment of able persons with liberal arts backgrounds to teaching, or to the retention of such persons in the field, is the lack of incentives in public school teaching. Ability and achievement are not rewarded with advancement in most school systems; in many schools all teachers perform substantially the same duties, superior teachers being burdened with the same time-consuming chores as the less gifted teachers and earning no better pay.

In 1956 Francis Keppel, then dean of the Harvard Graduate School of Education, urged a program for a "breakthrough" in education, one aspect of which was a suggestion about the recruitment and training of teachers. He pointed out that the innovation known as team teaching (considered in Chapter 7) was more than a technique for the more efficient use of teaching talent: it could also aid recruitment by offering powerful incentives to the highly capable student, and would establish teaching as a career with prospects of advancement and of financial reward. Team teaching, in essence, provides a way for a group of teachers to pool their knowledge and talents in the instruction of a larger number of pupils than any individual teacher would normally handle alone. It carries the old principle of the division of labor into the schools and takes the teacher out of the isolation of the self-contained classroom. Besides this mobility and better division of talent, the team principle arranges for the highly gifted teacher to be assisted by other teachers, trainees, and aides who perform such time-consuming duties as record keeping, the holding of drills, the administration and marking of tests, and many other essential, semiskilled tasks. Schools reorganized so as to employ several different levels of skill and competence would be able to pay teachers according to their clearly differentiated roles, as is done in business and the professions. And this prospect of attaining a superior position, and its attendant pay, would attract the more talented people and thus greatly aid in the recruitment effort.

The Fund supported projects in universities and graduate schools of education designed to train teachers for differentiated roles in partnership with neighboring public schools. These institutions included Brown, Chicago, Yeshiva, Harvard, Johns Hopkins, Stanford, and New York universities, the Claremont Colleges, and George Peabody College for Teachers. In 1959 some of these pilot programs received long-term grants from the Ford

Foundation, which gave approximately $20 million to thirty-one colleges and universities from Hawaii to Vermont, including private and public universities, liberal arts colleges, and teachers colleges.

But this could only achieve a limited effect. A major reason, Abraham Flexner pointed out, for the great difficulty of changing teacher education was the complete centralization of the teacher certification authority in the states. At the turn of the century there had been a mixed system of local and county and state controls, but the trend toward greater centralization was unmistakable. Before long state control was virtually complete; the certification process had taken charge of teacher education and stamped it with a rigid credit-counting "professionalism."

As numerous critics have observed, John Dewey and Henry Barnard and Horace Mann themselves could not be certified to teach in a public school today. Professor Edward Gordon, director of Yale's teacher-training program and an outspoken critic of certification procedures, has given this bill of complaint: (1) too often the process of getting certified to teach is only a matter of putting in time; (2) almost anyone can enter some teacher-training program somewhere, whatever his lack of ability ("since education courses are often tailored to fit the lowest level of ability, good students cannot sit through them"); (3) knowledge of the subject to be taught matters least of all ("in manuals on certification, the subject-matter requirements are nearly always in fine print"); (4) once a teacher is certified, he often winds up teaching in another field than the one he prepared for. It is significant that Professor Gordon could have included such charges in a cautiously optimistic appraisal he made, in the early sixties, of revisions in certification procedures that were going on. Since that appraisal further and more drastic changes have been made under the leadership of commissioners of education such as James Allen of New York, but much remains to be accomplished.

Certification originated as a safeguard against the laxity and corruption of nineteenth-century educational standards. Viewed solely as a force against evil, certification has a respectable history. Viewed positively, certification can take some credit for the steady increase in the sheer amount of education every teacher must receive. Since the beginning of this century every decade, on the average, has added a full year to the preparation required of teachers. Four years is now the almost universal minimum, for both elementary and secondary school teachers. By now there is a well-established trend toward a five-year requirement for all teachers. Granted: sheer increase in preparation time does not *ipso facto* mean improvement in preparation. But in comparison with the one- or two-year program of the old normal school, which was almost entirely on the how-to-do-it level, the longer term of modern teacher-training programs was bound to mean increased proportions of general education and subject matter specialization. In short, and to state the obvious, the added years count if they are filled with solid preparation.

Having given the devil his due, I must go on to say that by the 1920's and 1930's state certification, which began as a belated reform of the old nonsystem of local control, had developed into an increasingly unwieldy and stultifying superstructure that in turn cried out for change. The evils of the certification pattern were many. Chief among them has been the imposition of arbitrary professional standards, based on quantitative measures of courses taken and credits earned and unrelated to any measure of teaching quality or demonstrated competence. Furthermore, certification requirements have varied erratically from state to state, each system rigidly enforced with all the "narcissism of small differences." At its worst the certification structure has kept good people out of teaching, legalized mediocrity, and even made it difficult for a teacher to get work in any state other than the one that certified him originally.

So powerful became the certification process that it went far beyond the simple licensing function of other professions to assume *de facto* control over teacher education itself. Whatever professional courses the state departments of education required, these courses the teacher-training institutions perforce provided. At the same time the state certification laws kept to a minimum the requirements in academic subject matter and left prospective teachers free to pad out their professional training (at the expense of the more difficult academic courses) well beyond the minimum required. Dismayed by this unwholesome evolution, many liberal arts colleges and universities gave up any commitment they had to teacher education and abandoned the field.

State certification arrangements are now in the process of intensive study and reform. In recent years more than half the states have undertaken significant reforms, a few of them involving complete revision of certification structures. There has been a steady decrease in the number of education courses required and a steady increase in subject matter and liberal education requirements for high school teachers. The changes have also included some improvement in reciprocity, so that teachers—like the rest of mobile America—can move easily across state lines. A number of states are showing a marked interest in the use of teacher-qualifying examinations, long out of favor, which should help, as I have said, to open up teaching careers to able people with unconventional preparation.

Above all, current revisions point to a day when teacher education of high quality will determine certification requirements rather than the other way around. Specific course requirements are being reduced, as well as the number of different kinds of certificates. Many states have adopted the "approved program" approach, whereby colleges and universities submit their programs of teacher education to the state for approval, and graduates of satisfactory programs are automatically certified as teachers. The learned societies, which have at last addressed themselves to the shaping of public school curricula and the training of public school teachers, favor this approach and it now seems to be gaining support across the country.

Professor Gordon is not alone in finding current certification reforms inadequate and the pace of change too slow. On the one hand, there are professional educators—such as Myron Lieberman and Lucien Kinney—who deprecate any change short of removing certification control from the state and establishing it squarely in the profession. On the other hand, there are academic purists who will settle for nothing less than the transfer of the licensing power from the states to the colleges and universities themselves.

The biggest bombshell in James B. Conant's eagerly awaited report on teacher education, which came out in the fall of 1963, was his recommendation for the outright abolition of the certification system as now constituted. In its place he would set up a system whereby, for certification purposes, the state would require only that the candidate hold a bachelor's degree from a "legitimate college or university," that he submit evidence of successful and well-supervised practice teaching, and that he possess university-wide endorsement to teach in a "designated field and grade level." Dr. Conant based his *Education of American Teachers* on a two-year study of seventy-seven varied institutions in all parts of the country, and he made a persuasive case for his certification plan, calling the present procedures "bankrupt" and condemning as a "national scandal" the practice in most states of allowing teachers certified in one field to teach almost anything else.

None of these radical proposals for scrapping the present certification machinery, however, seem to be based on a realistic assessment of the teaching profession or of the dynamics of education. While there is every reason to hope that the certification structure will be simplified and stripped of its accumulated powers, it seems likely that the locus of control will remain with the states. Few scholars, after studying the record of the educational establishment of the past few decades, would approve the concentration of control within the profession as it exists today. Conversely, neither the profession itself nor in all probability the state legislatures would ever countenance the scholars' solution and agree to let the colleges and universities take over the licensing power, even in the modified form of the Conant proposal, with its various safeguards.

My own feeling is that, by and large, present revisions in

certification are in the right direction. The over-all tendency of these reforms is to cut certification down to size and reduce it to a simple legal device for maintaining minimum standards in the schools. There is a good argument in favor of framing certification codes that positively *encourage* experimental teacher-education programs, with the ultimate purpose of providing alternatives and making requirements sufficiently flexible and general that they no longer act as a barrier to experimentation. In the past certification tried to do too much, with damaging consequences to teachers and the institutions that trained them. The procedures have held back needed reforms in the mainstream of teacher education. On these issues the Conant report, as anticipated, stirred up a major—and wholesome—controversy. Qualified approval was the prevailing tone of the early reactions, with the sharpest disapproval coming from educational bigwigs and from would-be reformers—radical or conservative—who felt the recommendations went nowhere near far enough.

I regret Dr. Conant's decision to bypass the knotty problems in teacher education, and in particular his rather offhand dismissal of such promising developments as the new fifth-year plans in which Harvard played such an important role. But I can only applaud his attack on the stultifying quality of current certification practices and his well-documented emphasis on the urgent need for better subject matter preparation, better practice teaching, and better in-service training, and his insistence on joint school-university responsibility for teacher education.

In general, reformers of teacher education are concentrating on programs that include maximum education in the arts and sciences. They are trying to thrash out the difficult question of the precise professional training a teacher requires. There is a broad consensus on the relevance of studies in the philosophy and psychology of education and in education's place in American history and a fair consensus on the need for some instruction in methods and techniques of teaching. Again, the validity of practice teaching or the internship is generally accepted. How and when prospective teachers should be exposed to these components, however—and for how many semester hours—are moot questions. A number of considerations enter in. There is the perennial question of when a course is "professional" and when it is not. For example, there is an excellent case for integrating the philosophy and history of education into general courses in philosophy and history which, if taught "liberally," would be of value to all students, not just Education students. There was never much point to irresponsible attacks that lumped together as "method" or "methodology" everything in teacher education that was outside the mainstream of liberal arts. Certainly teacher education by the 1920's and 1930's had grown overfond of the methodological, but it always included professional courses of substance and, if taught well, of real value.

It would be inaccurate to claim great gains for the teacher-education and certification reforms of the past two decades. But it would be equally uninformed to underestimate them or to judge them strictly in bookkeeping terms—numbers of teacher graduates from the new programs, numbers of new programs, number of improved state certification arrangements, and the like. Most of the teachers coming out of the new programs appear to be exceptionally well prepared and superior practitioners, but they represent a small fraction of the total new teaching force and an even smaller fraction of the effective demand for teachers. It will be years before the returns are in on such programs and their graduates, and even longer before we can assess the impact of the new ways of preparing teachers on the children they teach.

What can be claimed, even if it is entirely unmeasurable, is a new spirit of open-mindedness and a new determination to improve teacher education. Promising results of the accommodation, however limited, between educators and scholars are beginning to emerge. This is evident in the new school curricula, in new programs to prepare teachers, in certification revision, in joint recruitment campaigns. One of the most hopeful manifestations of the new spirit can be seen in the until-recently moribund field of in-service training, both formal and informal. There is high potential in the federally sponsored yearlong or summer institutes connected with the curriculum revisions, and in diverse programs under joint university-school sponsorship. These engage the working teacher in continuing education of real substance, entirely different from the *pro forma* extras in education courses that teachers have been taking these many years to qualify for routine raises or administrative jobs. And most hopeful of all is the evidence—slight, still, but palpable—that young people of intelligence, imagination, and drive now look with favor on school-teaching careers.

At long last an array of forces in education and in society generally has converged to change the role of the teacher in America. The teacher of tomorrow will have to be more than a transmitter of knowledge; he will have to be a skilled deployer of diverse teaching instruments, of stored knowledge in many forms, of powerful new devices for self-instruction. He will have enough planning time, thanks to these new tools and techniques, both to design a program of study tailored to each student's individual needs and also to meet with students, when they can really benefit from the experience, in much more intimate groups than are now possible.

One thing will not change: the teacher of the future, like teachers of all time, must try to inspire his students to become all they are capable of being; the techniques of the future should make this goal more accessible than it has ever been before. Such is one vision of the school of tomorrow. It challenges teacher education in two ways: first, to help transform the teacher's role by working with schools and with prospective teachers toward the fullest utilization of every emerging opportunity to foster the learning of students; second, to devise ways of preparing teachers to fill their new roles.

Teacher education twenty-five years from now should reflect the changing organization of the schools. The emphasis should be on the student learning, not on the teacher teaching. The innovative approach would then become the dominant characteristic of teacher education in America.

5   The Innovative Approach to Teaching

Most definitions of teaching bear the mark of the psy-chologist, who equates learning with behavior (or potential behavior). Such definitions usually ignore the *substance* of teaching, though the dictionary indicates that the word itself means that which is taught or instructed, as well as "the act or profession of instructing." As soon as the "what" intrudes itself, of course, we find ourselves on the brink of that abyss labeled The Aims of Education, whither all paths seem to lead.

Any discussion of the teacher's job must, to be sure, include if only by implication the goals of teaching, but for the moment let us skirt this matter and focus on the *what* and *how* of the instruction: the consensus, if any, on what it is that teachers are to teach and the consensus, if any, on how they are to teach it to produce the best results. How close can we come to delimiting the act and substance of teaching?

I propose to set course toward that objective by circumventing as many obstacles as possible. In doing so I shall inevitably resort to simplification, but I shall try to resist the temptation to over-simplify. Simplification number one: the yawning question of the aims of education—which I unfashionably think is of critical importance—I propose to handle summarily whenever it crops up and get on with the business at hand. Let me simply restate an opinion already expressed: that the primary goal of formal education is intellectual; that the specialized purpose of the schools is to convey knowledge, the uses of knowledge, the ability to acquire and keep on acquiring knowledge, and the insights and understanding deriving therefrom; in short, to learn to learn.

However, to stress the *intellectual* objective of school teaching is by no means to assert that only the intellectual or scholarly competence of the teacher is relevant. Sensible educators recognize, as indeed all of us do in recollecting our school and college days, that the profoundest effects a teacher achieves in opening up a student's mind and imagination may be adventitious, unpredictable, personal, and wholly unrelated to the formal instructional context. The whole teacher, as well as the whole child, is involved in the educational process. But recognizing this fact is no reason to go overboard for personality and the intangibles of character.

Another cautionary note: in my brief statement, above, of the goal of formal education, I meant its parts to be coordinate and integrally related—in other words, the transmission of knowledge per se is an insufficient goal. The teaching function is far more complex and important than that. The modern world requires teachers to convey knowledge in such a way that it becomes part of the student's equipment for meeting, understanding, and appreciating the world he will grow up in.

Finally, let me add that more and more educators are coming to realize that the student is far more important in the process of learning than the teacher. Cumulative evidence from many sources —animal experiments, studies of how children learn, everyday observations of the way they really behave—has shown up the inadequacies of old notions of motivation, based on reward and punishment, by demonstrating that human beings are born with the desire to know, the urge to explore and to master their environment, to achieve. Professor Robert White calls this basic human drive "competence motivation." We see it in operation constantly outside the bounds of any formal educational setting—

babies learning to talk, small boys making themselves expert in their hobbies, teen-agers in their self-acquired knowledge of sports or automobiles, or dancing. In the light of this new understanding, it becomes clear that *how* a teacher taps this natural motivation is as important as *what* he taps it with.

The tiresome dichotomy of *subject vs. method* which for so long bedeviled educational controversy was a false dichotomy from the start. Its falseness and irrelevance become clearer every day as, in the current renaissance of interest in the schools, scholars and behavioral scientists pursue exciting new insights into learning and teaching and those who learn and teach.

In refusing to accept the separation of substance and method I thereby dissociate myself from the extreme advocates of subject matter as the be-all and end-all of schooling. Admiral Rickover, Robert Hutchins, and many of the basic-education enthusiasts are brilliant and eloquent men; by their very single-mindedness they have served an immensely useful purpose as gadflies and counter-weights.

But I believe that in the teaching of the future the correlation of method with results will emerge clearly. In fact, what seems to be emerging is a new and highly significant *synthesis* of substance and method. It is, indeed, for their new insights into teaching and learning that the current endeavors in curriculum revision hold greatest promise. To be sure, the most obvious recent change in the schools has been a new emphasis on subject matter, which to many people seems no more and no less than a return to the good (or bad) old preprogressive days. But if it is a return, it is a return with a difference.

In the uproar over schools and learning, the villain *methodology* has been a popular scapegoat. Critics have denounced its role in teacher education and its subsequent baleful influence on school teaching. I am among those critics, and it may surprise my more embattled adversaries in the educational establishment that I now seem to tolerate an erstwhile bête noire. There are several important distinctions to be made, however. It is not so much that educators—and especially the educators of teachers—took account of methodology; it is that they *over*emphasized it at the expense of content. Furthermore, objection has been legitimately raised against bad or indifferent and increasingly ineffective methods, rather than against methodology per se. Finally, it was the very separation of method from matter, in the indoctrination of teachers and to some extent in school practice, that marked the worst educational extravagances. It seems to me that a most significant aspect of the reforms under way, in curriculum and teacher education and elsewhere, is a restoration of *balance* between the substance and the methods of instruction, and, even more basic, a growing recognition of the special relations between given subjects and given methods. The new methodology beginning to emerge I am all in favor of, despite its bad old name.

A variation on the subject vs. method argument—another tiresome antithesis that sometimes makes debate over education sound like a defective phonograph record—presumes a contradiction between teaching subjects and teaching children. Fortunately, both sides seem to be largely cured of their infatuation with the sound of these words, having made the novel discovery that the verb "to teach" takes two objects, direct and indirect. Teachers teach subjects to students, we are now agreed. So far, so good. There is more to it than that, to be sure, but for the moment let's settle for this happy compromise.

The *matter* of teaching, then—the raw material, so to speak—is equally the student himself and the subject matter of the curriculum. The art (or science or craft) of teaching consists of blending these raw materials to make a new product: viz., an educated or a somewhat *more* educated child (let the definition of "educated" go begging for the moment). Now, at best, this is a hopelessly inefficient process. No manufacturer could possibly succeed in business if production involved so many imponderables, with no quality control over his raw material, and worst of all, nothing but the haziest specifications for the end product. If I may pursue the metaphor briefly, let us consider a single detail of such a production line. "Raw" is obviously a misnomer for the student material that confronts the processor. A teacher might more easily assess the possibilities and the outcome if he really had raw material to work with. But students from kindergarten on come to any teacher already semi-processed by earlier teachers, and at every stage by parents, by experience, and by hereditary forces unknown.

I don't know what the current expertise is on the optimum efficiency of American manufacturing, but my impression is that even the most highly rationalized plant, with the most up-to-date machinery and technique and the best management and work force, operates at considerably less than maximum effectiveness. At very best, human nature and the recalcitrance of matter being what they are, you always have to discount productivity by an X factor to cover low morale, slack, entropy, and general cussedness. Viewed in this ugly light, the American educational enterprise probably operates at a mere fraction of the learning capacity of most of its students. The slack is—and must always be—tremendous. While it is useful and provocative to apply businesslike concepts like productivity to education, we shouldn't fool ourselves that, *mutatis mutandis*, a school can ever run like an office or factory. The point is, rather, that in their own way and on their own terms schools and teachers and students could be immeasurably more productive than they now are or ever have been. It is a major purpose of this book to focus attention on likely ways to achieve this end.

Earlier chapters have reported a number of promising avenues to better education: a re-evaluation of accepted ideas about education, a public policy designed to make the progress of education less haphazard, the improvement in the preparation of teachers and the conditions of school teaching. But beyond all these critically necessary reforms, and even more central to the process of learning, we now have important evidence that there are changes to be made in curriculum and in methods of instruction that will bring us closer to the goal of better education. Change for change's sake will take us nowhere. We must make changes informed by an overriding and consistent purpose, organic changes with a lofty but attainable end in view. In part, these changes demand a new way of defining that end—or, if you like, a way so old it seems new. In part (and the parts are interrelated) the changes spring from new insights into the nature of knowledge, the potentialities of man, and the complementary roles of those who learn and those who teach.

The question of curriculum has been resolved down through the ages in a tug of war between the forces of conservatism and the forces of reform. In modern times—and especially in the United States—the pragmatic demands of an expanding industrial society, as seen in the land-grant colleges and technical institutes, have usually prevailed, however modified by philosophical concepts of the nature of man and by ideals of education. On balance, the prevailing force through the centuries has been conservative, and it has acted to keep the corpus of knowledge central to schooling.

Against the backdrop of conservative continuity, a long line of reformers has tried to reverse the order and to wrench the educational system around so that the learner, rather than what is learned, is central. This objective has motivated reformers at least since the Renaissance. Typical exemplars are Comenius, the great Czech bishop and educator, and Montaigne, the perfect spokesman of humanism.

In the sixteenth century Montaigne wrote:

The usual way [of tutors] is to bawl into a pupil's ears as if one were pouring water into a funnel, and the boy's business is simply to repeat what he is told. I would have the tutor amend this state of things, and begin straightaway to exercise the mind that he is training, according to its capacities. He should make his pupil taste things, select them, and distinguish them by his own powers of perception.

And he adds a tag from Cicero: "The authority of those who teach is very often a hindrance to those who wish to learn." A century later Comenius wrote that "the beginning and end of our Didactic will be to seek and find a method by which teachers teach less and learners learn more." So down the centuries, through Rousseau and Pestalozzi to John Dewey and Montessori and beyond, the reformers have tried to gear the content and methods of education to the nature and needs of the student. But, although the specific content of the curriculum changed with the changing years, there was always in any given period a set curriculum at the center of the formal process of education—whether it was the trivium and quadrivium of the medieval university or the three R's of the little red schoolhouse in nineteenth-century America.

Then, at the beginning of the twentieth century, something happened with no precedent in the history of education. There was a tide in the affairs of this nation that swelled to prominence the eclectic educational ideas of philosopher John Dewey and psychologist William James, and brought the idea of the student as center of the educational process into active service in American schools. It was, as Lawrence Cremin has said, a truly Copernican revolution. Describing the influence of reform at the turn of the century, Cremin wrote in *The Transformation of the School:*

> It helped shift the focus of teaching to the student, asserting that no education could be worthy, much less efficient, that persisted in ignoring his nature, his needs, and his development. Moreover, it threw new emphasis on the scientific study of feelings, dispositions, and attitudes as elements in which education has an undeniable stake. . . . Now, the "given" of the [educational] equation was no longer the school with its well-defined content and purposes, but the children with their particular backgrounds and needs. . . .
> The shift was truly Copernican, its effects, legion. . . . Reformers had a field day, as did sentimentalists, and American schools were never quite the same again.[1]

There is no need to review here the aftermath of this wave of reform. For better or worse, the schools were, as Cremin says, transformed. In the decades following the first surge of utopian reform that proposed to improve man and society through the schools, many forces acted to distort and divert the initial impulse.

---

[1] Lawrence A. Cremin, *The Transformation of the School: Progressivism in American Education, 1876–1957* (New York: Alfred A. Knopf, 1961), pp. 103–104.

Not the least of these forces was dissension and misunderstanding and opportunism on the part of the lesser men who tried to put the great new ideas into practice. John Dewey himself lived to disown the movement he had inspired.

In Cremin's words:

. . . Dewey sought to substitute for the older curriculum he so roundly criticized a new program that was better planned, better designed, better organized. Convinced that his own innovations were far from final, he saw the continuing quest for further improvement as the central task of a science of education. He was destined for disappointment; . . . later he pronounced progressive education a failure, a movement that had destroyed well but too soon abandoned the more difficult task of building something better to replace what had been done away with.[2]

It is noteworthy and ironic that John Dewey, while decrying the excesses of the traditional school and of conventional teaching methods, never denied the intellectual purposes of schooling nor the importance of scholarship. And early in his career he sharply censured the kind of fuzzy practice into which his own ideas would one day be translated. Dewey wrote in 1902: "Save as the teacher knows, knows wisely and thoroughly, the race-expression which is embodied in that thing we call the Curriculum, the teacher knows neither what the student's present power, capacity, or attitude is, nor yet how it is to be asserted, exercised, and realized."

America's growing industrial might, the flood of immigrants to her towns and cities, the steady buildup of universal compulsory education—these and other developments irresistibly spurred the transformation of the public schools. On the way to the modern schoolhouse some funny things happened to the curriculum. To begin with, the schools introduced all manner of new courses that were presumably attuned to the needs of youth. Many of them were utilitarian or peripheral; many were watered-down versions of the old disciplines. Since, in most cases, new courses were simply

2 *Ibid.*, p. 142.

tacked onto the old, schools were soon offering a bizarre hodge-podge of subjects and nonsubjects. At the same time, during decades marked by an explosion of knowledge and revolutionary new concepts on all fronts, courses in many of the old-line disciplines fell disastrously out of date, as did the teachers who taught them. The gap grew particularly wide in mathematics and the physical sciences, with the greatest deterioration in the high school but with intellectual slack diffused throughout the school system.

Concurrently—and paradoxically—this period saw the rise of a full-blown specialty known as curriculum development, which was to spawn thousands of experts and to pre-empt untold millions of teacher-hours for committee work in school systems all over the land. The reader who has only a casual acquaintance with public schooling and its history may be surprised to learn that this vast body of endeavor had little or nothing to do with *subject matter*. It had little or nothing to do with improving, or even updating, the *content* of school offerings, nor with improving the teacher's grasp and communication of subjects.

We find ourselves in a Lewis Carroll fantasy where words take off on their own and renounce their parentage. The word "curriculum," which once meant (and outside the educational pale still means) a course of study or a program of courses, grew and swelled under the ministrations of curriculum-development experts until it became synonymous with life itself. I am not exaggerating. Here are a few authoritative definitions from schoolmen in the best of standing (the quotations come from a textbook called *Issues in Curriculum Development: A Book of Readings*[3] which, though published as late as 1959, appears to be unaware of or indifferent to the all-important national curriculum revisions, then well launched). In 1936 Harold Rugg offered this definition:

The "curriculum" . . . is really the entire program of the school's work. It is the essential *means* of education. It is *everything* the

[3] Marvin E. Alcorn and James M. Linley (eds.), *Issues in Curriculum Development: A Book of Readings* (Yonkers-on-Hudson, N.Y.: World Book Co., 1959).

students and their teachers do. Thus it is twofold in nature, being made up of activities, the things done, and of the materials with which they are done. [Mr. Rugg's emphasis][4]

Twenty years later, this was the message from Saylor and Alexander in a book called *Curriculum Planning*:

The curriculum is the sum total of the school's efforts to influence learning, whether in the classroom, on the playground, or out of school.[5]

The editors of *Issues* note that the Dictionary of Education gives three basic definitions of "curriculum," plus a two-page listing for "some forty sub-entries, including activity, articulated, broad fields, child-centered, correlated, integrated, social, traditional, and vocational." On their own, the editors then add the following summary, which rather gives the show away:

Three basically different definitions [of curriculum] were identified in the literature: the first in terms of the experiences of children under the jurisdiction of the school, the second in terms of social need and design for institutionalized education, the third in terms of the psychological changes in children brought about by their school activities.[6]

In citing these quotations from the quite recent past, and in taking issue with the bloated concept of curriculum that came to prevail in the schools, I don't want to revive old animosities or indulge in the easy sport of burlesquing educational excesses. It is my purpose, rather, by stating the background baldly, to make crystal clear the import of the curriculum reforms now under way. Reform, to be effective, must go beyond a mere updating and reorganization of the content of school programs, imperative and difficult as these tasks are. The overriding need is nothing less than

[4] *Ibid.*, p. 4. Quote originally taken from Harold Rugg, *American Life and the School Curriculum* (Boston: Ginn and Co., 1936), p. 18.
[5] *Ibid.*, p. 4. Quote originally from J. Galen Saylor and William M. Alexander, *Curriculum Planning for Better Teaching and Learning* (New York: Rinehart and Co., 1954), p. 5.
[6] *Ibid.*, p. 4. Quote originally from Carter V. Good (ed.), *Dictionary of Education* (New York: McGraw-Hill, 1945), pp. 113–115.

to redress prevailing concepts of what and how the schools should teach. Those who are revising the curriculum are also revising the definition of a curriculum.

Before going on, I think it only fair to set down certain compensatory truths, obvious though they may be. What happened to the curriculum in prewar America was no sinister scheme foisted by an educational cabal on the unsuspecting public, but was a response to many pressing demands. The "transformation" of the schools, while sweeping, was by no means as complete or devastating as in summary it sounds; the power and extent of any educational change is modified by the inertia of tradition and the recalcitrance (or good sense) of individual teachers or principals. And, above all, the bloating of the word "curriculum" into a synonym for "life" had its origin, like so much else, in a seminal and highly meritorious idea of Dewey's; its ultimate distortion was a prime example of the untoward results of good intentions gone wrong.

This particular idea was, in simplest terms, to foster the learning and the development of the child by relating school subjects to the child's experience outside of school, and—with this end in view— to involve the whole community in the building of the curriculum. It was a provocative idea and could produce excellent educational results. But its built-in risks, in retrospect, are all too apparent. Dewey himself never intended to *substitute* community planning and real-life situations for the body of knowledge. And, of course, no school however quixotic ever tossed subject matter out completely, all the antiprogressives to the contrary.

What did happen, in far too many schools, was that curriculum developers were carried away by the techniques and apparatus of "planning" (another word with its own special meaning to educators); form displaced function. The change in the pattern of curriculum building was (to quote the *Issues* editors again) "from selection of materials by experts who organized them according to the logic of a field, to the participation of teachers, pupils, and the community in identifying goals to be achieved and ways to reach them." And observe, to clinch the point, that in the editors' summary of the "literature," quoted above, not one of the "three basically different definitions" of curriculum mentioned subject matter; all three of them construed curriculum in terms either of the child's experiences or of social need or of psychological change. This—in so far as real teachers and principals took it seriously— was de-emphasizing subject matter indeed.

The transformation of the curriculum in the two or three decades before World War II and the rise of the peculiar "science" of curriculum planning were matched and in part inspired by developments in educational theory and methods. These were the years when educational psychology came into its own. The idiom is sadly apt: for educational psychology was early cut adrift from its theoretical moorings and abandoned by the academicians to its own increasingly diffuse and unproductive devices.

At the outset teachers and educators looked to psychology as a source of wisdom that would throw light on dark corners of the learning process and would produce practical guidance on methods. No doubt there was considerable naïveté in these expectations, as William James gently tried to warn the teachers of his day. In any event, the "new science" evolved in a way that made its findings less and less available for the day-to-day needs of teachers. From around the turn of the century on, what had originally been a broad stream of research and speculation into the long-range aspects of learning gradually branched into two distinct channels, which soon were following quite independent courses. On the one hand, the academic psychologists pursued their pure research and investigations on a level remote from the imperatives of the classroom; unlike their great precursors and certain of their European contemporaries, they concentrated more and more on intensive laboratory studies of simple types of learning. It was the age of the rat. Well do I remember my own experiments on the relative effects of strychnine, caffeine, and just plain water on rats as they learned to run an early electrical maze. (I found no differences.)

Educational psychologists, on the other hand, under the dominant influence of Edward Thorndike, became increasingly absorbed in measurement per se—"the measurement of measurement"—and in studies of the social and developmental (i.e., nonintellectual) aspects of learning. "Whatever exists at all exists in some amount; if it exists in some amount it can be measured." Before long the typical academic psychologist and his opposite number in educational psychology belonged for all practical purposes to two separate disciplines.

In general, the psychological theory that chiefly influenced the training of teachers, teaching methods, and the conduct of schools in the first half of the twentieth century was compounded of elements of behaviorism and traces of the newer Gestalt and field theories. In reaction against the old "faculty psychology" of the traditional nineteenth-century school, which put a premium on the most dry and remote studies for their mind-and-memory-training quality, educators tried to take account of the "learning situation" as a whole and the interplay between child and society. They repudiated the now outmoded theory of transfer, which posited connections between one kind of learning and another, and they wholeheartedly subscribed to the Thorndike revision which limited transfer to the most marginal role. Inevitably the effects of all these theories, discredited or no, persisted in actual classroom practice.

Though by mid-century there was no claim to a unified theory of learning, there was considerable confidence on the part of educators, especially the teachers of teachers, that research had uncovered many of the basic components for such a theory and that the schools were well set on a course marked Truth. In his monumental work *Teaching-Learning Theory and Teacher Education, 1890 to 1950*, published in 1952, Walter S. Monroe wrote:

Although it is impossible to be certain in regard to the future, there is, in the opinion of the present writer, substantial support for the hypothesis that the current theory of teaching is sound in general outline and that future developments will be of the order of refinements and systematization of formulation. . . . In view of the large amount of research underlying the present thinking about learning, it seems unlikely that revolutionary discoveries will be made.[7]

Developments of the past decade and a half have made startling changes in this picture of comfortable assurance and conviction, even though no new and unified teaching-learning theory is close at hand, nor have all, or even many, of the old convictions been routed by new research. What is going on is more subtle and various: a statement closer to the facts would point to the discovery of new insights, a reformulation of old truths to suggest new meanings, the recognition that new means are now available to put well-established convictions into effect, and suffusing all, the sense that our educational system—whether "traditional" or "progressive" or the two in uneasy combination—has grossly underestimated the learning potential of students and the intrinsic educational power in the nature of knowledge itself.

Many elements have contributed to the present state of change and transition: the revolution in instructional technology, the heartening revival of scholarly concern with the school curriculum, the new or revived interest of behavioral scientists in the kind of learning that takes place in school. What all this activity on many different fronts can mean to schoolteachers and their students is the drastic revision of subject matter so that it has more meaning and lasting usefulness, plus a reordering of the roles of teacher and student that will release the individual student's potential power for learning (or "self-teaching," as the Montessorians call it) and the individual teacher's powers to inspire and guide the process in his particular way.

Work has now been in progress for some time on all the principal subjects of the school curriculum: the physical sciences and mathematics in the vanguard, the social sciences, the humanities, the arts trailing behind. In some cases—mathematics, for instance—reforms were initiated by diverse groups of scholars, at

[7] Walter S. Monroe, *Teaching-Learning Theory and Teacher Education, 1890 to 1950* (Urbana: University of Illinois Press, 1952), p. 79.

different times, with different objectives. Many of the revisions were started a good while back, in the early fifties or before, as projects of the various learned societies. But it took the educational anxieties that Sputnik caused to produce the sharply accelerated curriculum efforts of the 1960's, which are distinguished by national scope, joint involvement of scholars and schoolteachers, and important financial support from the federal government and the foundations.

In so far as reform was provoked by out-of-date curriculum in the public schools, the need can be readily illustrated. In physics, for example, few high school teachers had adequate preparation to begin with. High school biology was largely "a parade of animal and plant life with endless names" (in the words of Dr. John Moore of Columbia University), taking little cognizance of basic concepts like genetics and evolution. Dr. Paul Hurd of Stanford University, another biologist connected with the high-level program to modernize biology teaching, has said that science offerings in general were often "skimmings and smatterings, dribbles and dabbles of assorted facts and generalities . . . [with] facts . . . divorced from anything that might be called the processes of science, sterilized of their beauty and left dangling without a place in the scheme of things."[8]

In mathematics and the sciences, at least, it could be argued that the culprit was time itself. New discoveries in the twentieth century had revolutionized these subjects, and it is not surprising that the schools were left far behind. Not even this excuse, however, can help explain the glaring deficiencies in the typical English curriculum and in a shocking number of English teachers. In 1961 a nationwide study by the National Council of Teachers of English revealed "chaotic conditions"; among other dreary findings, the Council estimated that fewer than half of all teachers of English throughout the school system had adequate preparation.[9]

[8] Gene Currivan, "Teaching of High-School Biology to be Drastically Modernized," *New York Times,* May 24, 1960.
[9] Fred M. Hechinger, "Lag in English: Poor Preparation of Students Is Laid to 'Chaotic Conditions,' " *New York Times,* Jan. 29, 1961.

I should like to reintroduce at this point the name of a remarkable educational catalyst who is, of all things, an experimental psychologist. This is Jerome S. Bruner, the director of Harvard's Center for Cognitive Studies, and author of *The Process of Education*.[10] It had been a long, long time since a book about education had exerted such an extraordinary influence.

The Process of Education was the outcome of a government sponsored conference with Bruner serving as chairman, held at Woods Hole, Massachusetts, in 1959 to discuss the improvement of science education in the public schools. The jacket states that the author, in setting forth his views of the conference conclusions, also "outlines a challenging new philosophy of education." This, in essence, is what the Bruner book does. And it is the concentrated excitement of the book's ideas about teaching and learning that accounts for its quite remarkable impact. In less than 100 pages of polished prose, Bruner grappled with basic questions of education in the light of curriculum experiments that had been taking place all over the country for five years past.

"We begin with the hypothesis that any subject can be taught effectively in some intellectually honest form to any child at any stage of development." So begins Chapter Three. It is a famous sentence by now, which we have already had occasion to cite. It assailed the readiness-for-learning concept, and this was but one of the sacred cows of the "new" pedagogy that Bruner challenged. Other major themes emphasized the *structure* inherent in each subject, the essential role of intuition, curiosity, and *discovery* in the learning process, and the potential motivating power intrinsic to the subject matter itself.

In singling out Bruner's book I want to make clear my meaning. I certainly do not mean that this "challenging new philosophy of education" has swept the workaday world of schools and colleges. What I am stressing, rather, is the impact of this book—and subsequent exposition of related ideas—on up-and-coming school

[10] Jerome S. Bruner, *The Process of Education* (Cambridge: Harvard University Press, 1960).

administrators and on those who comprise the educational establishment.

Reaction to the Bruner book has been by no means all of a piece, of course. There was enthusiasm, even fervor, in some quarters. There was also skepticism, and a weary "so-what" response. I know first-rate superintendents and principals who saw the book as a beacon of educational light. On the other hand, administrators of equal caliber were unimpressed. I heard one principal, for instance, credit *Process of Education* for providing a "quick, philosophic glow" but no more. In general, the skeptical reaction stems from one of two objections, or both: (1) the ideas were nothing new; (2) the ideas were just that—hypotheses yet to be proved, only tangentially connected with the national curriculum revisions, and perhaps of dubious merit and limited application.

Bruner himself credited many of the ideas he presented with "long and honorable lineages in the history of educational thought." The prime source of the book's psychological excitement is the work of Piaget and the so-called Geneva school and of other European innovators. One could amass many references, European and American, attesting to the importance of "structure" in the learning process, and to the educational merit of fostering the sense of "discovery." Way back in 1947 there was even a presidential commission whose major recommendation was for more "emphasis on the student's acquiring familiarity with the processes of inquiry and discovery."

Granted, then, many of the ideas Bruner expounded are not really new. But to the thousands of people who took heart and inspiration from the book the ideas somehow conveyed a new spirit and a new hope. If nothing else, Bruner seemed to have achieved a small miracle of emphasis and timing in bringing together, at such a critical and receptive period in American education, old but untried ideas of tremendous power plus new insights into such areas as motivation and readiness.

The second objection—that the hypotheses were unproved and

up to then scarcely exemplified in the curriculum reforms—is valid as far as it goes. Of the major curriculum studies then in progress, only a few exemplified to any marked degree teaching principles based on structure, learning-by-discovery, and so on. (There are a good many more applications by now.) A close study of the Bruner book, as a matter of fact, reveals no explicit claims for the curriculum studies that formed the basis for the Woods Hole conference. Indeed, there is reason to believe that the Chairman's Report was considerably bigger than the sum of its parts and that Bruner's role exceeded the modest one he claimed for himself as recorder of "the sense of the meeting."

If Bruner was, in fact, projecting a philosophy that transcended the evidence, *Process of Education* soon began to assume the aspects of a self-fulfilling prophecy. Jerome Bruner himself was never in any doubt about the revolutionary nature of the events and ideas in which he became so actively involved. As he wrote to me not long after the publication of his book:

I do not think that the present product is a re-emphasis of old themes. I think our current conceptions are wildly revolutionary, way beyond my furthest expectations when I wrote *The Process of Education,* and that all of us feel as if we have a big bear by the tail. After two years of hard work on mathematics learning, for example, I have literally reached the point of being quite unable to say how far we can reasonably expect an ordinary 12-year-old to have progressed if he had been taught decent mathematics well during the five preceding years. The change in my view and in the view of others comes not only from a new conception of human beings as information processing systems but also from a radically changed conception of what is the nature of mathematics and what is worth learning about it first.

That many of the new ideas are untried and in need of experiment and verification is abundantly clear. No one claims otherwise. The Bruner book is larded with references to the need for further specific research—I counted close to fifty. There is no question that these powerful ideas for the advancement of learning and teaching must be tried out—and inevitably altered and refined—in the schools, by real teachers and real students.

Many new ideas, these included, are already under trial, with the momentum provided by the federal outlays back of the most important of the national curriculum revisions and, in the past few years, by the infinitely larger sums that Congress has voted for educational reform and improvement. Many of the curriculum reforms have been tested and revised repeatedly, and extended to many school levels. The impact of the curriculum-reform movement on teacher training—particularly in-service training—is potentially tremendous (in *pre-service* training the potential is largely unrealized). Inspired in part by the national movement, many local school systems have undertaken curriculum revisions of their own, sometimes incorporating and adapting the national programs.

The major curriculum revisions and the far-reaching implications of the ideas advanced by Bruner and other behavioral scientists have caused a tremendous stir in educational circles, with repercussions up and down the Establishment generally. I have a friend in education who advances the dictum: no educator ever admits publicly that he was wrong. Certainly the dictum applies to many of the bandwagon emanations from establishment dialecticians and unreconstructed progressive educators, which have run the gamut from denigrating the new movement as no more than a restatement of what every modern educator knows to denouncing it as rank retrogression to a dark pre-Dewey past. But these voices were in a minority, and are growing fainter. The predominant reaction from educators has been a recognition of the importance of the new curriculum revisions and the new approaches to learning, colored by wry gratitude for this belated attention from Academia and a troubled sense of their own part in making reform necessary. An encouraging official position has been that of the National Education Association, which in 1959 initiated the Project on Instruction "to define and state the views of the organized profession . . . on the directions, tasks, and quality of the instructional program in the challenging decade ahead." This project, which draws on scholars and experts outside the NEA's world, reflects a serious long-range approach to curriculum problems, taking full account of the new movements afoot. The NEA has now established the Center for the Study of Instruction which, building on the work and recommendations of the Project, is charged with the continuing study of educational questions, the search for new ideas, and the provision of information and active assistance to schools and colleges undertaking innovations.

Perhaps the most disarming reaction came from Arthur Foshay of Teachers College, Columbia, an outright spokesman for the "self-contained classroom" and an establishment stalwart. Retiring in 1961 as president of the NEA's Association for Supervision and Curriculum Development, he delivered a remarkably candid speech which, in effect, embraced the new curriculum ideas and their psychological base, and took his own group to task for what he called "flawed theory." Among other things, Dr. Foshay said:

> I have to say that the theory on which I was behaving now seems to me to have been true, but inadequate. Hindsight says that it was flawed from the beginning by a failure to acknowledge a third element necessary for the making of intelligent curriculum decisions. . . .
>
> I learned that curriculum decision should be based on a knowledge of the child and of society. . . . What was left out of this theory was the nature of organized knowledge. As professional educators, we have taken organized knowledge . . . for granted.

Since that speech Dr. Foshay has done much—over television, in conferences and workshops—to push beyond the tiresome futility of name-calling and blame-assigning to pull all forces together toward better education.

As someone remarked not long ago, the 1960's saw education restored to academic respectability as a field for psychologists after a quarter century or more of obloquy. By way of counterpoint, juxtapose the following statement, made at about the same time in the *Review of Educational Research*: "After a quarter-century of virtual neglect, during which educational and developmental psychologists have emphasized personality and social development in teaching and research, cognitive development has emerged as an important focus of research and general interest for the educator." One of the hopeful auguries for improved education is not only the rapprochement between schoolmen and scholars, but also that between scholars in the behavioral sciences, especially psychology, and the field of education. A new unity of substance and method is, I believe, emerging that holds great promise for the future.

What seems to be coming, at long last, is an attempt to relate important findings on the nature of knowledge and the process of learning to the complicated practical needs of average teachers and average students. There is the real possibility that more than half a century's psychological insights derived from highly simplified laboratory conditions, plus the new European-inspired findings about intelligence and mental activity, may be transmuted into exciting classroom achievement. To this end, widespread and imaginative *classroom* experimentation is essential. It is still true, as William James told the Cambridge teachers seventy-five years ago, that "psychology can state the laws: concrete tact and talent alone can work them to useful results."[11] But if the so-called laws of learning cannot be applied wholecloth and directly to the classroom, it is only there that they can be tried and modified to serve education.

In general, we still are ignorant, not so much of processes and conditions that promote learning nor of human growth and development but of general theories to explain these processes and practical ways to exploit them. As Ole Sand, director of the N.E.A. Center for the Study of Instruction, says, "Nirvana is a long way off in curriculum land." In particular, we really know little about the complex forms of learning, about the kind, for example, that goes on in classrooms; the revived interest of academic psychologists is shaking up the whole accepted body of "principles" and "laws." Certain basic findings about *learners* will doubtless withstand the shakeup (individual differences, growth, rates of learn-

[11] William James, *Talks to Teachers on Psychology; and to Students on Some of Life's Ideals* (New York: W. W. Norton, 1958), p. 68.

ing, mental age, specific aptitudes), but new concepts about *learning* and the nature of knowledge seem to be in the making that may greatly alter and improve our management of teachers and students in the classroom. These new (or refreshed or restated) concepts embrace such matters as structure, reinforcement, readiness, and motivation. New ideas about motivation, especially, are bound to affect education and its psychologists. As the late Gordon Allport once wrote:

> I think our educational psychology has been mostly wrong about the process of learning—or perhaps not so much wrong as woefully incomplete. . . . Love and social reward (as well as some fear of punishment) sustain the processes of attention and retention. . . . All these incentives are extraneous to the subject matter. . . . It would be going too far to put the blame for intellectual apathy onto our current teaching of educational psychology. Yet I am inclined to feel somewhat punitive about the matter. Psychology has not yet settled down to the problem of transforming matters of fact—whose acquisition current learning theories explain fairly well—into autonomous matters of importance [Allport's phrase for "value"]—which they do not explain at all.

Opinions differ on many of the "new" hypotheses, on the extent to which they actually do (or should) influence curriculum reform, on the degree of hopeful innovation involved in all this, and on many related points. My own view is sanguine. I set it forth tentatively, not because it lacks conviction but because it is inevitably based on numerous yet-to-be-proved assumptions and hypotheses. I believe that the current efforts of scholars, school-teachers, educational organizations, administrators, and behavioral scientists—if continued and strengthened—will lead to profound improvements in the way the schools convey knowledge and understanding. Even though much of the early curriculum revision has been confined to updating and is subject to valid criticism (for imbalance, for instance, and for concentration on subjects in isolation), I am convinced that more radical and coordinated revision—to make the "substance" of education more learnable and teachable—will come increasingly to the fore.

6 · Education's Technological Revolution I: New Tools For Learning

Technology can set the teacher free. In an educational future which is possible but by no means inevitable I see the teacher raised to a role of dignity and distinction that will draw on all his human resources: intellectual, cultural, temperamental. Technology, in the broad sense that includes organization, can be harnessed to this human purpose. It can also, in its own right, aid learning and immeasurably enlarge the scope of knowledge and experience for teacher and student alike.

With the current surge of public interest in education, the subject matter of this chapter is bound to have a familiar ring. The mass media have made nearly everybody aware of teaching-by-television, language laboratories, "teaching machines," other mechanical and electronic marvels, and to a lesser degree of organizational innovations like team teaching and nongraded schools. Cartoons that play variations on the theme of the robot teacher and computerized learning have replaced, in *The New Yorker* and elsewhere, cartoons and jokes about the little monsters of progressive education. I shall not try, then, to review in the compass of a single chapter the item-by-item progress of educational technology. Instead, assuming some familiarity on the part of the reader, I shall try to interpret that progress, and such projections as can be made from it, as it affects school improvement. Since I have been closely identified with the recent history of technology in the schools, and in particular with the encouragement of television and of team teaching, it should surprise no one that I am biased in their favor. What may be useful to the reader in this chapter is my effort to explain *why* I am biased in their favor—what a decade and more of personal involvement in the movement to use technology in education has taught me about its benefits for students and teachers.

The resistance of the schools to the forces of technology is a clear example of cultural lag. As suggested earlier, the industrial revolution that transformed every other phase of society in the eighteenth and nineteenth centuries left education and the world of teaching virtually untouched. If now at last modern technology reaches the schools, it is with the compounded force of what is variously called the second industrial revolution, the electronics revolution, or simply automation. Now we expect schools to make a tremendous leap forward and to skip a whole stage of evolution that has already brought the rest of industrialized society to the brink of automation. What confronts the schools is not unlike the prospect before the underdeveloped countries of the world that strive to change overnight from a pastoral or farming economy to a full-fledged industrial society.

Until recently, the schools had scarcely altered the instructional pattern of centuries which had persisted since the introduction of the printed book. The basic elements of this pattern were and to an unfortunate extent still are teacher, students, and books within the four walls of the classroom. Before the educational ferment of the postwar years, the twentieth century wrought little change on this pattern. Radio, film, all the apparatus subsumed under the title "audiovisual aids," were mere embellishments to the age-old triad.

Many causes explain the long technological backwardness of education. Among the more important are these: inadequate financial support for schools; the decentralization of our school system, which, as I said, slowed the spread of innovations; the insulation of the world of education from influences at work in the world outside; the lack of competition and of an accepted criterion of efficiency; and—least tangible but perhaps most important of all—an implicit feeling shared by teachers and laymen alike of the irrelevance, or even downright impropriety, of applying technology to the closed society of the schools and to the traditional teacher-pupil relationship. These conservative forces melded to form a block to the use of technology in education. As a result, the schools never organized for change.

Industrialization, as industry quickly came to recognize, means much more than the mere introduction of machines; it also requires profound changes in policy and in the organization of work. When the schools did deign to use a little technology, perhaps radio or motion pictures, they simply tried to fit it into the conventional instructional system just as the motor was originally attached to a horse-drawn buggy, without realizing that to get the good of a major innovation entails redesign of the whole enterprise. So the experiments petered out, and Edison's dream, for example, that the motion picture would bring the best teachers to every pupil never came to pass.

The resistance of educators to technology involves many ironies, of course. One is the spectacle of an institution admittedly central to the age of technology ignoring technology in its own operation. Education preaches what it doesn't practice, and fails to apply its own precepts. The teachers on whom we depend to satisfy America's endless need for technically sophisticated manpower have themselves been frozen into molds of "conventional wisdom" and time-tried inefficiency.

At last we are seeing the belated and often still reluctant acceptance of technology by the world of education. Again, a variety of factors are at work. To start with, all the elements mentioned earlier that created the postwar educational crisis also acted to break through educational conservatism, open the way to innovations, and lend urgency to the search for new ways to use available teaching talent fully and to augment it by effective means however unorthodox. The public, at first uneasy and, after the Sputniks, really alarmed over the inadequacies of the schools, was willing to spend more money on education. Furthermore, the layman's distrust of technology in education was mitigated in part by the massive wartime use of large-group and mechanized instruction in the armed services. Millions of servicemen had directly experienced high-speed indoctrination in languages and complex techniques of many kinds. They and their kin were open to the idea that what worked in teaching how to transmit the Morse code or how to troubleshoot a tank's engine might also work in teaching multiplication or electronic circuitry. (As director of the Standards and Curriculum Division, Bureau of Naval Personnel, during the war, I was among those who saw and devised new procedures for training men rapidly.) Servicemen's testimony, the wide publicity given to these military educational achievements, and the accelerated use of similar methods in industrial training made the public favorably aware of the innovations.

Other postwar developments helped to encourage change. One was the availability of new communication instruments with exciting potential for teaching, such as television and electronic tapes, and of an older instrument in a new form specifically designed for teaching, namely, programed instruction or the self-teaching "machine." Finally, the postwar application of substantial sums of money to educational technology gave needed impetus and support to all the varied factors that favored change.

There are signs that an instructional revolution may finally hit the schools. Its force and potential are tremendous. Yet what has been accomplished so far is the merest beginning. It will be years before the full impact of technology makes itself felt in the far reaches of America's vast educational enterprise. But make no mistake: the forces at work can, could, and might radically transform the schools and the role of the teacher. We shall need to find out much more than we know now about the best ways to use the new technology, about timing and specific application and organization. In the process we shall doubtless do many things wrong before we do them right; we may abandon devices that now seem promising for others that cannot now even be imagined; we may eventually arrive at patterns of school organization and deployment of students and teachers wholly different from present experimental designs. In the process we shall without question violate hallowed traditions and shibboleths. No true reform is possible otherwise, nor can it take place without its inevitable concomitant of dispute, misunderstanding, resistance, hostility. All these and more are present now as the revolution gets under way and will doubtless gather force as it proceeds.

When I speak of a *radical* transformation of the schools and of teaching I am using the word in its simplest dictionary sense. The potential power of the instructional revolution can alter the very roots of formal education; what is afoot is no mere tinkering with the peripheral attributes of schooling; and that is why "revolution" is the proper word. Technology fully and wisely exploited will force a re-examination of the essentials of learning and teaching and make us look anew at the content of formal education, at the standard arrangements of classroom and grade level that frame the content, at the respective roles of student and teacher. The reappraisal, frequently quite agonizing, has begun, and is gathering momentum. Out of it should ultimately come—if the gods grant us luck, wisdom, and time—an educational system better in every way.

For the technological revolution is matched by the re-examination of curriculum and the learning process summarized in the preceding chapter. Indeed, it is arbitrary to divide these developments as if to suggest that here, on the one hand, is technology, and there, on the other, curriculum and concomitant methods to be applied like separate remedies to the ills of education. Obviously this is folly; the reforms are inextricably related. In fact, one of the dangers in the present educational ferment is the very tendency to treat as separate these modes of improvement. They are separate only in the sense that highly specialized knowledge and talents are involved in their respective development and application and in this sense, and for clarity and convenience, they can be talked of separately. But they must flow together in the life of the school, as wise administrators know. Schools sometimes try to apply reform superficially, like a poultice: a bit of the new math here, a little TV there. The mistake is fundamental, but in many cases self-correcting: for, as we shall see, so interrelated are curriculum and technology, method and matter, that changing one almost always leads to changing the other. Thus, for example, a true improvement in a high school's science program is almost bound to utilize television, tapes, a variety of technological devices. By the same token, schools that seriously do undertake programmed instruction soon find that the rearrangement of staff patterns inexorably leads to a review and improvement of the substance that the staff and the machines teach, to say nothing of their ways of teaching it.

This chapter and the next will observe the convention that the technology and organization of instruction can be discussed apart from its substance and methods, asking the reader to compensate for the flaws of human communication by letting his mind's ear attend to a contrapuntal refrain that says: form and substance are bound together, and woe to the educator who forgets it.

In education's long and often unformulated resistance to technology we can isolate certain recurrent themes. Paramount is the instinctive, almost atavistic opposition of man to machine. To convey, for instance, the depth of feeling in some quarters against technological instruction, commentators often invoke the image of the Luddites who tried to stem the Industrial Revolution by smashing labor-saving machinery. It is a precise enough image to express the opposition of those teachers who see in television or programed instruction or language laboratories a sinister mechanistic threat to their own livelihood. That technology has provoked real uneasiness and even fear on the part of teachers is undeniable.

It is also sad. For such reactions bespeak both misunderstanding of technology and a deep-seated insecurity among teachers as to their own roles.

It would be wrong to impute these anxieties to the generality of teachers. At their height perhaps they affected only a minority, made up of the least competent and the least self-confident. At the other end of the scale, many teachers of high competence, young and old, sometimes have tended to take a critical view of technology, putting it in its subhuman place. Teaching machines, television, films, tapes, computers, and projectors they dismiss as mere gadgetry, specious adjuncts to the high business of teaching and learning. But between these extremes, many teachers are open-minded and intellectually curious enough to want to learn more before making up their minds.

In lieu of trying to tell the full story of the development of educational technology since the war I propose to set the stage with an over-all summary as backdrop for singling out a few examples of educational innovation that illustrate the range of technology's utility and its versatility in enhancing both teaching and learning.

Those of us whose schooling goes back to the first decades of the century or earlier are not apt to recall that teachers of our youth used any audio-visual aids beyond the immemorial chart, chalk, and blackboard. But as parents or innocent bystanders we do recall the emphasis placed on audiovisual aids in the decades just before World War II. Forward-looking educators spoke highly of them at PTA meetings and in print; up-and-coming school systems appointed assistant superintendents or specialists in charge of audio-visual aids and colleges and universities created special audio-visual centers. Part of the scrap bag legacy of progressive education was the notion that any teacher really on his toes would make use of the latest films and such. The emphasis throughout was on the *visual* in audio-visual; radio and the phonograph made scarcely a dent in the relentless orthodoxy of the schools except, perhaps, in the primary grades. And the strange metamorphosis that overtook textbooks in those days stemmed in part from the effort to make them compete, in garish illustrations and abbreviated text, with the most visual of the visual aids. It sometimes seemed as though the true audio-visual enthusiasts were really out to destroy the book. In some circles, "audio-visual" became a swearword.

As is often the case, the cure that was designed to remedy a real defect (in this case, the schools' overemphasis on the verbal and bookish) went too far and proved worse than the original disease. The banality of many of the earlier teaching aids has been widely exposed. Intellectuals and impassioned humanists were not the only ones who defended the book and the printed word to the death; many a working schoolteacher even more effectively preserved the bookish tradition of the schools by giving the merest routine obeisance to the audio-visual aids that were in vogue. In truth, many of them deserved a fair trial. I do not want to give the impression that the whole audio-visual movement in education was futile. It was no such thing. But in its proliferation of finicky aids with no organizational or philosophical changes to utilize them to the full the movement did little more than add to the store of textbooks an impressive roster of hardware (much, perhaps most, of it unused or underused). Radio, film, and recordings played little or no *integral* part in the classroom; they did not act to release the classroom teacher for the peculiarly human values he alone could provide.

In short, by the 1950's technology had scarcely gained a toehold in the school system. The technological innovations that had been adopted were usually ill-used and ineffective. In contrast to this record of slow stagnation, the progress in the past decade and a half has been much more promising. A few specifics are in order.

By 1969 schools and colleges all over the United States were making use, large or small, of such technological teaching aids as language laboratories, self-teaching machines, films, recordings, overhead projectors, tapes, computers, and computer-assisted instruction (CAI), as well as a multitude of lesser mechanical and electronic devices. On the horizon are new technologies with un-measurable potential, such as Peter Goldmark's EVR—Electronic Video Recording—that will provide, at small cost, a 7-inch reel holding a half-hour show in color, with stereophonic sound, or the entire Encyclopaedia Britannica.

And there's an astonishing renascence in the educational use of film. It comes in two parts. The first consists of determined new efforts to breathe life and inspiration into the moribund "class-room film." One straw in the wind was the emphasis on films manifest at the 1968 meeting of the American Historical Associa-tion. Professor William B. MacNeill, chairman of the University of Chicago's history department, reporting on a project the as-sociation had undertaken with funds from the U.S. Office of Education to improve films for high school and college use, de-clared that films eventually could carry the main burden of con-veying information and a "sense of sequence" to students. This millennium, however, could come about only with the production of worthwhile films of historical validity, and this in turn de-pended, Mr. MacNeill pointed out, on getting film makers and historians to work together and on expunging the traditional atti-tude of history teachers that film is an "intrusion" in the class-room. The currently available history films sampled by Mr. Mac-Neill and his committee were strikingly defective, falling generally into three categories: costume re-enactments of famous events, newsreels, and travelogues.

Meantime, a small New York publishing firm has incorporated a film company called the University-at-Large, working with his-torian Arthur Schlesinger, Jr., who, with other luminaries, will make ninety half-hour films to be ready for classroom use by 1970. Others are John Kenneth Galbraith, Jerome Bruner, Buckminster Fuller, Robert Lowell, and Stephen Spender. One of the first productions on the schedule is a film of Marshall McLuhan making a film of Marshall McLuhan making a film.

So maybe, after all, Thomas Edison's dream will come true. Far more exciting than this potential belated triumph, however, is the second aspect of the current revival of films in education. This is the virtual passion young people now display for movies—not just looking at them but *making* them. It began with college students, now it's getting into the high schools, and the first national Young Filmmakers' Conference, which was convened early in 1968 in New York City, really meant "young": it featured the products of kids, even toddlers. The source of this astonishing widespread interest of the young in film making is too complicated to explore here. What makes it feasible to indulge this interest is the fact that nowadays there is film-making equipment available that is at once inexpensive and easy to operate. Films can be made for almost any amount of money, from a few dollars to a few thousand. (One member of this newest wave of film-makers called his film 8½, to commemorate not Fellini but his $8.50 budget.)

All kinds of projects are in train to capitalize, in and out of school, on this phenomenon and to plumb its almost unimaginable possibilities for education, formal and otherwise. They range from university projects, such as one at Teachers College, Columbia, where Professor Lou Forsdale has long been pushing the great potential of 8mm equipment in education, to programs and contests sponsored by companies in the field (like Kodak and Bell & Howell), to small neighborhood enterprises. One of the patron saints of the whole movement is a McLuhan disciple named John M. Culkin, S.J., director of Fordham University's Center for Communications. Writing recently in the *New York Times* on the subject, Father Culkin said:

In general, the below-college groups look on film as a way of communicating something about themselves and their world. Film gives them a way of illumining and controlling their environment. It forces them to see, to select, and to interpret. It gives them a valuable experience in working as a member of a team. And for many students it opens an avenue of expression for feelings which otherwise might never have been communicated. Too often the schools give up on kids who can't scale the alphabet barrier and withhold experiences from them which could be communicated through other media. The likeli-

hood is that if you bring a student alive in one medium, he will come
alive across-the-board. Film seems to be a privileged medium for such
eye-to-eye resuscitation.

In the same piece Father Culkin singled out some of the young
people and *kinds* of young people caught up in the film-making
fever:

Tim Page is a filmmaker. He is ten years old. He has a problem. His
mother won't let him see any of Fellini's films. [Author's interruption:
I happened to see Master Page on an ETV program, along with some
of his works. His aplomb and sophistication were formidable.] Cristina
Rodriguez has just finished "My Movie," perhaps the first film ever
done by a three-year-old. A legend is already building around one 14-
year-old who has more than 80 films in the can. He now talks about
his "early period," the influence of Truffaut on his work, and his fear
that he may be over the hill by 16.
    And in the urban ghettos almost every city boasts of its crew of teen-
age filmmakers who are "telling where it's really at" on celluloid. The
word is out: film is in.

To turn to an entirely different kind of technology, the language
laboratory, unheard of before the war and a rarity even ten years
ago, has become a commonplace. It is essentially an arrangement
using tape recorders and an intercom system to provide individualized instruction in foreign languages by enabling students to
listen extensively to first-class accents and to record and check their
own pronunciation. The first language laboratories were concentrated in the colleges and universities, but in the aftermath of
Sputnik and the Conant reports the idea began to take hold in
the more up-and-coming high schools. By 1969 thousands of language laboratories were in operation in the public schools.
    In some cases they made strong language departments stronger
by making it possible for students to drill themselves, at their own
pace, so as to get the extensive practice that mastery of a new
language entails but that classroom teachers seldom have time for,
and to achieve much more precise pronunciation than the classroom teacher could usually provide. In other cases the language

laboratory, plus perhaps cooperative ventures among schools in sharing scarce specialists, made the difference between language study and no language study. As America became painfully aware in the 1950's, the postwar teacher shortage was most acute in foreign languages, mathematics, and science where the lack before the war had been greatest. The successes of the language laboratories have been tarnished by many disillusioning experiences deriving from the practical difficulties involved. But I believe the promise is there and will be fulfilled.

Valuable and promising as are all the new devices, two technological innovations in particular caught the public imagination during the 1950's. In very different ways they seemed to open up a whole new era of teaching and learning. In the ensuing years of wide experimentation, we have found out all manner of things about the potential—and the limitations—of both television and programed learning. We have found out how much more there is to find out, as well. But experiment has proved beyond any doubt the most important basic assumptions about the two devices: (1) that television is an instrument of almost unimaginable potential for *mass* instruction[1] and (2) that the self-teaching machine, or programed learning, is an instrument for *individual* instruction of at least equal potential.

Together they have not solved the teacher shortage, though some of the impetus behind their use sprang from this hope. They have yet to put a teacher out of a job and, in my view, they probably never will. But together, and in combination with other mechanical and elctronic devices, they can spread the influence of the best teachers and, by relieving them of tasks that technology could do as well or better, set teachers free to spend maximum time with students. This relationship between teacher and student has constituted the ideal of education since Socrates' day—concentrated interchange with small groups, work with individual students, discussions, probing, improvisation, and all the intangi-

[1] Recent developments suggest that TV can be flexibly adapted, as well, to *individual* instruction.

ble human values that the teaching process, at its highest, generates. Instructional television, as the Appendix indicates, has not yet realized this lofty goal, although it has progressed surprisingly far considering the sheer weight of dead tradition it has had to push aside (or push into motion). Programed instruction has fared somewhat better, though measured against its *potential*, its impact has been minimal, quantitatively and qualitatively.

By now one would suppose that every literate American has heard about the "teaching machine" (though only a few years ago a large percentage of teachers had not). Full-page ads in leading newspapers and magazines have promised to teach anyone anything in five minutes. If it were not for the inherent soundness of the basic idea, a person might have been tempted to dismiss the whole movement out of hand as a fascinating case study of faddism among professional educators and of commercial exploitation.

Behind the garish publicity, however, stand several compelling facts. Programed learning is based on distinctive, coherent, and thoroughly validated laboratory findings. It exemplifies psychological principles which have proved their effectiveness in the schools. The uniform results of diverse research studies show that students learn about twice as fast with programed instruction as with conventional methods.

The most succinct explanation of the basic idea behind programed learning that I know has been offered by Professor Eugene Galantier, who describes it as a new way of writing textbooks in interrogative rather than declarative sentences. Students learn best when their minds are engaged and active, and not by sitting and passively trying to "absorb" page after page of material. And they learn even better and faster if some kind of immediate feedback tells them they are actually learning. The message is: keep the student's mind active and responding, keep him mentally ducking and weaving to get the point and make the correct response, then give him the immediate reward of knowing he is right.

The writer of a program, then, begins by working out the most logical presentation of his subject matter. Then he breaks it down into the smallest possible steps to be learned. By exposing one of these units of information to the student, and immediately making him respond on its content, attention is riveted and the student's intellect engaged. The student can breeze through the program as fast as he can read it or he can ponder each question. But when he has finished it he will know the material, because his progress will have been controlled by constant correct responses to challenging questions.

This example consists of three frames from a linear program, *Basic Mathematics: A Problem Solving Approach* by R. H. O'Malley.[2] The linear format is used in this program, but the frames make extensive use of multiple-choice responses as well as constructed responses.

EQUATIONS

1.

An *equation* is a mathematical statement showing that two quantities have the same value. In an equation we use the equal sign (=) to show that the quantity on the left of the equal sign is equal to the quantity on the right of the .... sign.   equal
Decide which of the following expressions are equations. (Write *yes* or *no*)

	Yes or No	
a) $2 + 3 = 5$	....	yes
b) $3x + 2y$	....	no
c) $3 + 2 = 6 - 1$	....	yes
d) lwh	....	no
e) $0 = x - \dfrac{3}{2}$	....	yes

Problems "b" and "d" above are *not* equations because they do not have an .... sign.   equal
The word "equation," and the word "equal" are both derived from a Latin word which means "level" or "equal." This may help you to remember that an equation ALWAYS has an equal sign.

[2] *Basic Mathematics: A Problem Solving Approach*, by R. H. O'Malley (1963). Reprinted by permission of Addison-Wesley Publishing Co. All Rights Reserved.

2.

At this time, we do not have to know which numbers the letters in our equation represent, but we do know that our equation must include an equal sign. There should also be something on the left of the equal sign and something on the .... of the equal sign.   right

xy is NOT an equation, but $x = y$ IS an ....   equation

If it does not have an equal sign, then it is/is not .... an equation.   is not

See which of the following expressions are equations. (Write *yes* or *no*)

	Yes or No	
a) $4x = B$	....	yes
b) $a + b$	....	no
c) $m + n = z$	....	yes
d) $3x = 12$	....	yes
e) $7 - x - y + 2$	....	no

3.

In order for an equation to be a true statement, the left-hand side of the equation must have the same value as the .... -hand side of the equation.   right

Decide which of the following equations are true statements. Determine whether the right-hand side has the same value as the ....-.......... side.   left-hand

(Write true or false)

STATEMENT	TRUE OR FALSE	
a) $3 + 2 = 6$	....	false
b) $5 - 3 = 2$	....	true
c) $4 + 6 = 12 - 2$	....	true
d) $5 + 8 = 24 - 13$	....	false
e) $57 + 119 = 200 - 24$	....	true

Two additional features distinguish a program from most other instructional materials. First, the goals which the program is to achieve have been set forth very clearly, in specific terms of the student's response. The skills and understanding to be mastered through the program must be defined with precision. Second, the program is developed through constant testing on students, frequently in large numbers. These two processes—sharply defining the ends desired and testing the materials on students—mean that programs have a much more solid empirical foundation than the usual teaching materials.

How does this work out in actual practice? The answer to this question is best suggested by some of the case-study reports from schools which have actually used programed instruction. Assume, for example, that you have a fourth-grade class of average young-sters. How might programed instruction be useful in teaching them mathematics and science? The two reports which follow, the first from the Baldwin-Whitehall Public Schools in Pennsylvania, the second from Charlottesville, Virginia, are cited from *How to Use Programmed Instruction in the Classroom*.[3] Together, they indicate the concrete results which might be achieved in such a situation.

1. *Baldwin-Whitehall Public Schools, Pennsylvania*

This case study is taken from the report of a project carried out by the Learning Research and Development Center of the University of Pittsburgh under the direction of Dr. Robert Glaser. The aim of the project was to study the use of programmed materials within the classroom structure. The project involved grades 1, 4, 7 and 9. The work with the fourth graders is described here, for it provides the most useful information about the use of programs.

The fourth graders were given programs dealing with multiplication, division and fractions as well as programs in spelling. The multiplication and division programs were given to six classes over a period of six weeks. The students worked at their own pace four days each week, 45 minutes each day. The programs were divided into ten subsections for the purpose of measuring the students' progress periodically. As each student completed a section he was given a test and allowed to go on to the next section if he passed the test with a grade of 70% or better. If he failed to pass the test, he was required to repeat the program and then pass a retest at the 70% level. One day each week the teacher presented review and practice materials dealing with the programmed sections that most students had completed. Some students finished the

---

[3] Robert E. Silverman, *How to Use Programmed Instruction in the Classroom* (Cambridge, Mass.: Honor Products Co., division of Bolt Beranek and Newman, Inc., 1967).

entire program before the end of the six-week period and were given enrichment material to work with.

The students were pre-tested and at the end of the six-week period were given post-tests. The post-test scores showed clearly that the programs were effective instructional instruments.

After the multiplication and division programs were completed, one-third of the students were given programmed instruction in fractions and the remaining two-thirds went on with regular classroom instruction in the normal arithmetic curriculum. At the end of the school year, all students were given tests in multiplication and division and fractions. The test results showed that the students who went on to the fractions program were equal to the other students in their multiplication and division skills and exceeded the other students in their ability to work with fractions. These results indicate that the students who went on to the fractions program learned significantly more arithmetic while they retained the skills required by the normal curriculum. For these students, the programmed material served to extend the curriculum effectively.

2. Charlottesville, Virginia

This study is part of a two-and-a-half-year project conducted by W. D. Hedges under the auspices of the Division of Educational Research of the University of Virginia. The project involves the use of programmed science materials together with simple science experiments at the fourth-grade level. The programs, prepared especially for the project, are linear in format and deal with heat, light and sound.

The first phase of the project was a pilot study with two fourth-grade classes that used the programs and two that did not. Each class studied science for 30 minutes on Monday, Wednesday and Friday for five weeks. Less than the full 7½ hours was needed by the classes using the programs; the average time required for them was 5 hours. In spite of the fact that they took less time, their achievement was higher than the students who did not use programs. Furthermore, their interest was very high, even enthusiastic.

The second phase was an expansion and further development of the work begun in the pilot study. Six fourth-grade classes from four rural elementary schools were involved: Gordonsville, Unionville, Orange and Barboursville. The preliminary findings indicated that one class, consisting of able students (mean IQ of 115, S.D. 18), progressed particularly rapidly. The children worked "avidly" on experiments that they had prepared themselves. Their attitude toward science was very positive, and the teachers expressed pleasure at the results of the children's efforts. In the other classes, the results were less dramatic, but still positive; the pace was slower with considerable spread within the classes.

The tentative conclusions . . . were that programs can be used as an effective method of teaching science for the following reasons:

- a. "Interest is high and remains high."
- b. "Students can and do work responsibly while doing experiments by themselves."
- c. "Students can proceed at varying rates of speed and they really enjoy this."
- d. "The inservice value for teachers is high."

In discussing his experiences with this project, Hedges states:

"In short, it is now possible for the enterprising teacher to sort of feel her way into this new method of teaching science. She may find it is just what is needed for her very fast or very slow students. On the other hand she may find that a unit here or one there is exactly what she has been looking for to supplement a TV science unit for the entire class. There are many other possibilities. As indicated initially, it is doubtful if programming will or should constitute the whole of teaching elementary school science. Just as the textbook, the field trip, the science telecast, the radio, the film, et al, have a part in a good elementary school science program, so is it probable that programming will take its place with a role to play as the nature of that role becomes better understood through research."[4]

It may well be that the "teaching machine" idea spread faster than any other educational idea in American history. A 1962 NEA survey revealed that school principals around the nation expected it, of all innovations, to make the greatest strides in the shortest time. By 1964 a catalogue of completed programs then available listed close to 200, covering subjects from algebra to psychology; many times that number were in preparation. Today the number of programs available in the United States is over 3,000. By early 1967

[4] W. D. Hedges, in *Science and Children*, October, 1964, p. 23.

Peter Cavanagh and Clive Jones compiled a list of approximately 1,350 programs on the market in England.

To try to gauge the impact of programed instruction by sheer quantitative measures is, of course, fallacious. As in the case of instructional television, there has been a lack of solid *quality* in many—perhaps most—of the programs available. Many of the machines themselves have also been shoddy and inefficient. As suggested earlier, one compelling reason was the rush of new companies and established publishers to get machines and programs on the market, usually without taking the time for the extensive field tests that are essential. Today, however, specialists in programed instruction are encouraged by the rapid development of sophisticated computer-based teaching machines, which bear little resemblance to the crude devices first offered to the schools. Another hopeful sign is the increasingly individualized way that a given school adapts programed instruction to its own special needs, fitting it flexibly into a network of innovation. In 1965 psychologist Robert Glaser head of the Baldwin-Whitehall project and a scholar in the field, wrote: "A few years ago, I was greatly concerned that the uncritical rapid acceptance and too-ready use of programed instruction would accomplish two things: that high expectations coupled with awkward usage would result in disappointing outcomes and that the rush toward immediate practicality would pull the field away from its loose ties with the scientific study of behavior. As is usually the case, things were neither as good nor as bad as expectations. There were disappointments, but there were more successes." Professor Glaser went on to speak of the gratifying increase of interest, on the part of scholars and behavioral scientists, in the techniques of programed learning as "instances of the ways in which behavioral science might contribute to educational practice."

Just as television provides, it seems to me, an unprecedented way of bringing the most inspiring lectures and demonstrations by the finest teachers to the largest possible number of students (not to mention history as it is made, scientific experiments, dance and dramatic programs, art demonstrations, and films of historical events that would obviously be impossible without television), so programed learning, I believe, offers the complementary chance to reach the individual student with a precision, force, and certainty never before attainable. The Appendix examines instructional television in some detail, showing that the application of a really major innovation to an educational system mired down in established procedures is far from simple. While less complex innovations fit easily—perhaps too easily—into the traditional classroom, television necessitates basic changes in education that many teachers and administrators are not willing to make.

I remind the reader at this point of our contrapuntal theme: that schools will not be reformed by technology alone, however broadly conceived, but that there must be concurrent advance in the substance that the schools convey. We must avoid at all costs what an effective educator I know calls "capture by gadgetry"; we must not, as he says, merely exchange the old for a new orthodoxy. Instruments for mass and for individual instruction and for the gradations between can have profound effects on nearly every aspect of education. But the mere superimposition of television or programed instruction on the status quo would grievously dilute the contribution technology can make to learning and teaching.

Clearly technological devices can greatly aid the learning process. Their potential is enormous. Technology can free the teacher to make the maximum use of his special talents for teaching. And it can help, along with able teachers, to set free in the student his curiosity, independence, and inherent desire to learn.

7 Education's Technological Revolution II: The Reorganization of Teaching

New ideas about the organization of teaching and schools are an inseparable part of the new technology of education, as I've said. Again, for the sake of clarity, however, I'll separate the inseparable and confine this chapter to some aspects of the *organizational* status quo that must yield before optimum learning situations can be provided. These include the self-contained classroom and the isolated teacher, the rigid schedule with the grade-level pattern and unit of instruction, and schoolhouses built to the measure of these anachronisms.

Even though fifty years of research have failed to prove the correlation of educational excellence with a particular class size, a specific low student-teacher ratio is still the unquestioned educational ideal. Estimates of teacher shortages are based on this "ideal" ratio. Shop talk in teachers' lounges resounds with comparisons of "loads" (that repellent term). The vast majority of teachers and administrators now at work in the schools are sincerely convinced of the inviolability of the small class as an educational ideal. In certain critical situations—with children damaged by heredity or environment, let's say, or with the children of big-city ghettos—there is no denying that a lone teacher can accomplish much more the fewer the children she has to "handle." From the teacher's point of view, a small class is certainly easier to handle than a big class. But even from the teacher's point of view there is much more to the problem than this rather elementary criterion would suggest. Enterprising school districts all over the country are experimenting with new ways of organizing staff and students and subject matter. Finally, under the negative impetus of the teacher shortage and the positive impetus of new technological devices, there has developed a strong movement to put to pragmatic test the old clichés about class size and teacher-student ratios.

One hypothesis being tested is that the concept of "ideal class size," like that of the "good teacher," is not simple or absolute but relative: the ideal instructional unit depends on many variables including the nature of the subject matter, the purpose of the lesson, and the age, aptitude, and other characteristics of the students. For instance, the organization of students in large groups (of 50 to 100 or more) is appropriate for introductory lectures, exposition, some demonstrations, procedural instructions, and the like; the older the students the more apt they are to respond well to instruction in large groups. The best thing about large-group instruction is that it saves teaching time and talent for all-important work with small groups and with individuals.

In effect, schools are breaking out of the old forms and devising *systems* of instruction flexible and ingenious enough to meet the present urgent demands on education. A variety of experimental systems are now in operation. Hundreds of schools, most of them elementary schools, have been working toward a nongraded system in which advancement will be keyed to individual progress in given areas, rather than to cut-and-dried progress by grades and standardized norms. "The hold of the graded system—and the grading system—will be broken. Learning will be a continuous process, stimulated and supported by personal satisfactions in learning rather than by grades and degrees. . . . School and classroom organization will provide the flexibility needed to support the idea of continuous progress for each child." It is an excellent token of changing times that this statement was made, early in the sixties, not by a maverick reformer but by the NEA's Department of Elementary School Principals.

The most extensive series of organizational experiments in secondary education was sponsored by another NEA department, the National Association of Secondary-School Principals (NASSP). In 1955 the NASSP's curriculum committee succeeded in interesting a number of strong school systems in experiments combining several new techniques for the better use of teaching time and talent. With foundation support, the committee started a four-year program under the direction of a newly appointed Commission on the Experimental Study of the Utilization of Staff in the Secondary School, the members of which were top-ranking secondary school administrators and specialists.

When the commission held its final meeting in November, 1960, it could look back on a highly encouraging four years. In that period of time it had sponsored, helped, and studied experiments involving 100 junior and senior high schools in eleven states. Some schools had chosen to experiment with only a single aspect of staff utilization, others with a combination. There was frequently a chain-reaction effect in which a single experiment in a school led to the introduction of additional and different projects.

The commission's work embraced all kinds of schools, large and small, and in many varied settings. There had been no blueprint; all the schools had been invited to participate and to devise their own experiments based on local needs. A number of projects had operated in consultation with nearby colleges or universities or with state education departments. The commission's projects produced evidence indicating a salutary influence on teacher training, on the design of school facilities, on the use of community resources, and—most encouragingly—on teacher salaries. The commission has spread the word of its findings via four major publications, the final one its 1961 publication, *Focus on Change*.[1]

[1] The author of all four reports is J. Lloyd Trump, director of the commission, formerly professor of education at the University of Illinois, and now an

In these publications Dr. Trump projected a "school of the future" in which the student would spend about 40 percent of his time in individual study, with minimum supervision but with instant access to a wide variety of learning devices and materials: teaching machines, tape-recorded lessons and drills, scientific apparatus, books. Another 40 percent of the school day the student would spend in large groups, where teachers would use mass media of instruction, including television, films, a variety of projectors. The teacher time saved by these two arrangements would be reinvested in seminars or individual instruction for the remaining 20 percent of the typical student's time.

In much of the experimental work now in process the organization of teachers into teaching teams plays an important part. Team teaching is a highly imprecise concept, and a controversial one. The name itself is so controversial that such euphemisms as "cooperative teaching" are often used instead, even in schools enthusiastically engaged in this staff innovation. Essentially a teaching team consists of at least two professional teachers, working with or without aides or novice teachers. The team as a whole is responsible for a large group of students, in all phases of instruction, including planning, teaching, and evaluation. I myself would add the further stipulation—and here is the chief locus of controversy—that one of the professional teachers be recognized, if only *de facto*, as the team leader. Good schools with wise principals and confident teachers have, of course, utilized this concept in the past, without formality or fanfare. But it is only in the past decade or so, with leadership from Harvard and other universities, that the idea has spread and that experiments have been mounted to try out its many permutations.

associate secretary of the NASSP. Dr. Trump is a leading spokesman for new directions in American education. The titles of the four reports are: *An Exciting Profession: New Horizons for Secondary School Teachers* (NASSP, 1957), (now out of print); *Images of the Future—A New Approach to the Secondary School* (NASSP, 1958); *New Directions to Quality Education—The Secondary School Tomorrow* (NASSP, 1959); and *Focus on Change—Guide to Better Schools* (Rand McNally, 1961).

In considering true innovation in education, a passage written long ago by Charles A. Beard has direct relevance:

What then is this technology which constitutes the supreme instrument of modern progress? Although the term is freely employed in current writings, its meaning as actuality and potentiality has never been explored and defined. Indeed, so wide-reaching are its ramifications that the task is difficult and hazardous. Narrowly viewed, technology consists of the totality of existing laboratories, machines, and processes already developed, mastered, and in operation. But it is far more than mere objective realities.

Intimately linked in its origin and operation with pure science, even its most remote mathematical speculations, technology has a philosophy of nature and a method—an attitude toward materials and work—and hence is a subjective force of high tension. It embraces within its scope great constellations of ideas, some explored to apparent limits and others in the form of posed problems and emergent issues dimly understood.[2]

This is a useful definition to bear in mind in considering technology's impact on the schools and on teachers and students. For, as Beard's definition makes clear, technology is a dynamic, ever-changing force that constantly breeds new forms. More important than understanding a particular technology is an open-minded point of view keyed to the unknown and challenging, a special attitude toward materials and work. Furthermore, as Beard indicates in passing, technology embraces processes and procedures as well as machinery.

When the Industrial Revolution swept over plants and mills in the eighteenth century, managers soon found that it was not enough to install new machinery; once installed, the machines compelled a radical transformation in the industrial use of time, space, and people. The mechanization of manufacturing, mining, and farming imposed a companion revolution in management and control, the invention of whole new *systems* of operation.

2 "Introduction to the American Edition," in J. B. Bury, *The Idea of Progress* (New York: Dover Publications, 1955; first published as the American edition by Macmillan in 1932).

In order for the instructional revolution to transform education as industry has been transformed during the past three centuries, in order for technology to advance the quality of teaching and learning, the institutional status quo must undergo far-reaching and fundamental changes. The key concept here, of course, is productivity, a word that until recently was anathema in educational circles. Teachers and administrators and parents shuddered at the application of this crass marketplace measurement to the subtle, complex, value-encrusted business of teaching the young.

Fortune magazine was probably the first to come right out in print and chide the schools for low productivity. That was ten years ago, in 1958, and generated quite a stir. *Fortune*'s dollar-and-cents analysis of education compared the number of pupils instructed with the time and staff required; it concluded that the schools' efficiency was low and that educational "productivity" had been declining for more than half a century. By now Sputnik and related forces have catapulted education into a major industry, with a total budget second only to national defense and fraught with grave implications for survival; it no longer seems crude to expect education to make a decent return on the dollars (and energy and hopes) invested in it.

How educators can put this productivity concept into practice is the focus of thousands of experiments and developments now under way. Obviously there was a basis for the traditional reluctance to apply economic precepts to education. They cannot, of course, be applied mechanically: the educational system is not a business enterprise, it is subject to public policy, it does not operate for profit, its product is in part genuinely intangible and imponderable. To this extent the old reluctance is understandable, and it is no wonder if the teaching world becomes indignant when faced with brisk managerial talk of education's input and output.

Schools, as I have said, can merely add technological devices to their programs with no change in organizational pattern, much as one would add a kindergarten. They can introduce one or more of the new curricula. Similarly they can superficially revise their conventional organization, instituting team teaching, a system of non-professional aides, some flexibility in the shape of nongraded classes or dual progress plans all without benefit of mechanical devices. Schools *can* do these isolated things, and unfortunately some of them do, just as during the heyday of scientific management in the 1920's schools tried to conform to the superficial criteria of "efficiency" imposed by businessmen-dominated school boards.

Halfway measures may show good results if the school is blessed with gifted teachers (who always produce exceptions to any rule). But, more often than not, the compromise produces meager results and no net educational gain for the students (which, after all, should be the goal of educational change). The school has perhaps won itself a federal or foundation grant; the superintendent or principal in his annual report to the board can point with pride to the innovation; the public feels self-satisfied at being in the vanguard of educational fashion. But the chances are that no substantial improvement in teaching and learning is taking place.

The resort to gimmickry is one of the pitfalls that beset the instructional revolution. Like the Viennese in the old proverb, I regard the situation as desperate but not serious. For, as noted earlier, there is evidence that flawed endeavors like these are often self-correcting. If team teaching is inaugurated with public fanfare and little fundamental preparation, team members of caliber and integrity are sooner or later bound to study anew the subjects they are teaching and in all probability to make basic improvements in curriculum and techniques. If a school makes its concession to the times by, say, employing well-educated housewives to correct English examinations and themes but with no particular preparation for the change, the discipline of exposing one's work to accomplished outsiders before long forces the conscientious English teacher to review the basis for his assignments and examination questions and to sharpen and improve his procedures.

If a principal decides that the very model of a modern high school demands a bit of television and so decrees, he may or may not discover that a lecture course on kinescope adds no more and no less than the addition of a conventional lecture course. But wise teachers in the particular department involved are bound to realize that to get the full value of the televised course they must exploit the staff time saved and use the course to build up more lively and rewarding sessions with small groups or with individual students.

The illustrations so far have dealt with the interaction between technology and organization. There is also a seepage or a chain effect, if you like, *within* these two aspects of technology. I mean that the school that embarks on reform by buying one teaching machine is very apt later on to add television or the experimental use of tapes. And the school that tries out contract readers or some other type of nonprofessional teachers' aide is a very likely candidate for team teaching. In recent years countless examples of both these chain reactions have come to my attention.

If the danger in superficial or opportunistic experimentation with technology seems less than alarming, there is a long-range danger that is not so easily dismissed. It inheres in technology itself, whatever the application, and is reflected in man's residual, ineradicable fear that machines will take on a life of their own and ultimately prevail. In the previous chapter I referred to this fear as "atavistic," which it is, but dubbing it such makes it no less real and no less understandable. The world has not yet seen the machine surmounting man; but the world has only the briefest experience in living in an environment of machines which are different in kind as well as degree from their predecessors of even a generation ago; and the world has seen the awesome, if not total, triumph of the machine in the field of agriculture, for instance, where it helped achieve miracles of productivity while in the process fast removing the values of the old family farm. In the dawn of the space age, what we casually read in our daily papers is enough to make the antiutopias of Huxley and Orwell look old-fashioned.

Professor Harry Broudy, of the University of Illinois, has squarely set forth the problem:

We have not yet learned to enjoy the blessings of automation without sacrificing human values in any area of activity. . . . The automobile may be an adjunct to living, but one can see that we are reaching a stage when one's mode of living is shaped by the fact of automobile transportation. Is there reason to believe that we can do otherwise in automated instruction? . . . From using television to supplement the classroom teacher, it is only a step to arranging classes so that one can take advantage of the most efficient use of teaching machines. Given enough investment in automated instruction by manufacturers, publishers, and school boards one can expect strong efforts to protect and exploit that investment.[3]

Broudy concluded that "we have no real choice but to try to outwit the machine age, to seek therein the potentialities for human values that it undeniably has." Here, I think, is the heart of the matter. The machine age has the power to set education and teachers free, but eternal vigilance is the price of that free-dom—vigilance in educators and laymen alike to harness tech-nology to the human values of learning and teaching.

The full use of technology will require extraordinary control, imagination, and discrimination on the part of teachers and school executives, together with great flexibility in school organization, so that the new devices in their great variety and adaptability may be fully integrated into the daily life and basic purposes of the school. But it is becoming clearer every day that the procedures that will realize the greatest educational return from technology are in general the very procedures that will best safeguard the intrinsic human values of the schools.

It is an axiom of the instructional revolution that no flesh-and-blood teacher should be wasted on procedures that technology can do as well or better. Evidence mounts daily in the schools that technology, properly used, impels the restoration of real learning by putting the learner front and center. The role of the teacher, then, becomes what it has always been at its best—the knowl-edgcable and sensitive guide of learning.

If the revolution prevails, the teacher in his role as guide will command a whole battery of extremely versatile new aids to learn-ing, from scrambled text to push-button kinescope libraries.

[3] Quoted in Ronald Gross, "Education's Industrial Revolution," in *The Progressive*, Vol. 27, No. 9 (September, 1963), p. 40.

Even more important, and thanks to the rationalization that technology requires, the teacher will have a battery of human assistants to help him to cultivate and deepen learning. Some of these assistants will facilitate the process by relieving the teacher of manifold clerical and other nonteaching chores; others—not only his colleagues but also specialists from the community as well as outstanding teachers and artists via television—will augment the teacher's own experience and background by bringing their own special gifts to the students. In the schools of the future the master teacher (by whatever name) will act as director of this whole complex system. The teacher as purveyor of information, as drillmaster, as Jack-of-all-trades, is obsolete. His new role, that only technology fully realized can create, will be that of a master of the resources of learning, at last afforded time and opportunity for the cultivation of students as individual human beings with a potential to learn.

To sum up: technology wisely exploited and controlled will at once increase educational productivity (i.e., the output of truly educated children per input of time, energy, and money) and restore to the art and science of teaching its uniquely human and personal pre-eminence. There will be a further result for teachers, as this book has suggested elsewhere. Out of the instructional revolution may come such a realignment of the teaching force that new career patterns will open up. No longer will teaching be circumscribed on every side by the convention that treats all teachers alike and makes no differentiation, in pay or opportunity, for quality and originality and individual talent. We may yet be able to attract more of the best and liveliest young people into teaching with the assurance that they can fulfill their highest potential and be suitably awarded in the process, in self-respect, a sense of purpose, and even money.

The present experiments in staff deployment offer many hopeful prospects, but these may be the merest sample of what experience and ingenuity may one day devise. The organization of teachers into instructional teams in itself suggests a range of different careers, some of which were mentioned above. The full development of devices like television and programed instruction will open up another wide range of careers, for example, in the science of programing and in many other specialties. And these suggestions, embracing as they do scores of different teaching roles, hardly begin to cover the rich opportunities teaching could offer once technology helps to pry the dead hand of tradition from the schools. Other fresh areas for the subject-matter teaching specialist will open up as schools find it possible to give proper attention to the pressing need for on-the-job training of teaching interns and student teachers and beginning teachers. With a wise and sensitive division of educational labor it will be possible for many schools to do what a few enlightened schools do now and make provision for experienced teachers of high competence to take the time needed to guide and nurture the inexperienced.

Francis Keppel, when he was dean of the Harvard Graduate School of Education, argued thus:

It is painfully obvious that American education needs more clearly defined career patterns. The lack of such patterns is responsible for much of the turnover in our teaching force, and for the shortage of able young men who enter classroom teaching and stay there. What is needed is a visible "career line" beginning with recruitment and continuing through initial training, intermediate experience on the job, further advanced training, and ultimate placement in positions of leadership. This, in turn, calls for the creation of new teaching roles in the schools, with suitable responsibilities and salary levels.[4]

Young people debating the choice of teaching as an occupation and all the teachers now at work (barring only the timeservers and outright incompetents) should welcome the exhilarating changes that the instructional revolution, through the uses of technology in all its implications, may effect in the role and prospects of the teacher. *"Occupation: teacher"* may yet mean a true profession and a rewarding career.

[4] Francis Keppel and Paul A. Perry, "School and University: Partners in Progress" (Manuscript written for Phi Delta Kappa and undated). p. 8.

8 The Humanities: New Frontier of Curriculum Reform

We are well into second, third, and even fourth "genera-tions" of curriculum reform in math and science—each building on the achievements (and striving to remedy the defects) of the ones which came before. Now it is time for a strong shift of focus, going far beyond the efforts noted in Chapter 5. The new fron-tier, I believe, lies in the humanistic area of the curriculum. In this chapter I shall attempt to appraise the present state and to discern the immediate future of the humanities in public educa-tion, in the light of a new climate of opinion almost comparable to the impact of Sputnik on the American mind: the so-called "cultural explosion."

We must take account of two contrasting sets of facts. First, *the American people are today concerned with humanistic and cul-tural matters to a degree unprecedented in their history.* And, second, far from reflecting this new concern with humanistic and cultural matters, *the schools of the nation have let the humanities and arts languish.* I do not believe we can long permit such a discrepancy between what people want, and very badly need, and what the schools offer. Educators must stake out a role in the forefront of the new American concern for the intellectual, aes-thetic, and spiritual dimensions of life.

Before suggesting how educators might fill such a role I had better make clear what I mean by "culture." I cannot help but equate culture with the humanities in the broadest sense. In this view the humanities are not simply words and books, nor are they just the humanistic fields of study such as philosophy, literature, languages, history, comparative religion, and the arts. Words and books are the invaluable records of the past. But they are dead unless they are interpreted and expressed in the lives of human beings today.

The humanities suggest to me man's ability to contemplate uncertainty, to resist dogmatism, to take delight in the differences between men, nations, cultures, and ages. The humanities reflect man's capacity to plan, to set goals, to work toward rational ends rather than being governed by instinctive urges. The humanities directly touch the life of man. They encompass man's beliefs, his ideals, many of his highest achievements.

Any person with feeling, any person who is truly concerned with his conduct toward others; any person with ideals to achieve; any person who thinks about the basic ideas that make a difference in the lives of men; any person who creates something, whether in art, music, literature, or scholarship, that vitally affects the way people live; any person who is working in the interest of mankind—any such person is in a vital way dealing with the humanities.

Understood in this way, humanistic study constitutes what Frank Jennings of the New World Foundation calls "one of the most profound, mind-shaping experiences in the life of man . . . [making] it possible for Plato and Christ to instruct us from thousands of years away. It joins minds and times together for the better management of our universe . . . it is through the record that others leave to us in fact and fancy that we human beings live so richly in so short a time."[1]

Most people today, from college onward, are inevitably caught

[1] Frank Jennings, *This is Reading* (New York: Dell Publishing Co. [Delta Books], 1966), pp. 88–89.

up in the busyness of making a living rather than in the rewards and delights of living. The outcome of such preoccupation can be disastrous to us as individuals. The sum total could be disastrous to the world of men. For only as each of us strives to carry forward humane values can mankind understand and control the vast forces unleashed by science and technology.

I do not think any man has ever been converted *to* the humanities, though I know a great many who have been converted *by* the humanities. Let me just say, then, that the man who is a stranger to any tongue but his own; who believes what he likes and likes what he believes without ever having submitted his ideas to scrutiny; who has never dwelt with Homer and Shakespeare; who is deaf to the exaltation of music, blind to the eloquence of paint, marble, and metal—that man is so much the less a full human being.

The American people are today concerned with humanistic and cultural matters to a degree unprecedented in their history. That is the first basic fact we must consider.

It is no exaggeration to say that we are in the midst of a cultural renaissance in this country. Alvin Toffler deserves much of the credit for bringing this trend to public attention through his book *The Culture Consumers*.[2] Since the end of the war consumer spending on the arts has risen precipitately, far more rapidly than spending on recreation or sports.

There are more art galleries in New York City today than there were in the entire country in 1950. We can see similar developments in the fields of music and literature. LP records—embracing an incredible repertoire old and new—are, along with FM radio, bringing music to new millions every year. A paperback revolution is going on in publishing. It makes scholarly books, formerly passed from hand to hand by faculty members, available

[2] Alvin Toffler, *The Culture Consumers* (New York: St. Martin's Press, 1964).

to millions of students, and literature of every variety available to the general public. Book sales as well as library circulation are increasing far more rapidly than the population.

Even the mass media have contributed to the cultural explosion. A nationwide broadcast of *Hamlet* was seen by more people, in one evening, than the total number who have seen it performed since it was written!

Perhaps it may seem wrong to speak of the arts and the humanities in quantitative terms. Numbers, of course, are no indication of quality, and the fact that millions of people watched *Hamlet* over television tells nothing about what benefits, if any, each of those millions derived from the experience.

But in another sense sheer quantity is very significant. For there cannot be a great flowering of art or of the humanistic studies unless audiences, facilities, and resources are available. Just as students and scholars need books, so painters need galleries, dramatists need theatres, and musicians need orchestras. It is certainly clear that the great cultural epochs of the past were firmly rooted in certain material conditions. When we think of the greatness of Greek drama, we think of the great theatres of Athens and Epidaurus. When we marvel at Shakespeare's achievement, we cannot overlook the challenge that shaped his art: the Elizabethan theatre and the London audience avid for rich language and exciting action. The sculpture of Michelangelo and the music of Bach both drew their inspiration and their material support from the church, the great patron of the arts in their times.

In short, quantitative trends are important because they show whether or not a culture is ripe for certain kinds of development. The public relations chief for a large Detroit manufacturer recently summed up the attitude of the more enlightened corporations toward supporting culture. "We have to be interested in the shape of the arts in cities where our plants are located," he told me, "because if there are none, engineering and scientific people won't come."

What accounts for this ferment in American culture? The basic reason, I think, has been accurately discerned by Peter Drucker in his projection of American trends during the next decade. Professor Drucker, whose predictions of social, political, and technological developments have been singularly prescient, sees the United States moving into a period of political turbulence in which "domestic politics will be dominated by unfamiliar issues—not only new, but different in kind from the things we have been arguing about since 1932. [We] will be concerned, not primarily with economic matters, but with basic values—moral, aesthetic, and philosophical."[3]

The interests, tastes, and even the basic concerns of Americans are changing. As more and more of the population achieve higher levels of education, stable careers, and relative economic security, there is quite naturally a waning of purely economic motivations. The climb to the top was thrilling for the father, but his son cares more about taking in the view—or perhaps in discovering an entirely different kind of mountain to climb. America seems to be reaching a stage of individual and national development that transcends material achievement. We are experiencing the emergence of new needs, just as pressing, that cannot be satisfied by material things alone. These needs can be met only by understanding ourselves and our world. The pre-eminent means to such understanding is humanistic study.

Do the schools today reflect this growing American concern with humanistic, cultural, and artistic matters? The answer is NO. As one looks back over the past decade of ferment and innovation in the schools, it is striking how much of the experimentation has concerned the sciences rather than the humanities. The terrifying gap between America's strides in scientific knowledge and limping progress in humanistic understanding is reflected in our schools and colleges. As the Report of the Commission on the Humanities stated in 1964: "*Without major efforts in all the schools of every*

[3] Peter Drucker, "American Directions: A Forecast," in *Harper's Magazine*, February, 1965, p. 39.

state, the status and influence of the humanities in the schools will inevitably decline in the years ahead."[4]

It is good to be able to note that American educational leaders are increasingly cognizant of this new responsibility, and of the schools' present failure to cope with it. Harold Howe II, former U.S. Commissioner of Education, in an address[5] in 1967, said that "it is a major function of education to foster humanistic values, to help create the kind of social and intellectual climate in which the aesthetic sense will flourish." But Commissioner Howe added at once, "Our educational system is failing to discharge this function with anything like the imagination and ingenuity the task deserves."

What will continuation of this failure mean? Why should the humanities and arts be strengthened throughout American public education? The answer is simple and compelling. We must do everything we can to help our children deal with problems of value and problems of meaning such as have never before faced mankind. Already we can glimpse a new social order in which work, leisure, family, education, and social organization will be vastly transformed. This new world will be the world of the computer and the automated factory. It is a world in which diseases that have scourged mankind for centuries will have been conquered. It is a world which will know enough about those two great mysteries of life—the living brain and the immortal gene—to control, with frightening ease, the thoughts of individuals and the direction of the human race.

We cannot tolerate another generation that knows so much about preserving and destroying life, but so little about enhancing it. We cannot permit our children to come into their maturity as masters of the atom and of the gene, but ignorant and barbarous about the ways of the human mind and heart.

[4] Report of the Commission on the Humanities (New York: American Council of Learned Societies, 1964) p. 20.

[5] Harold Howe II, "Aesthetics and the National Interest." Address before the Annual Commencement, Ohio State University, June 13, 1967.

If the schools and colleges fail to rise to these challenges, there will be a steady slippage in our ability to cope with life-and-death problems in the world and in our own country, in our standards of morals and civility, in public taste, in people's capacity to wrestle with complex ideas and to weigh competing values. If the schools and colleges let the humanities languish, Americans' new-found leisure is likely to become a vacuum to be filled with boredom and frustration. Automated factories will churn out lipstick and tail fins. All the great media of communication will be keyed to the uncultivated mind. People will inhabit—but scarcely *live* in—an environment of increasing ugliness.

American schools have a particularly difficult role to play in reviving the humanities. For our public schools have traditionally devoted themselves to meeting the expressed needs of their students and their communities. Private schools can emphasize the arts or the humanistic fields if they wish, but public schools must relate what they teach to the lives of the constituents. They must constantly demonstrate the human relevance and utility of their activities. Therefore the public school is not able to emphasize the humanities just because the teachers or administrators have a predilection for those studies. The institution is constrained to show that humanistic studies are of real value to the majority of the students.

Here is where the sheer dimensions of the "culture boom" are highly significant. They show the rapidly growing demand of Americans for cultural satisfaction. People are speaking up in the most effective way they can—they are voting with their pocketbooks. What they are saying is that music has become as important to them as baseball, that books and recordings are as desirable as boat trailers, that art in its multiple present-day manifestations is getting to mean as much to them as cosmetics and liquor. The voice of the American people is saying this more urgently each year. In short, more and more Americans are devoting more and more of their time to learning and appreciating rather than merely being entertained, to cultivating their own tastes rather than merely following the leadership of others. It is time the nation's schools came to the forefront with plans based on the recognition that intellectual, academic, and cultural pursuits have achieved a new respect and status in American society.

What will be required to raise the level of public school instruction in the humanities to meet this challenge?

First, we will need *teachers* who themselves exemplify the humanistic ideal we wish to inculcate in students. Fortunately, we are in a better position than ever before to get them. As noted in an earlier chapter, more and more teacher-training programs emphasize broad liberal education and depth of study in a major subject field.

Second, *we need to utilize the whole range of new media to bring home to the student the power and relevance of the humanities to his life.* Filmed plays, televised performances of music, art reproductions, new curriculum materials for teaching history and archaeology—all are essential. In the words of the Commission on the Humanities: "Most classrooms in the country are twenty years behind what they might be in the power to communicate ideas."

Third, *new programs of study* will be required as was the case in the sciences and mathematics. A recent survey by Frank Jennings of recommended reading lists for high school students revealed that one book appeared on virtually every list. This title clearly dominates the field of English teaching in American high schools. The book is *Silas Marner.* It has been the favorite for decades— despite the fact that contemporary literary critics and scholars hardly consider it worth their attention. Here is a fantastic situation like that which confronted Professor Jerrold Zacharias of M.I.T. when he discovered that one of his youngster's physics textbooks was based on a concept of science which was fifty years out of date.

If curriculum is the heart of education, what are the most important short-range and long-range curriculum needs in the humanities and the arts? There is an immediate need to improve the courses now being offered. The problems of upgrading the vast scope of the humanities are too complex for schools to wait until entire new integrated courses have been developed. Until the U.S. Office of Education's English Program and other current efforts bear fruit, schools can avail themselves of various piecemeal efforts of significance like the Encyclopaedia Britannica films of *Hamlet*, *Oedipus Rex*, and other classics. Moreover, many schools and school systems are embarking on promising developmental programs on their own. For example, the number of California high schools which offer courses in the humanities has tripled in the past five years. Almost a quarter of the state's high schools now offer such courses and many more are interested in doing so. In most of these courses the subjects drawn from include not just English, art, music, and philosophy but also anthropology, semantics, architecture, and drama.

But such local efforts are not sufficient. To make the humanities the force they should be in American education requires more than piecemeal, local effort. It requires more than the research and experimentation supported under the USOE's English Program. It requires more than the fine work that the John Hay Fellows Program did in upgrading teachers of humanistic subjects. It requires, in fact, a realization that *the humanities, properly conceived and taught, constitute the great integrating force in the school curriculum.*

I think we have lost sight of the power of the humanities to unify all school subjects around the whole man. This is in large part the fault of the humanist scholars, who have chopped up their field into its component "disciplines," a necessary classification for advanced scholarship but one that is useless if not actually harmful in the lower schools.

Moreover, many of the humanists themselves have permitted their disciplines to become divorced from the vital concerns of contemporary men. A British book, *Crisis in the Humanities*, edited by J. H. Plumb, puts the matter succinctly: "The humanities are at the cross-roads, at a crisis in their existence: they must either change the image that they present, adapt themselves to the needs of a society dominated by science and technology, or retreat into social triviality."[6]

How, then, can the humanities become the great integrating force in the school curriculum? To achieve this they must transcend the traditional subject matter categories by which the schools organize the curriculum. Schools must center their teaching on major ideas with which students will have to grapple throughout their lives. Only the insights of the humanities can illuminate such themes as freedom, responsibility, and the aims of life.

The "Ideas Curriculum," for example, is one way of using the humanities to integrate the school curricula by overcoming the fragmentation into "disciplines" and their divorce from men's real lives. Focusing directly on major ideas which students will be grappling with for the rest of their lives, it builds the groundwork for a spiral of lifetime learning, in which students periodically, throughout their school careers and later in life, return to reconsider the most important concepts from increasingly knowledgeable and experienced perspectives (an adaptation of the "spiral curriculum" espoused by Jerome Bruner).

Nothing would alarm me more than the improbable prospect of having the Ideas Curriculum, as set forth here, adopted by every school in America. For I offer it not as a panacea but for the very purpose of provoking and even angering others to the point of coming up with even better, more constructive, and more creative ideas. This much is clear: previous efforts to adjust humanistic or general education to the contemporary explosion of knowledge have proved unsatisfactory. The assumption that a student can sample all significant fields of study and thereby come out with a "well-rounded" education has proved fallacious. Efforts at survey

[6] J. H. Plumb (ed.), *Crisis in the Humanities* (Baltimore, Md.: Penguin Books, 1964), p. 8.

courses have not really satisfied most scholars. Existing general education programs in higher education were conceived and developed, for the most part, by generalists with very little collaboration from our really first-rate scholarly minds. So survey courses are little, if any, improvement on traditional subject segmentation.

In developing curriculum educators have been concerned about cultivating students' maturity in almost every area, but not in their grasp of major ideas. Long ago we worked out levels of achievement in simple skills—reading, writing, etc.; we do not regard them as adequate, nor do we have confidence in our measuring instruments. But we do have tests of attainment; we have established norms so that we can identify the deviants in one direction or another, high or low.

There are similar standards in subject matter areas: in mathematics, for example, educators have defined very carefully the concepts students are expected to acquire at different grade levels. Traditionally pupils are led first through simple arithmetical concepts and calculations, then in high school they are "taken through" algebra, geometry, and in some cases, trigonometry. College continues with advanced algebra, calculus, differential equations, etc.

Yet even though there has been a fairly intelligible progression in mathematics, we have become dissatisfied. The accumulation of knowledge in the field plus what we have learned about motivation and the psychology of learning have caused us to start rethinking the mathematics curriculum. As a result, the students are dealing with more "advanced"—but essentially simple—concepts at an earlier age. In the same way, physics scholars have now devised new courses to deal with modern ideas of time, space, and matter. The Physical Science Study Committee at M.I.T. has provided such a synthesis, with the result that college physics courses have had to be revised to challenge graduates of the improved high school offering.

I could go on in this way through every discipline, many of which are now being reorganized on the assumption that we have been shutting our eyes much too long to contemporary discoveries in the subject fields and in the psychology of learning. We are now convinced that children can begin substantive learning early. Furthermore, they want it. Many behavior problems disappear when children are challenged intellectually. As we saw in an earlier chapter, experiments today are testing whether elementary school-children can grasp concepts heretofore thought only suitable for college students. Over and over again we are finding that our assumptions of what and how children learn are based on what and how we learned and what the teacher understood a generation or two ago.

The world is now moving at such a rapid pace that our expectations of what children are capable of learning are antiquated. Our educational system is still tied to axioms that shaped the schools our parents and great-grandparents attended. We assume that we can correct this glaring deficiency by reorganizing and updating subject matter to encompass the new world of knowledge. But there are so many new facts that learning them has reached the point of diminishing returns.

We need a new approach to the intellectual mastery of our environment and ourselves. We need a new focus for the curriculum. I propose that schools make a direct, continuous, and intensive effort to teach students *to think*. But this is insufficient as a principle of curriculum construction. For thinking can't be taught in the abstract, just as you can't teach "writing" or "speaking" without giving students something to write or speak *about*. To my mind the most suitable *substance* for the schools to help students think about is the realm of ideas—the major ideas that have made a difference in civilization.

If we are to reconstruct our curriculum to deal directly and thoroughly with the cultivation of maturity in thinking about critical ideas, we need to answer at least three basic questions:

1. Which ideas are so significant as to justify systematic treatment throughout the educational system? Energy is one, as important as any with which man is struggling today. Work is

another. Equality is yet another. Power, the state, justice and freedom are others.

2. With each of these ideas, what elements should successively
engage the child as he matures? By what criteria or types of observation can we judge the level of maturity a student has reached
in grasping ideas? For example, how should a high school graduate's understanding of freedom, energy, or space differ from that
of a sixth-grade pupil?

3. What kinds of materials would have to be developed to aid
pupils in going from the relatively simple levels of thinking to the
more complex?

The answers to such questions cannot be derived from any
single discipline, for every major concept cuts across the fields into
which, for the sake of convenience, we have classified knowledge.

Take the idea of energy, which looms so large in the world
today. It certainly has been basic to the Cold War—we have
learned how significant is the difference between "high-energy"
and "low-energy" societies—and it is basic to a sensible contempla-
tion of a Hot War and its consequences. Obviously, too, a comprehensive understanding of energy can't come just from studying
physics. Nor should we wait until a student studies physics before
he begins dealing with energy. The pupil starts with a simple
understanding when he observes the function of a wheel. He goes
on through a variety of experiences, which are not at present
systematically planned, and we hope he gradually develops greater
competence in thought about this idea.

Energy is a basic concept not only in physics but also in chemistry, biology, geology, psychology, sociology, economics, and even
philosophy and history. As the eminent historian Allan Nevins has
written: "From the material point of view, history is primarily the
story of the increasing ability of man to reach and control energy."
We must study this complex question in attempting to determine
how historical eras, like the Renaissance, the Reformation, and the
Industrial Revolution are born.

We can also think of the kinds, sources, conservation, development, and uses of energy—whether for war or peace, whether controlled by the individual or by a group or the state. We should not just assume that individuals will mature in their understanding of energy any more than we assume they will mature in under-standing physics if they approach it incidentally rather than sys-tematically. In both cases our approach needs to be well ordered and appropriate to the student's age, whether it is in the under-standing of an idea, a subject, or a skill.

Or consider another basic idea of our culture, which is about to undergo radical change—change which will be comprehensible only to those who know what this idea has meant to men through the ages. I am thinking of the idea of work.

Students do learn a considerable amount, in history and eco-nomics, about how the conditions of work have been changed in the course of human development—the agricultural revolution, the rise of the guilds in the Middle Ages, the industrial revolu-tions, etc. But what about the *idea* of work?

In primitive societies there is often no rigid distinction between work, play, ritual, family life, and other social activities. A radical change occurred by the time of the Greeks. For them work was drudgery and nothing more—a necessary but galling evil. The Romans adopted this idea. Early Christianity, in contrast, regarded work as a punishment laid upon man by God. But it gradually added the notion that labor could be a way of sharing the gifts of fortune with one's needy fellows. In other words, work might have some value as a means to charity, but it still had no intrinsic value of its own. Thomas Aquinas decreed that a man who has the means to live without working is under no moral obligation to work.

The Reformation brought a highly dramatic change. Work came to be a means of self-discipline and a visible token of grace. Luther was the great innovator here, with his concept of work as a form of service to God.

Finally, with the Renaissance, a new idea of work began to emerge. Man came to be viewed primarily as a worker, and labor is seen as the chief activity of a society, replacing religious activity or warfare at the center of life. This idea of man figures prominently in many Renaissance writers, as it does in Bergson's equation of Homo sapiens with Homo faber, and in Marx.

At the present moment of history we face a great crisis in the idea of work. Heirs to the tradition just briefly surveyed cannot easily overcome the notions of sacredness and significance which have accrued to the idea of work throughout Western history. Yet we are rapidly creating, through advancing automation, a society in which it may be quite impossible to provide work for everyone. The result is that the debate over the meaning of work has burst out of the philosopher's study and become one of the issues on which men will soon have to take sides.

Now let us consider the idea of work from the viewpoint of the individual student. As a child matures, and begins to interest himself in particular work roles, his idea of work changes considerably. We all know how hard it is to explain to children what we do when we're at work. No one is quite prepared for the real meaning of work until he is committed to it full time. Even then, growth should not stop, though frequently it does. As the years pass and one progresses in one's chosen field, the idea of work takes on new meanings—meanings of service and dedication. David Riesman has pointed out that one of the critical distinctions between men and women in American society is that men have careers, while women only have jobs—two different ideas of work with vastly different consequences.

In both the individual and in history it is possible to trace a developing maturity in the capacity to think about work. We can discriminate, roughly but persuasively, between a simple, static, egocentric, materialistic viewpoint and a complex, fluid, socially conscious, idealistic one.

Another key idea in our lives today is equality. Here history, philosophy, anthropology, literature, political science, and other fields can bring the student to a mature understanding. He might begin with Plato's Republic, the classic Greek picture of a state based on the natural inequalities between men. For Plato, who assumed that men were unequal, the ideal state was one that organized men according to the true and most relevant order of inequality. Thus his utopia is realized when every man has been put in the place dictated by his nature. Aristotle, too, insisted that justice is proportional and, in passages which were quoted widely in the American South before the Civil War, defended slavery on the basis of natural inequalities.

Christianity injected a new idea of equality through its concept of an individual's worth. Created in the image of God, each individual was equal in the eyes of God despite any inequalities in his capacities or worldly status. Thus spiritual equality superseded the Greek notion of natural inequality. This complete about-face was a chief turning point in Western history. Yet Christianity, by stressing the salvation spiritual equality would make possible in the afterlife, often had the effect, especially in the Middle Ages, of resigning men to social and economic inequality here on earth.

A further stage was reached with the notions of political equality that emerged during the Enlightenment. The revolution against privilege that it produced emphasized a secular and activist equality which contrasted with the spiritual equality of the Middle Ages.

In the twentieth century two concepts of equality took shape which still largely guide the world. In America the idea of equality of opportunity became a cardinal principle of social policy. In Russia the notion of economic equality was adopted from Marx and supposedly put into operation—though, as we now know, it quickly degenerated into another form of privileged hierarchy.

In our own country we are on the verge of social cataclysm over this issue of equality. We have all seen the buttons distributed widely by civil rights groups: they consist merely of an equal sign. This reveals how central to the civil rights struggle is the idea of equality. No one can fully understand the historical significance of this movement without a firm grasp of the history of equality. Just as important is an acquaintance with the insights into this idea which are contributed by philosophy, psychology, sociology, economics, anthropology, and the other disciplines.

Yet our conventional academic programs make no attempt to achieve such understanding. Each of the academic disciplines touches on the subject at some points, but nowhere are the strands brought together, examined for contradictions, and woven into one fabric of significance.

We may say we want to encourage students to think maturely about the chief ideas of our culture. But as long as we merely hope that this power will take shape as a by-product of instruction in the conventional academic subjects, we will be disappointed in our results. If we really think that students should develop this power while in school and college, then why not devise meaningful programs and place them right at the center of the curriculum? If we examine our current offerings closely we will find, despite the renowned explosion of knowledge, that much can be deleted. For this very explosion of facts has, paradoxically, made them *less* important in education than they used to be. We must, of course, teach students how to go about acquiring the facts they will need and how to tell which facts are accurate and relevant. But much of what we teach students will be obsolete before they can put it into practice. Thus we could eliminate large parts of the curriculum without impairing the students' intellectual development. But this is only worth doing if we know what we want in their place.

I recognize that the programs I am suggesting would raise serious problems. One of the hardest to crack would be the school-teacher's traditional stance of neutrality. A curriculum built around major ideas would inevitably bring controversy right into the classroom. Today, in many communities, the teacher who led a discussion on such topics as black power, the Vietnam war, or Communism would be committing political suicide. Plainly, if we believe that schools should do more to generate thoughtful understanding of crucial ideas, then we would have to mobilize strong community backing for administrators and teachers willing and able to tackle controversial issues.

The key ideas of our culture animate and control men and women in both their day-to-day activities and in their larger social and intellectual lives. The set of basic ideas which each culture develops constitutes one of its major features. In short, the development of ideas constitutes a chronology of man's life style down through the ages.

I suggest adding a new dimension to our total school and college curriculum. Schools and colleges have dealt systematically with students' development in skills and subject matter. Now they need to deal systematically with students' grasp of major ideas. (And here, incidentally, would be a magnificent opportunity to plumb the potential of television, which could come into its own at last through imaginative programs designed to convey the sweep and power of the humanities and to stimulate thought and discussion. Television must cut loose from its present educational restraints. As Lucien Kinney says, using TV to teach arithmetic is like using a machine gun to kill mosquitoes.)

In no sense am I recommending indoctrination or a preordained way of coping with ideas. I am emphasizing the thinking process, which is creative and inherently hazardous. We never know where thinking may lead us; it is adventurous by definition. Thinking about ideas and ideals founded this nation. And now with the rapid expansion of knowledge we need to be sure that the major ideas that have contributed so much to the progress of civilization, to freedom and happiness for man, should not be lost in a mass of detail.

William S. Learned, the late staff officer of the Carnegie Foundation for the Advancement of Teaching, commented to the author:

> Good education selects large, simple ideas which transcend the limit of terms or years; good education builds these ideas gradually into his [the pupil's] permanent possession and shows how they fit and control other ideas; it teaches where to hang the details on these main conceptions, and by constant review, as the sculptor reviews his clay, it gives the pupil a sure feeling for what is important and what is irrelevant—a genuine philosophy.

For such an achievement, innovative education can become the key once it develops a new focus on the mastery of ideas.

9 The Need for Innovation in Higher Education

While it is true that some colleges and universities have conducted experiments and demonstrations designed to improve instruction, the cumulative and enduring impact is practically imperceptible.

For example, the Fund for the Advancement of Education devoted millions of dollars over a decade to demonstrations aimed at improving our colleges and universities. Hundreds of institutions were involved in these experiments. But in many cases, even after the demonstrations proved successful, the institution returned to its traditional teaching procedures.

Teaching by television is an example. After a few colleges had demonstrated its effectiveness, a nationwide program of instruction was launched—Continental Classroom. Professor Harvey White of the University of California taught the first course, in atomic-age physics. Although it was offered at 6:30 A.M., over a million teachers, students, and parents viewed it regularly throughout an entire academic year. During that year, six Nobel prize winners—Brattain, Kusch, Rabi, Seaborg, Anderson, and McMillan—and other distinguished scientists helped to teach the course. They represented an array of talent that no single university could possibly have offered its students. The following year a chemistry course was offered by Professor John Baxter of the University of Florida, likewise chosen as an outstanding teacher. He, too, was aided by eminent chemists from academic, industrial, and governmental laboratories. Other courses in biology, government, economics, and the humanities followed in rapid succession on national networks.

Every study made of the effectiveness of these courses indicated that the professors were, for the most part, superior, and the students learned as much as or more, according to test results, than others who pursued similar courses in the self-contained classroom. Enterprising institutions and communities have since adopted the idea with notable success: Chicago's hardy televised junior college curriculum and New York State's recently inaugurated University of the Air are outstanding examples. But Continental Classroom itself was allowed to wither on the vine and no comparable college course is now being televised nationally.

There are a number of reasons for the attrition of promising innovations. Here are a few of the most important ones. First, there is no mechanism whereby colleges can offer instruction cooperatively. Therefore, after an experiment involving a number of institutions has been successful, there is no agency that is responsible for carrying it on.

Another major reason that must be faced is that many innovations have been given insufficient trial and all too often have been mounted with little imagination or skill. This flaw undoubtedly explains in part the halting progress of instructional television (as the Appendix indicates) and probably accounts for much of the resentment among college students to televised courses as just another manifestation of vast impersonal education.

But if television and other promising innovations have been slow to catch on in the colleges and to fulfill their potential, I think the major obstacle lies in the faculty. This fact emerged very clearly from a study conducted some years ago by Professor Richard I. Evans of the University of Houston and Peter Leppmann, and it is still substantially unchanged. The study was published under the title *Resistance to Innovation in Higher Education*.[1] When professors rated various teaching procedures in order of preference, the five top-ranking procedures turned out to be the following:

1. Myself conducting a small class
2. Myself as a professor
3. Myself conducting an advanced course
4. Myself conducting an introductory course
5. Myself conducting a lecture course

Down 18th on the list is:

18. Television instruction supplemented by small discussions

Twenty-third on the list is:

23. Television instruction in introductory courses

And at the bottom of the list of procedures:

29. Television instruction in advanced courses
30. Straight television instruction for large classes

Obviously there is no relationship between the achievement of students under different teaching procedures and the preference for these procedures by professors.

In this connection, one conclusion of the study is especially worth noting:

. . . the faculty was, on the whole, self-confident about its instructional skills . . . We can note further that they ranked all items dealing directly with ITV in the lower half of the list . . . However, when the professor was asked to project himself into a teaching situation using television, his opinion of the medium rose significantly.[2]

Clearly, a very large majority of our institutions of higher learning and faculty members have no commitment to change or to improve college and university teaching. Is it any wonder, then, that one of the most noteworthy innovations in college teaching in

[1] Richard I. Evans and Peter K. Leppmann, *Resistance to Innovation in Higher Education* (San Francisco: Jossey-Bass Inc., 1968).
[2] *Ibid.*, p. 51.

recent years came about through student initiative rather than faculty enterprise? I am thinking of the so-called "Experimental Colleges" (or "Free Universities") which have now been established by students at some forty institutions, from San Francisco State College to Dartmouth. These universities consist of certain courses designed, organized, publicized, run, and largely taught *by students*. Naturally, they are extraordinarily responsive to the students' own interests. The subject matter tends to come from outside the standard college curriculum: some favorite topics are sexual behavior, LSD, contemporary radical (and conservative) thought, and jazz. In teaching techniques these free universities are also innovative: they place much more responsibility on the student than does the regular college, casting aside the whole apparatus of one-way lecture-teaching, tests, grades, credits, prerequisites, etc. The desire to learn is all the motivation these courses need, and apparently much learning does occur. It speaks well of American colleges and universities that the best of them have encouraged this movement and tried to learn from it.

For the most part, however, college faculties and administrations have remained impervious or hostile to change. This conclusion presents us with a curious paradox. The "best," the most sought after, college and university professors are those conducting research and pushing forward the frontiers of knowledge in specialized fields. Research means discovery and application of new principles, and thus implies change and improvement. And yet, even though research is carried on largely by university faculty members—or former faculty members who have gone into industry or government—institutions devote virtually no money or effort to experimentation and innovation in college teaching itself. On the one hand, they are vitally concerned with exploring the unknown, with challenging every old principle and with finding new insights in their fields of specialization. On the other hand, they accept wholly the traditional methods or old wives' tales about teaching, without any thought of improving procedures.

Sir Eric Ashby, vice-chancellor of the University of Cambridge, speaking in 1963 on "Investment in Man" in his presidential address to the British Association for the Advancement of Science, stated the issue poignantly:

> The very word "efficiency" applied to universities is anathema to some academic men. But of course there is no reason why our instruments for investment in man should be immune from the criteria of efficiency any more than our instruments for government or for the administration of justice are immune. Nor is there any reason why we should regard research into the production of educated people as any less important than research into the production of steel or artificial fibres. But we shy away from the idea of education as a technology. The techniques of education in Britain have scarcely been touched by the scientific revolution. This is particularly true in the universities: although dedicated to the pursuit of knowledge, they are reluctant to pursue knowledge about themselves. . . . The introduction of technology into teaching and learning at the university level evokes such emotional reactions that it is difficult to persuade some people to comtemplate it objectively.

Why is there such resistance to change, to innovate, to improve our teaching procedures? The reasons, I think, can be simply stated:

1. Tradition: the customs of Academia are notoriously conservative.

2. Motivation: the faculty have no interest in being more efficient.

3. Laziness: teachers follow the methods of those who have taught them.

4. Comfort: following the same procedures year after year is much easier than changing.

5. Economy: the old methods seem to save time and effort which can then be used in other activities such as research and writing which are valued more highly than teaching by universities in promotions and salary.

6. Technology: the outmoded construction of buildings and other facilities freeze instructional procedures.

7. Timidity: why stick out your neck and be criticized, when your present procedures are adequate by current standards?

These are the chief causes of resistance to change in higher education. The resistance is expressed not in these terms, however, but in terms of certain assumptions about college teaching not unlike those which block progress in the lower schools, but with their own salience.

The first assumption is that *effective college teaching must be carried on in small classes.* We have elevated this into a criterion of over-all institutional quality, usually assuming that a low student-teacher ratio is a sign of high-quality education. Yet the available research, as I have said, gives no support whatever to this assumption. In fact, the burden of proof is squarely on those who equate small classes with effective teaching, even though the traditionalists always try to reverse the procedure.

The monumental University of Minnesota studies of the 1920's are classics in this area. Small classes, mostly of 25 to 30 students, were compared with large groups ranging from 35 to 150 students. Most of the criteria used were tests of knowledge, but some attempts were made to measure more elusive intellectual changes. Out of fifty-nine controlled experiments involving a wide range of subject matter courses, forty-six favored the large classes. In the light of these and other studies, class size seems to be a relatively minor factor in educational efficiency, measured in terms of student achievement.

Very little significant research on this question has been conducted since the Minnesota studies. Even more significant, there has been little effort to apply these findings. Until very recently virtually nothing had been done to make class sizes suitable to various subjects and teaching methods.

A second fallacious assumption is that *there is a direct correlation between what the professor says in the classroom and what the students learn.* Just as the ideal of Mark Hopkins on one end of a log and a student on the other is belied by the facts regarding small and large classes, so here we are bemused by another ideal that is unrealistic. Our ideal is the scholarly, well-organized, fluent, entertaining, inspiring lecturer. But we must begin by recognizing that very few faculty members have this gift of eloquence, poise, and personal magnetism. Even with those who do, it is dangerous to assume that student learning follows as a matter of course. Students, I must stress once again, learn only from their own mental effort and activity. The professor's words are interpreted by each student according to his own experience, knowledge, and capacities. Since no two students are identical, they do not learn exactly the same things even though they are exposed to identical instruction.

The third assumption which impedes progress is that *the student learns only, or best, when he is physically in the room with the teacher*. Here again an ideal haunts our thinking: the small seminar or the image of disciples strolling with their master in some Socratic academy. But the facts are that much effective learning goes on without the presence of the teacher. Consider the student pursuing a research topic which has really engaged his curiosity and concern—or perhaps something totally removed from formal education, like skiing or a political campaign. This student can learn many things without supervision of any kind. Or recall the academic achievements of students studying by correspondence or of servicemen in the Armed Forces Training Program.

As Henry Steele Commager once told an interviewer:

We still refuse to learn what Oxford and Cambridge, for example, have taken to heart, that lectures often interfere with learning, that professors cannot be expected to do all the teaching, and that a major part of education is and should be performed by the students themselves.

In a sense, the final goal of any student's education should be the capacity to learn without the teacher, to continue his intellectual life on his own initiative and with his own resources. Increasingly, this is becoming not only an educational ideal but a social necessity. I think everybody realizes today that if graduates have not learned to learn on their own, then they have learned nothing of enduring value in a rapidly changing world. The time is past when we can indulge the notion that gives the student a body of knowledge during his four years of attendance, and then graduates him into a world where he can apply that knowledge for the rest of his life. Now the reverse is true: the moment he's off the campus the young man (or woman) who wants to win a place in the world must learn on his own—which was always true but never to the extent it's true today.

A final disabling assumption is that *there is an inverse correlation between technology in teaching and individual freedom.* People assume that the more machinery the less flexibility. This is the fear already mentioned, shared by students and teachers, that the introduction of technical devices on the campus will destroy individuality.

The reverse is true: in an era when students come in tidal waves, the vigorous, flexible, and *imaginative* use of technology may be the only hope for avoiding regimentation. To meet the needs of the individual student and to enable him to proceed at his own pace in a tailor-made program of studies, there is no choice but to bend to educational purposes every device and technique of modern communications science. If colleges want to preserve precious time for small group discussions and individual tutorials, then they will have to use labor-saving technology to release professors from teaching elementary material and acting as drill-masters.

The emerging technology of college teaching provides unprecedented opportunities for individualized instruction. Language laboratories can enable students to master foreign tongues with new ease and accuracy. Programed learning permits them to proceed at their own rate, with constant reinforcement and testing. A wide variety of audio-visual materials can stimulate students to self-study which is quite as effective as classroom instruction.

I believe we will soon discover that the more technology is properly and creatively introduced on the campuses the more the individuality, flexibility, and effectiveness of the total program is increased. Far from enslaving the student and professor, modern teaching tools and techniques can liberate them from the rigid compulsions of conventional instruction.

These unexamined assumptions, then, are the four walls of the box which blocks our access to the most promising innovations in higher education. If colleges and universities could break out of this box, if they could institutionalize innovation and invention on the campus, they would find a new freedom and flexibility in exploiting the limited resources available for instruction.

For years the voice of reason has gently implored Americans to examine fixed ideas about how college students learn. Now, however, the strident voice of necessity is demanding it. We must reconsider our penchant for small classes, our myth of the potency of the lecturer, our prejudice that instruction must be transmitted through a professor's larynx, and our assumption that technology and freedom are incompatible. College enrollments are soaring. New students come from the generation born during the postwar baby boom, but new faculty members come from the low-birth depression period. (In early 1968 the prospect of graduate schools greatly depleted by the draft greatly compounded the problem.) American higher education is caught in a demographic bind, and no amount of rhetoric will enable us to match students and professors in the conventional way in the years ahead. Either institutions will devise new ways of extending the influence of the best available faculty members or stand by and watch the quality of instruction steadily decline.

This is the kind of dilemma which can only be solved by moving to a higher level in educational planning. It means using television to bring outstanding lecturers to all students who can benefit from them. It means tapping the reservoir of the best instructional films available and creating new ones. It means using the long-distance telephone to bring outside lecturers to the campus, as when the late Professor Moses Hadas of Columbia lectured to students on five campuses simultaneously. Every modern medium of communication must be similarly harnessed to expand and strengthen the process of instruction.

Sitting in an office in New York City, Professor Hadas delivered a series of lectures on classical studies, which were transmitted over telephone lines to classrooms in five colleges in the South. After hearing each lecture, the students could talk with Dr. Hadas and get answers to their questions immediately. Thus they had the advantage of studying under one of the most distinguished classical scholars of our time, despite the fact that a scholar of such eminence could not usually be brought to their campus to lecture in person.

There are many ways in which students can learn—from lectures, from motion pictures and television presentations, from audio tapes or records, from books or discussion with their peers, alone or in small groups. There are many media of communication which can enrich students' education, many ways in which the faculty's knowledge and wisdom can be placed at the student's disposal, many opportunities for tailoring each youngster's program to his individual needs and aspirations.

The best way to realize these potentialities is for each institution to make a positive commitment now to innovation in teaching. Along the lines suggested in Chapter 2, every college should establish a program of research and development in the art and science of teaching. One lead worth following here is that of the State University of New York, which under Samuel Gould's leadership has designated one of its new college campuses as an experimental center. This college is free to question any practice in the current system, test out alternatives, and then help other units of SUNY to adopt what is worthwhile on their own campuses.

What would happen at representative institutions if they devoted a mere ½ of 1 percent of their instructional budget to this purpose? I think the results would be just as significant, if not more so, as those that have come from research in science, medicine, and industry. M.I.T., which through the Physical Science Study Committee has already revolutionized science instruction in American high schools, could have a dramatic impact on collegiate education. The University of Chicago, which has been experimenting with different ways of grouping students in secondary school, might update and extend the pioneering Minnesota experiments in college class size. Antioch College, which has done so much already in independent study, could explore the limits of independent study for the able student.

Some very provocative questions could also be studied through this procedure. For example:

Why is it that one of our best liberal arts colleges, such as Columbia College, could provide a very good education by offering less than 500 courses, and other colleges not nearly so well regarded need to offer over 1,000?

Why is it that a graduate school of education, such as Harvard's, could turn out exceptionally able teachers by offering about 100 courses, while other professional schools of lower quality need to offer 500 or even up to 1,000?

Why is it that among ten of our best universities and liberal arts colleges, one institution can carry on (nonlaboratory) instruction

- in biological sciences with an average class size of 130 whereas another does so with an average of 12?
- in chemistry with an average class size of 169 whereas another does so with an average of 6?
- in psychology with an average class size of 271 whereas another does so with an average of 15?

and so on through the various subjects in the curriculum. Yet the currency in academic credits is readily interchangeable among these institutions which include the University of California, Indiana University, Purdue, Vanderbilt, Michigan State University, and the University of Minnesota. Or, to state the issue in different terms, why is it that faculty salaries cannot be raised in order to attract more able people into the profession when it has been demonstrated by these institutions that high faculty salaries are not necessarily associated with high costs per student?

Why is it that the Free University of Berlin, as I mentioned in Chapter 1, can start from scratch and in less than two decades become an outstanding institution, particularly in the sciences, with one professor for every 50 students, when American institutions feel they cannot develop quality unless they have one faculty member for every 15 students or less?

What is the meaning of a college education when it has been shown over and over again on comprehensive examinations that many college seniors know less than many high school seniors?

If a liberal education is meaningful, what is it we should expect from a liberally educated college graduate in breadth of knowledge and understanding, depth of analysis, writing abilities, intellectual interests, etc.? Are there no minimum standards by which we can judge, aside from four years of residence in an accredited college?

And if accreditation is so important, why is it that students from nonaccredited colleges do as well in some of our best graduate schools as students of comparable ability from accredited colleges?

Furthermore, if education is basically the process of communicating the culture of one generation to the next, why is it that we do not make greater use of modern means of communication in extending the services of our ablest teachers?

These are only sample questions. One might go on and on illustrating the kind of inquiry that needs to be made if America is to build institutions of quality for the students bound to arrive ten years from now. We can no longer build in the image of the past. Even though we had the financial resources, we could not find and educate the teachers required to continue "higher education as usual."

We recognize, of course, great diversity in our institutions of higher learning. We have over and over again reiterated our belief that in diversity there is strength. And we have demonstrated in many ways that this is the case. But diversity does not mean watered-down or diluted standards; it is not a rationalization for mediocrity; it means differences. Underlying the differences there must be a sound rationale. Our concern for diversity must not lull us into accepting low quality. Instead, it should renew us in our strivings for excellence in developing to the fullest the variety of human talents which a society of free men so urgently needs.

10 The Requirements for Quality Education

The innovative approach I have been describing always provokes one basic question from boards, parents, and even professionals in the field of education. "Do these new techniques and approaches really improve the quality of teaching and learning or will experimentation endanger the quality of our schools?"

To assay some general answers to this perplexing question, we must begin by considering briefly the meaning of this word "quality" in education. What are its components? How can a community judge whether or not it is achieving quality in its schools? Second, we must consider coming changes in education and how one can plan for the future in the new situation facing the schools. Quality and innovation, as we shall see, are closely bound together in education today. The school system which does not constantly experiment, change its program, shift its emphases and methods, really cannot sustain quality.

First, then, what do we mean by quality in education? Each of us has something in mind when we talk about education of quality. This is a perennial question at all levels. Some time ago the *Christian Science Monitor* ran a series of articles on education. One of these articles was entitled "The Quest for Quality." In this article the education editor of the *Monitor* said we need to start at the top of the system. Thus, the ideal mix at the level of the public school system comprises an informed school board guiding the school system in a searching self-examination; a superintendent as interested in teaching and instruction as in organization; and principals who permit and encourage experimentation and innovation. This combination, the record shows time after time, produces excellent education. In other words, the author is saying that education of high quality flourishes in an atmosphere created by leadership, a leadership that comes from within the community.

But there are other aspects, other questions people raise when they talk about quality education. What is a "good" teacher? Merit pay plans continually stumble over this poser. Is college education "effective"? Effective for what? The question keeps coming up in community after community and throughout the nation. What constitutes a superior elementary school program? Public school educators struggle with this one as each new generation of parents enrolls its children with fervor and apprehension. Are "our" schools as "good" as those in other communities? Who has not asked or been asked this disturbing question? The whole agitation of recent years over "excellence" and national standards testifies to the continuing concern with this elusive problem.

A little semantic sophistication is helpful here. "Quality" is one of those high abstractions about which people can work up a great head of steam.

There are a number of quite different criteria which are commonly used to measure educational quality. Among secondary schools, for example, it is the criterion of academic success that distinguishes such schools as Scarsdale High School, Andover, Winnetka from other public and private institutions. But everyone realizes that the background students bring to these schools has much to do with their academic records. A moment's reflection will suggest that first-rate vocational or technical schools, like the Dunwoody School, are doing just as good a job for *their* students, even though few of their graduates achieve the academic distinction that characterizes graduates of the first type of school.

Some other criteria by which schools are often evaluated are worth listing here, just to get them out in the open where we can see their deficiencies. In consulting with school boards, superintendents, and communities I most often hear the following evidence adduced to suggest the quality of education:

- The ratio of teachers to pupils is way above the average.
- A large percentage of our high school graduates go on to college.
- Our pupils score high on comparative tests.
- The teachers have been trained in "good" colleges.
- The teachers have had "fine" experience; they have come from other "good" schools.
- When our teachers leave they get positions in some of the best schools of the country.
- Our schools have an excellent reputation in other communities; many visitors come to see what we are doing; we are really setting an example for others.
- The school buildings are impressive; they have all the newest and finest equipment.
- Our costs per pupil are relatively high; our community is willing to put much money into schools.
- Our children "like" school.
- We just "like" the superintendent and the teachers we know.
- The pupils who took vocational courses in high school get good jobs in industry.

Every reader can readily expand the list. Witnesses who produce "evidence" like this usually sidestep any attempt to define quality, or trouble themselves with how it can be measured in publicly verifiable ways. There is no single entity, nothing that you can put your finger on specifically, corresponding to the word "quality" against which to measure a specific school system. Of course, some general guidelines have emerged from experience. But there is little profit in trying to discern, through endless discussion, the "true" meaning of a very abstract term like "quality." What we must do is make clear what we want it to mean and then get on with the work of judging where we stand. Quality of education is not an absolute. It is the degree of relevance between ends and means.

When we come to judge the quality of a particular college, school, or school system we need to take into account a number of interrelated factors. *First,* what are the major purposes or objectives of the educational institution or system? The goals toward which we are working need to be clear in order to have a basis for judging whether or not we are reaching those goals. And frequently, as I have said, our goals are too indefinite, obscure, or global. *Second,* what particular problems does the school or college face in arriving at the goals and is it making progress in the solutions of those problems? *Third,* what resources are available to do the job? *Fourth,* what is the quality of the people who are carrying on the jobs, both students and teachers? To compare two schools or school systems, then, will require far more than looking at test scores, marks, entry to prestige colleges, physical plant, or any of the cruder rules of thumb cited above.

Lest I be misunderstood, I want to make clear that I am not saying that the definition and appraisal of educational quality is too complicated for laymen to understand. That excuse has been used all too often to cover incompetence or lack of imagination in school management. It is possible and necessary for laymen to satisfy themselves about the quality of their schools. But it is hard work, and it cannot be done through seasonal debate.

To discuss quality in the abstract will not get us very far. But to find out whether quality is being achieved in specific ways, to meet specific purposes, through the best use of our resources, can be fruitful indeed. It is a continuing, arduous, profound exercise for board, superintendent, staff, and concerned citizens. But it is the most rewarding possible work, because it forces constant attention to the real heart of the educational process.

An ambitious project has started to come to grips with some of the tough problems involved in appraising what really happens to pupils in schools. The National Assessment of Educational Progress must not be confused with nationwide *individual* testing programs; it presages no federal control of curriculum nor will it inhibit innovation. Primarily its purpose is "to provide the intelligent, lay public with census-like data on the educational levels of important sections of our population." The project will attempt to measure educational attainment using an intricate sampling technique that includes 256 "populations" (classified by age, sex, socioeconomic status, region, and type of community).

But let's make no mistake about it. Let's not be too optimistic that at last through the National Program on Assessment we will have a means of judging the quality of education offered through our public schools. Until we have a chance to examine the tests, until we can note whether the tests measure what we regard as important goals for the schools, until from the evidence we can judge whether the tests are valid and reliable within a small probable error, until then we will not know whether this National Program will add one modicum to our present means of judging quality.

But I do believe it possible to assess quality in education, and I also feel strongly that the results should be used as a basis for formulating policy. Consider this as a statement about how board members, presidents, deans, and superintendents make decisions about education:

Educational requirements tend to be stated in absolute terms, without reference to their costs. But the educational effectiveness or educational worth of any given procedure cannot logically be considered in isolation. It must be considered in relation to its cost—and, in a world in which resources are limited, to the alternative uses to which the resources could be put. Educational requirements are meaningful only in terms of benefits to be gained in relation to their cost.

Accordingly, resource costs and educational worth have to be scrutinized together. . . . We need educational studies which compare alternative ways of accomplishing educational objectives and which try to determine the way that contributes the most for a given cost or achieves a given objective for the least cost. . . . Neither cost nor effectiveness alone is a sufficient basis upon which to make educational policy. . . . Purpose, program, and budget are all aspects of the same basic decisions.

If that sounds sensible, then you agree that the measurement of quality is necessary for educational policy making. But, again, you can't apply a yardstick to an abstraction. Only through defining goals and purposes, formulating and examining programs, and estimating the results and costs can we develop all the information needed for wide decisions. The question of quality thus pervades the whole process of educational decision making.

The statement just "quoted" is actually a description[1] of what former Secretary of Defense McNamara took into account when he introduced modern program-planning techniques in the Pentagon. I have merely substituted the word "educational" for "military" throughout. In other words, in judging quality we can move from one field to another and use essentially the same techniques. I believe that "cost-effectiveness" studies, systems analysis, and coordinated consideration of purpose, program, and budget are just as necessary to education, if quality is to be achieved, as they are to national security.[2] (It is perfectly possible to be hardheaded about education, for all its sensitive and imponderable aspects, without being cold-blooded.)

Let us look more closely at the technical considerations basic to measuring the productivity of school systems. Even a brief consideration will indicate the feasibility and promise of such an approach.

---

[1] By Charles J. Hitch, in *Decision-Making for Defense* (University of California Press, 1965).

[2] The fact that our present knowledge and skills are inadequate to the task of applying this kind of analysis to education merely heightens the urgency of developing such abilities.

Productivity can be defined as the relationship between selected imputs and selected outputs.[3] The mathematical relationship between inputs and outputs is called a production function; the operation of the educational enterprise thus may be defined as a series of production functions.

While the suggested procedure is analogous to the analysis of a business enterprise, there are, of course, some important differences. In business and industry inputs and outputs can usually be evaluated in monetary terms, so that the profit of a business organization can be measured. The inputs and outputs of education include many variables which cannot be expressed in dollars and cents; furthermore, inputs and outputs cannot readily be expressed in the same unit; hence, there is no concept in education corresponding directly to the "profit" concept in business.[4]

Research at the University of Chicago and elsewhere does suggest three types of input-output relationships in education and three ways of looking at the concept of productivity. In the first place, schools and colleges may be looked upon as service-producing agencies. The services may be defined in such a way that they are comparable among types of activities (for example, one student-hour of Biology I or one hour of individual counseling) and the costs of providing these services may be compared from school to school. In this case, therefore, the input-output relationship is the cost, in dollars, of a unit of a given service.

The second type of input-output relationship is considerably more complex. Here the output is the increment in student learning (for example, an average gain, for a group of students, of seven grade points in reading ability—or, if we chose to devise appropriately sensitive testing devices, a measurable advance in maturity and power to cope with important ideas). Input is the resources used to produce these increments—time of teachers,

---

[3] *Productivity* is considered to be a term which is synonymous with *efficiency.*

[4] Recent research and analysis in business firms shows that here also there is not the single-minded dedication to the profit motive that was once presumed.

time of students, space, equipment, and materials, including books. The input variables must be weighted for quality. Most of these inputs can be given a monetary value—the major exception, of course, being students' time—but there is no way at present of expressing the outputs in monetary terms. However, it is possible to express the input-output relationship in statistical terms, and then we can ask such questions as: (1) How much money should be spent in order to obtain certain desired results? (2) How should a given sum of money be allocated within the school or college in order to produce maximum results? (3) What are some of the ways in which substitutions can be made among inputs without losing the desired results?

I now turn to a third type of input-output relationship, which is more akin to the research in the economics of education than the preceding two types, and admittedly a highly special and narrow measure of educational values. This third production function measures the relationship between the costs of given educational programs and the incomes students receive after graduation. Thus we might compare the costs of junior colleges and those of advanced technical training institutes with their respective *benefits* (in terms of additional income received by graduates). This last measure is useful in comparing different types of schools or curricula within a particular school (for example, the general and vocational curricula of a comprehensive high school).

I turn now to consider what this concept of productivity in education might mean for the improvement of schools. In the first place, it is very likely that there are gross differences in productivity among and within schools. Although there is no proof as to the magnitude of these differences in any given instance, experience suggests that:

1. The cost of producing certain specific services (such as, again, instruction for one student-hour in Biology I) varies among schools, even when controls are introduced for the quality of the services. In particular, certain services are produced at a much higher cost in very small schools than in larger schools.

2. Schools differ among each other in productivity. That is, even when inputs are held constant there are differences in average performance among schools. Among the most important inputs are the socioeconomic characteristics of communities; many studies show these characteristics to be closely related to mean performance. A regression line can be drawn, relating the major inputs (socioeconomic status of the community and amount of money spent per pupil), and schools of high and low productivity can be identified depending on whether they fall above or below this line (Figure 1).

Figure 1

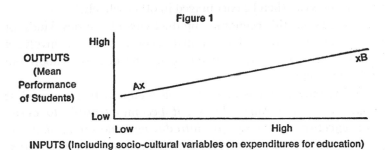

OUTPUTS
(Mean
Performance
of Students)

INPUTS (Including socio-cultural variables on expenditures for education)

NOTE: Even though the performance in school B is superior to that in school A, the former is under-productive, and the latter highly productive.

3. The various aspects of an educational program differ in their value as investment in human capital. (That is, they differ in the returns, in the form of increased income on investment in schooling.) For example, I would expect that some of the more expensive forms of vocational education, where research into the relationship between training and the market for skilled persons has been inadequate, are relatively poor investments. On the other hand, properly developed technical and vocational programs may provide a handsome return on the money invested in them.

There is evidence that the returns on investment in education can be increased by carrying out productivity studies of the following kinds:

1. Studies of the cost of producing specified services in different kinds of schools. The alleged inefficiencies of small high schools can be investigated in this manner, but these studies should not be confined to attempts to measure the effects, on cost, of differences in scale.

2. Attempts, through methods suggested above, to identify schools of high and low productivity throughout each state. Once such schools are identified, the factors related to high and low productivity should, wherever possible, be identified. The state can then provide inducements for low-productivity schools to improve their performance. The methods shown effective in high-productivity schools can then be encouraged in other schools.

3. Studies of the economic productivity of various kinds of schools, but especially of vocational schools. This will involve a longitudinal study of the income of graduates of these schools and studies of program costs.

Finally, once methods of measuring productivity are arrived at (even on an approximate basis), *it becomes possible to devise more effective procedures for introducing innovations and improvements into the system. As examples, research can be aimed at developing better input combinations to achieve the desired outputs and the value of new procedures in education can be evaluated.*

But isn't quality determined by more basic things than innovation—by such things as teachers' salaries, resources, facilities? And isn't innovation, on the other hand, something to be elected or not *after* schools have met the basic requirements of education? Isn't experimentation, in fact, a luxury for the school which has already achieved quality, a bonus for the affluent suburban school but irrelevant for schools in poorer communities? I think this "common-sense" view is incorrect and obsolete.

So is, in my opinion, another notion which equates innovation with educational emergencies. Indeed, a recent study of Systems Development Corporation indicates that innovations are most likely to take place in schools which are new or undergoing rapid growth. Typical of the pressures which seem to trigger innovation are rapid population growth, major changes in the composition, structure, or economy of the community, the pressures of organized groups, or challenges such as Russia posed when she launched Sputnik. But today rapid growth, major changes and challenges, and pressure from people vitally interested in the schools are becoming the standard conditions of the typical American community.

Change, in other words, *is* the status quo. Growth is the factor we can count on. Pressure is the natural environment of school policy-making. So, if innovation is the fruit of "emergency," we had better adjust to the idea that our society and our schools are in a permanent state of emergency and that innovation is a continuing responsibility. In my view, to achieve the quality of education which our children need today, schools must innovate.

Now, with this focus on change and innovation, what should we expect as we plan for the future of education in our communities? My answer is: we should expect change and we should welcome innovation. Quality and innovation are closely bound together in education, as closely as they are in industry. I don't think you can exaggerate the benefits that would accrue to a school system or a college or university willing to spend 3 to 4 percent of its total budget on new developments, on planning improvements for the future. It is a human problem that we're dealing with when we're concerned with the product of the schools. Show me a school which is not experimenting with new ways of improving education, and I will show you a school which, however good its present reputation, is likely slated for decline. Today good education is in large part synonymous with innovative education.

The process of innovation can, interestingly enough, have certain beneficial effects per se, regardless of the particular new practice involved. This phenomenon is an aspect of the so-called Hawthorne Effect, which has been widely observed in industry. Well-documented studies show that the productivity and morale of workers often increase when changes are made in the environment—quite regardless of what the changes are. When efforts are made to determine the source of the improvement, the critical factor is often the simple awareness of the workers that they are part of an experiment, that someone is interested in improving their environment and in learning their reactions. The same effect has been noticed time and again in schools. Teachers involved in a team teaching project, for example, operate at top effectiveness just because they are part of a new, fresh approach, and because they realize the administration is interested in helping them improve their performance. An atmosphere of stagnation is demoralizing; an atmosphere of challenge is exhilarating.

11   Innovative Education and the Deprived

The special problem of educating the deprived—particularly the children who live in big-city ghettos—constitutes the single most critical challenge facing American education today. What is the relevance of the innovative approach to this challenge? The answer to this question is complex, but boils down to three propositions: (1) experimental approaches are too recent and limited for educators to know which ones are of greatest value; (2) despite insufficient data, there is considerable evidence suggesting that the innovative *approach* does hold the key to meeting the needs of urban schools, but (3) its potential contribution to solving the over-all problems besetting ghetto youngsters is necessarily limited because these problems cannot be solved by educational programs alone.

The innovative approach has not as yet been vigorously applied to urban schools, though America by now has had several decades of experience in applying this approach to traditional educational procedures. I have been concerned, therefore, to show the success of the innovative approach in meeting various educational problems, but only to suggest its promise in helping to solve this critical "new" problem we have come so tardily to recognize. Only in the past several years has serious and sustained thought been given to it. And among the diversity of proposals which have been put forward none has been given sufficient trial to establish its efficacy.

Perhaps the most ambitious program in the nation is the New York City schools' More Effective Schools program, which pumps enough additional services and resources into slum schools to provide the equivalent of a good private school education. Proponents like Joseph Alsop claim that the program, though costly, is *the* answer to the problems of our big-city schools. Unfortunately, the available empirical evidence does not yet bear out—nor conclusively disprove—these claims. Rather, opinion is sharply divided on this controversial program. And the same is true of the other notable efforts. The most widely heralded "compensatory education" programs—More Effective Schools, New York's Higher Horizons, and the Great Cities School Improvement projects—have not significantly improved the academic performance of pupils.

But at least there are some issues for us to disagree about. And that means that fairly soon we should begin to see emerging some documented wisdom within the educational profession as to the right ways to tackle this bedeviling problem.

One thing, I believe, is clear already. The innovative approach seems to be the most rewarding one. Rather than merely give the deprived child more of the same—to "catch him up" through compensatory education programs—the most promising proposals envisage entirely new ways to reach such children. Here, as everywhere in the educational enterprise, the way forward must be an *innovative* way.

For example, as regards curriculum, many educators now favor a distinctive curriculum for the deprived. It would be quite different from the traditional or "reformed" curricula, however effective they have proved with middle-class youngsters. This curriculum would apply the techniques of individuation and flexibility, which I have stressed throughout this book, to the special needs of these students. Learning would be promoted through study which engaged the emotions as much as the intellect, which built up from concrete experiences instead of down from verbal abstractions, which involved participation and social action rather than mere passive reception of facts.[1]

The idea of the educational park, too, has gained widespread support. This centralized, richly programed environment would bring together students from a wide geographic area, thus moderating *de facto* segregation to some extent. At the same time centralization would offer opportunities, including funds for a much richer, more varied instructional program of benefit to all pupils.

A final example, having to do with organization. Late in 1967 a panel appointed by Mayor John Lindsay of New York and headed by McGeorge Bundy, president of the Ford Foundation, issued a plan for trying to resolve the problems of New York's schools. The controversial Bundy Plan involved a sweeping decentralization of the public schools of that city, giving to new, largely autonomous community school districts those critical powers over hiring and firing, curriculum, and teaching methods which had hitherto been held inviolate by the city's Board of Education. Mayor Lindsay, with the Bundy panel's agreement, presented a modified version of this plan to the state legislature. As this is written, the board has countered with a compromise decentralization plan of its own, and the debate rages anew. Whatever the outcome, to me the significant point is that the proponents of reform in the big cities are no longer remaining content with additive programs, extending the accepted techniques to the deprived neighborhoods. In school administration, as in curriculum and facilities design, the innovative approach is emerging as the key to solving the problems of educating the deprived.

As Mario Fantini of the Ford Foundation and Gerald Weinstein of Teachers College, Columbia (probably the most influential thinker on this whole question of education for the disadvantaged) have written:

[1] See Mario Fantini and Gerald Weinstein, *Toward a Contact Curriculum* (New York: Anti-Defamation League of B'nai Brith, 1967).

Our goal in improving the education of disadvantaged children has been to bring their schools up to the standards of the schools attended by their economic and social "betters." We strive to create middle-class schools in the slums.

But the middle-class school is not the best of all possible educational worlds. It is, in fact, a fortress built mainly of inherited, fixed concepts and practices. It is founded on the notion that the I.Q. is fixed. Its rhythm is a fixed system of grades based on a child's age. (All third-graders study the same material at the same time, varying abilities and interests be damned.) Most curricula still treat knowledge as fixed, with only lip service given to the concept that "truth" in any given field is more subject to change than not; the student has only to adjust to the school and learn the truth as it has been captured by the curriculum and he becomes an educated man. Similarly, the rules and regulations governing the profession and institutional practice are fixed—from class size to the credentials of a teacher.

Few of these fixed patterns were jolted by the clamor of Sputnik or the civil-rights movement.[2]

But, despite a strong temptation to do so, there is an overriding reason why I have not attempted any detailed examination of how the innovative approach can be applied to the problems of the disadvantaged. These problems are in large part problems of society as a whole, not strictly educational problems. This does not mean that the schools should not do all in their power to counteract the disastrous effects of environmental forces. There is no excuse for the all too familiar phenomenon of the schools actually aggravating the learning disabilities and handicaps of deprived youngsters. In many ghetto neighborhoods the children enter school in the first grade brighter, more willing to learn, more receptive to adults, than when they graduate twelve years later or drop out. This is the most devastating criticism which can be leveled at any educational institution: that it augments ignorance, stifles intelligence, and perverts fellow feeling.

Yet there is danger, too, in taking a grandiose view of the potentialities of formal schooling. The teacher can have only a limited

[2] "Taking Advantage of the Disadvantaged," *The Record* (Teachers College, Columbia University, November, 1967), pp. 103–104.

influence on a child's growth and development. To claim more is to court disenchantment. If the whole environment, the family, the mass media, the police and welfare agencies, and the other institutions of the society are all conspiring, knowingly or not, to trample the egos and to destroy the intelligences of minority groups in the population, the school—while it is inevitably concerned and must try to help—cannot offer a panacea. Rather, educators owe it to their fellow citizens and themselves to say frankly that more is required than schools can provide.

School programs, however advanced and potent, will never avail against environments which hammer away at children's self-respect, sensitivity, and intelligence. Until we alleviate ghetto conditions, until we break down the walls of *de facto* segregation in the central cities, we will not succeed completely in demolishing the learning handicaps of deprived youngsters.

To really meet the needs of the impoverished and discriminated against in our society, every one of us will have to make a real commitment and real sacrifices. Only then will education be able to augment our collective commitment to end misery and destitution in our land.

12 Education as a Futurist Enterprise

The focus of this book has been on schools and colleges and how we can make them run better and more humanely. I have argued that certain proposals for changing and improving education would be good for youngsters, for teachers, and for society—in measurable ways.

But education must be considered in broad perspective. If there is any human enterprise that engages man's deepest values, his highest hopes and most profound responsibilities, it is that of nurturing the young—and taking care in the process not to do them more harm than good. Looking to the future of education therefore inevitably means looking to the future of society. In fact, one needs to look to the future of society even for a clear vision of *present* educational needs and opportunities: what America does *now* about children and young people, in the schools and colleges of this country, will in large part determine the kind of future society these youngsters build in the decades ahead.

I believe that the innovative approach to education is in tune with the most powerful—and positive and admirable—trends in American society. America is essentially innovative, and this characteristic has not even yet reached the height of its expression in our culture. In almost every area of life we crave the new and better. New houses, new refrigerators, new automobiles, new fashions, new kinds of entertainment. On a higher level we aspire to new forms of expression in the arts, new achievements in science, new cures in medicine, new patterns for our social and political institutions.

Some time ago Erik Jonsson conducted me through the Texas Instrument Company, of which he is the creative genius. In the Dallas plant approximately 10,000 people were working on new developments in the electronics industry. While we were touring the plant, Mr. Jonsson observed: "You know, 80 percent of the specific products we were manufacturing two years ago we no longer make." A striking sample of the tempo of technological change.

It is no wonder that attitudes toward the future have changed radically in recent years. Many institutions are now engaged in serious, objective projection of the future, in order that they may deal systematically with the implied problems and opportunities. "Planning," it is now hard to remember, not so very long ago was a provocative word, suggesting foreign ideologies and doctrines. "The idea that a large country should be able to predict its future even half-way correctly five years in advance," writes Dr. Richard Lewinsohn in *Science, Prophecy, and Prediction,* "would have struck 19th century capitalists and socialists alike as utterly fantastic, as an idle play with figures." But now all major corporations have advanced-planning units that predict and plan for future economic developments. Government agencies are constantly creating and revising projections for various areas of society. Even universities, long resistant to rationalization of any sort, have begun to realize the necessity for long-range "master plans" for their future development.

In this chapter, then, I would like to look closely at the degree to which America is now increasingly focusing its attention on the future, on planning and charting purposeful change leading to a better life. For I think that all those concerned about education need to be aware of the degree to which innovation in the schools and colleges—and planning for innovation—is mandated by the new approach to innovation in society as a whole.

The latest technological innovation augmenting our ability to deal with the future is the computer. These machines have already been used to increase the accuracy of prediction in public affairs, most notably in projecting election results from a limited sample of returns. The potentialities here are well conveyed by Harold Lasswell's remark that "the critical procedure is the rehearsal of the entire range of imaginable options." It is now technically possible to simulate the behavior of a missile, a school system, a business, an electorate. Even more important than these particular instances of direct prediction by computers, computer technology has sparked a revival of concern with predicting and planning the future in general.

There are several projects afoot under corporate, governmental, scholarly, and philanthropic auspices. These are attempts to figure out the probable shape of the future with a precision and scope hitherto unknown. They are not mere speculations. Rather, they are rigorous, disciplined projections of future possibilities in a wide number of significant, interrelated fields. The resulting projections differ from previous ones in man's history because they are: group, not individual, efforts; systematic, not intuitive; based on data, not speculation; related to concrete policy, not idle speculation.

One of the most interesting of the group projects, directed by Professor Bertrand de Jouvenel and supported by the Ford Foundation, is called "Studies in Conjecture." De Jouvenel has written:

> The object of the venture is to promote surmising in the social and political fields, that is to formulate future developments which at present seem likely. It is hoped that such exercises in foresight may, in the course of time, make some contribution to political prudence, give warning of dangers to be avoided, or opportunities to be seized, or problems to be coped with.

Another effort to coordinate and refine expert projections of the future in more quantitative terms has been conducted by the Rand Corporation, under the direction of Olaf Helmer. The so-called

"Delphi Technique" has been described by one participant, Theodore Gordon, as follows:

> Experts were questioned individually by interview or questionnaire. In addition to questions relating to the central theme, each expert was asked what data would permit him to arrive at a more accurate answer. Between rounds of questioning, these data were made available to all experts. This was a type of controlled interaction which prevented direct confrontation. RAND found . . . that the opinions of the experts converged markedly. On the first round of questioning, their answers differed by a factor of one hundred; on the fifth round, their answers differed by a factor of two. The question asked had no discrete answer; the precision of the answer could not be evaluated. Yet, here were a group of experts essentially in agreement. . . . They had formulated a group prophecy.[1]

Perhaps the most celebrated outcome of such deliberations has been *The Year 2000*, by Herman Kahn and Anthony J. Wiener. This book grew out of the work of the Commission on the Year 2000, organized by the American Academy of Arts and Sciences, with Daniel Bell as chairman, and supported by the Carnegie Corporation. The commission has drawn on a great variety of talents and specialties—biologists, economists, political scientists, government people, among many others. Through the preparation of diverse studies and working papers, through meetings large and small, the commission has been engaged in the "complicated and subtle art of defining alternatives." The words are those of chairman Bell, who sees this as the commission's role as contrasted with sheer prediction. The commission takes very nearly the whole range of human concern as its province—from individual privacy to the mass media to the international order. In defining the premise of the Commission on the Year 2000, Mr. Bell has written:

> Time, said St. Augustine, is a three-fold present: the present as we experience it, the past as a present memory, and the future as a present expectation. By that criterion, the world of the year 2000 has already

[1] Theodore J. Gordon, *The Future* (New York: St. Martin's Press, 1965), pp. ix–x.

arrived. . . . The future is not an overarching leap into the distance; it begins in the present.[2]

Studies of the future are bound to gain importance and support as the need for long-range planning on a national or global scale becomes apparent in virtually every field of human endeavor.

What basic approaches and techniques are of specific use to the educator to help him think about the future and examine predictions and alternatives?

Perhaps the first thing the educator must do is, using as raw material the various predictions, forecasts, and projections in the field under consideration, to name and describe those developments that seem both most probable and most salient. He will be seeking to discern the lineaments of the future—to envisage those developments which, if they do materialize, will have the sharpest and most profound consequences for the educational problems which concern him.

Just as in a typical corporation 20 percent of the people may make 80 percent of the decisions, and 30 percent of the orders may account for 70 percent of the volume, so a few highly significant developments will have a disproportionate impact on the educational environment of the future. The late C. Wright Mills described such developments as "the pivots of history . . . points around which managed structures swing in new and unforeseen directions."

There is no need to arrive at a consensus on *the* future: the educator in many cases will want to consider a *range* of possible futures—in fact, this is obviously a more prudent and ultimately more fruitful procedure. Gordon and Helmer of the Rand Corporation usefully distinguish between "prediction" (of a single future) and "forecasting" (mapping out several possible futures). Some of the most sophisticated predictive enterprises currently in

[2] Daniel Bell, "The Year 2000—The Trajectory of an Idea," *Daedalus*, Vol. 96, No. 3 (Summer, 1967), Proceedings of the American Academy of Arts and Sciences, p. 639.

use employ the latter technique, including the Hudson Institute's "scenarios" of future military and social situations and the so-called "Monte Carlo" prediction technique. This technique, used at Cape Kennedy to map the flight of rockets, uses a computer to predict events on the basis of probability of occurrence. Safety requirements at the Cape demand accurate prediction of the flight path of each projectile. But all the variables affecting the flight simply cannot be known beforehand. So the computer samples the possible factors that would affect the rocket in flight, and plots a flight path based on each set of variables. What results is a family of flight paths ranging from the least to the most probable. This procedure illustrates how the computer becomes essential when prediction and planning reach the stage of operational details. The principle can equally well be applied to policy discussions in education.

In many respects it is relatively unimportant in education to predict exact time schedules for future occurrences, if general patterns of change and even directions of change can be foreseen. Such tendencies are much easier to foresee than the exact course of developments or the time schedule for future events.

If a general consensus can be achieved on (1) the factors that will largely determine significant aspects of the future and (2) their most likely effects, the next step might be to consider how these factors and their effects relate to the basic conduct of the educational enterprise.

Having considered the most probable and important changes and their implications, the educator might next explore the policies or actions most likely to influence the course of events. What kinds of policies and actions in a given area will shape selected aspects of the future to his best hopes and aspirations? For example, if available jobs in a certain sector of the economy are due to increase significantly, then a large investment in training for such jobs might be shown to be an economical use of public funds.

Still another route to fruitful discussion is the identification of "change of phase" points. In science, for example, we are clearly due for a distinct change of phase as the rate of growth of the past few decades inevitably slows down. (If expenditures for research and the number of scientists in the population both continued growing at their recent rate, by 1980 the entire national budget would be devoted to science and every adult in the United States would be a scientist.)

Projection of geometric curves to absurd extremes suggests one limit to the uses of extrapolation. There is another and almost opposite danger to this kind of projection: it can obscure the possibility of revolutionary upsurges. For example, the fine studies done by the Twentieth Century Fund and published in USA *and Its Economic Future* (1964) envisage only evolutionary changes, as indicated by typical phrases from the projections: "Even at its present moderate rate of growth, the nation's prospects are promising. . . . Assuming that productivity increases year by year at about the same rate as today . . . If the work week remains unchanged, and if employment and productivity reach anticipated levels . . ." Clearly such an approach to the future fails to take account of wholly new forces or quantum jumps in certain pre-existing areas. An example of this first kind of development would be the use of programed learning in American education; of the second kind, the unpredictable escalation of the civil rights movement after the Montgomery bus boycott.

These are some of the useful ways (as well as some of the pitfalls) of thinking about the future of education. I'd like to touch as well on some general methods of analysis that might make these ways of discussing the future even more fruitful. Are there significant characteristics of any discussion of the future that transcend the particular topic under discussion? If there are, how can they be usefully applied to sharpen discussion in a variety of fields?

We know some things about any set of observations, predictions, descriptions, or recommendations about the future, simply by virtue of the fact that they *do* relate to the future. Let us think of them as a map of the future.[3] Needless to say, the utility of any such map depends on its correspondence to the territory it purports to represent. As Harrison Brown and his coauthors of *The Next Hundred Years* put it with engaging candor: "The chief pleasure of a forecaster of future events lies in finding that his predictions are correct; that he has properly weighed trends and limits and has in fact foreseen the future."

What do we know about any map of the future per se?

1. We know that a map of the future cannot be certain, only highly probable. Later, when we overtake the future, we can look back to see whether the map was right or wrong. But when we make the map, in the present, it can only be characterized by some degree of probability. It behooves us, then, to keep continually aware that our pictures of the future are merely probable, to reflect this awareness in statements about the maps, to designate wherever possible the rough *degree* of probability attributable to various features.

2. A map is a human creation—it implies a map-maker with a purpose and a map-reader with a similar set of interests and preconceptions. The various projections of the earth's surface used by cartographers are quite different in appearance, yet each is useful for its specific purpose.

Similarly, different educators with different interests will create maps of the future dealing with their special concerns. Inevitably, neither the map-maker nor his professional audience realizes the selective nature of these maps; rather, it is assumed that a highly specialized map of the future portrays the most important and all-determining factors. Thus educators project a future in which

[3] This analogy is central to some of the most sophisticated managerial systems for dealing with the future. "A plan is a map of the future," according to Gabriel Stilian in *PERT: A New Management Planning and Control Technique* (New York: American Management Association, 1962). These systems have not, however, considered the implications of the analogy, attempted in the text.

schools and colleges are the dominant institutions of society; scientists like the late Lloyd Berkner foresee a "scientific age"; statesmen (with perhaps the greatest justification) see the international conflicts of the future as the all-pervasive force; population experts envisage demographic trends as the great molder of the future. Each of these experts has a keen grasp of one dimension of the future, but each of their maps overstates that dimension to the virtual exclusion of the others, as if one were to draw a highway map of the U.S. and claim that it gave a "true" picture of the country. Similarly, within their own fields, too, experts emphasize the aspects of the future that they themselves consider important; one educator might stress the number of teachers, another the spread of televised teaching. (My projections of Higher Education in the 21st Century, in the next chapter, are undoubtedly a case in point.)

No map covers everything in the territory it purports to represent. Each map is useful for its specific purposes. Judgment on a map of the future must deal not just with its accuracy, but with its relevance for the purpose at hand. Where a map purports to plot the probable future for a whole society, the criterion of "comprehensiveness" becomes paramount. As Nigel Calder has pointed out:

". . . isolated forecasts by individuals tend to center on a few ideas and overlook the fact that the world of the future, like the world of the present, is a complex system of many technical and human elements. A comprehensive approach is required if important factors are not to be missed."[4]

3. The purposive, highly selective nature of any map of the future suggests other questions that might well be raised in the examination and refinement of such projections:

    (a) When? Roughly what *time scale* does a given discussion span? (World government is perhaps on the way *ultimately* —but when is it envisaged as coming into existence?)

[4] Nigel Calder, *The World in 1984* (Baltimore, Md.: Penguin Books, 1965), Vol. I, p. 8.

(b) Where? What are the *limits of the territory* that a given map purports to describe? In making a prediction about college students in the future, for example, one might specify whether one is talking about students in Ivy League schools, large Midwestern universities, junior colleges, etc. Is a separate projection necessary for each of these?

4. Documentation in general is quite important in making maps of the future. In Europe during the early Renaissance there were two entirely different kinds of maps in currency, known to historians today as "churchmen's maps" and "sailors' maps." Churchmen's maps conformed to the ecclesiastical prejudices of the day and were accepted by scholars in the universities. Sailors' maps were heretical because they violated what the church said was true—but they conformed to what sailors knew of land and sea and were therefore used for navigation.[5] Is it possible that our maps of the present and future are frequently more like churchmen's maps than like sailors' maps?

Let me turn now from *how* to think about the future to *why* the educator in particular should and must look ahead. Educational change is an idea whose time has come. The innovations I have been analyzing in this book are, it would appear, on the brink of widespread adoption—and adaptation. Ten years from now American education may have changed beyond recognition. But how will it have changed? For if educators do not *plan* for the changes that are inevitable in the near future, the changes will take place at random, in response to specific crises and to pressure from special interest groups. Instead of a tapestry we will find ourselves with a badly made patchwork quilt.

In planning for the future of education, in mapping out alternatives, educators must keep in mind the importance of the comprehensive approach. As society grows daily more complex, the re-

[5] R. E. Dickinson and O. J. R. Howarth, *The Making of Geography* (New York: The Oxford University Press, 1933), pp. 61–62.

sponsibility it places on its schools and colleges is daily growing greater.

Educators must then look to the future with a particular style. They should approach it, not as do so many ideologists of one persuasion or another, with a fixed idea of its basic character. Nor should they eye it from the technician's viewpoint, as a mere "problem" in resource allocation or systems design. Rather, they should envisage the future as a challenge—a challenge demanding the most flexible, comprehensive, precise judgments of which they are capable.

13   A 21st-Century View of
American Higher Education

(This chapter projects the possibilities that can now be foreseen into an imaginary system of higher education for the beginning of the 21st century.)

In this year A.D. 2000, we live in a world very different from that our parents knew. Travel time to Europe and other parts of the globe has shrunk to only a matter of an hour or less. Shortly we will have our first manned lunar base fully equipped for indefinite stays, and will land manned spacecraft on both Mars and Venus. We are on the verge of extending our explorations into the infinite universe.

The International Telecommunications Satellite Consortium now operates on a worldwide basis, and Macy's has long been selling walkie-talkie video sets not much larger than a wrist watch. Our national data center makes technical information in virtually every field readily available to individual scholars. Indeed, our home facsimile systems have made newspapers obsolete. Satellites give us very accurate weather predictions and we are on the verge of controlling typhoons and hurricanes.

Our population has expanded far beyond the estimates of thirty years ago, when we numbered nearly 200 million persons. Even though our birth rate slowed up, we are today approaching 300 million, with over 30 million in the New York Metropolitan area alone. Our population growth and our emerging electronic technology have forced many changes upon us in the field of education. During the first half of the twentieth century, we established universal elementary and secondary education. During the second half we provided for all children equal educational opportunities regardless of race or economic status. (Of course, much of today's education is carried on in business, industry, and government, rather than exclusively in the context of the classroom.) We needed the additional skills and we had to protect the labor force in a market which no longer had jobs for untrained young people. In the process we restructured our educational system.

The New Shape of Higher Education

Many of our former liberal arts colleges—there were once 62 in the state of Pennsylvania alone—were unable to solve their pressing financial problems in the years after World War II. Since their physical facilities were still urgently needed, local communities transformed many of them into junior colleges. In addition, new institutions of that kind were being established for a period at the rate of 100 per year. The result is that a two-year college is now available for every young man and woman within commuting distance from home.

These colleges prepare some students for more advanced college and university work; they also train most of the technicians essential to the professions. The Rochester Institute of Technology under Mark Ellingson's presidency set the pace. After several periods of expansion, it now enrolls more than 50,000 students. Its graduates are serving throughout the world. Many of them, for example, have played important roles in developing the photographic computer systems which translate written messages from one language to another. The Institute's cooperative work-study program—now almost 100 years old—was among the first in the nation. At present nearly every technical training institution follows this plan with the students spending half their time at study and the other half at work.

During the thirty-five years following World War II, teachers colleges disappeared completely from the American scene. Their place has been taken by multipurpose institutions which, together with the strong liberal arts colleges and the universities, have discontinued the first two years, since these now come almost wholly within the province of the junior colleges. The transition took place with surprising smoothness. Once college football, basketball, and other sports became completely professionalized and the social fraternities and sororities vanished from the scene, such changes were easier to make. California and Florida took the lead.

The new multipurpose institutions, following the pattern first set by Florida Atlantic University, now admit qualified graduates from the junior colleges and offer three-year programs, culminating in the master's degree. During the last quarter of the century, there were heated debates at meetings of the Association of American Colleges on the question of whether or not the baccalaureate degree should be granted at the end of junior college work. The traditionalists won; the junior colleges continued to award the Associate of Arts or Associate of Science degree, while the baccalaureate of arts or science fell into disuse because students going beyond junior college pursued a program leading directly to the master's degree or a professional degree.

The largest universities, with their clusters of professional and graduate schools, research institutions, environmental and health institutes, have now become university cities. Education has truly become "big business," with all aspects of the large metropolitan university closely linked with every phase of urban development. Some, like New York University, enroll more than 200,000 full-time students (we continue to wonder whether these institutions are getting too big!) and offer some type of education for virtually every citizen.

And now we have two completely new types of institutions emerging. With the increasing complexity of our technological society, it became essential for most adults to take special courses periodically in order to comprehend and adjust to the sudden changes taking place during very short periods of time. Whereas during the seventies major changes still took five to ten years to be accepted, today they are becoming operative within a year or less.

Consequently every community now has neighborhood continuing education centers. Since more and more instruction is now offered over the computer-Telestar system, and since even examinations are administered over special two-way telecommunication instruments, the continuing education centers primarily offer the opportunity for small group discussions directed by able moderators to supplement robot instruction.

The second new type of institution was first proposed by Athelstan Spilhaus. In urging the creation of "sea-grant colleges," he pointed out that the need for them was comparable to that for land-grant colleges to experiment in agriculture at the middle of the nineteenth century. However, it took two decades after the proposal was submitted before the Congress finally acted to establish them. Only after the sand beaches were being swept into the sea, the shorelines eroded, and the water polluted to the point where it threatened to exterminate all sea life did public pressure mount forcing the Congress to take action. Now with seven sea-grant colleges well under way, we are belatedly developing the new field of ocean engineering which promises to both harness and quiet wave power. When this is finally achieved, floating cities in the oceans will become possible. Also for the first time it now seems that enough seafood resources can be developed to meet the world's protein needs. The availability of seafood and the new ocean mining resources are thus rapidly creating a great new market.

New Aims for Education

Our economy of abundance and our better system of distributing goods have made us less concerned with the strictly professional or vocational aims of education. Pressed by the rebellion of college students, we have overcome the temptation, prevalent earlier, to judge the value of a college degree by the additional earning power it confers. We now minimize the time spent on acquiring practical skills and factual knowledge. We no longer seek to produce a person "crammed full of knowledge" or (as the old *New Yorker* magazine expressed it in a cartoon more than a half century ago) the speaker who "knows nothing but facts." Our system of computers makes any and all facts readily and accurately available. We place more emphasis on developing wisdom; on leading our young people to higher levels of maturity in dealing with ideas such as liberty, energy, and beauty that have made a difference in the progress of civilization. We also concentrate on instilling ideals and cultural interests that help to make leisure time more satisfying than it was in the early days of the affluent society, when men were consumed—to the point of boredom—with strictly materialistic pleasures. We now recognize the truth expressed by Mark Van Doren fifty years ago: "Freedom to use the mind is the greatest happiness."

As part of this change we have seen the resurgence of philosophy as a key academic discipline. Like other subjects in the curriculum it has had its ups and downs. During the early part of the twentieth century it lost its vitality and degenerated into a study of philosophical systems and the microscopic analysis of language. After several decades, however, antiquarianism and logical positivism seemed equally sterile. No great philosophers emerged; the sciences grew to dominate the college and university campuses.

Those were the days when physicists, chemists, biologists, and aeronautical engineers with a bent for research could get almost any amount of money to advance their projects. The federal government, through the National Science Foundation, the National Institutes of Health, the National Aeronautics and Space Agency, the Department of Defense, and other agencies greatly accelerated research and development. As a result of this stepped-up effort, we added to our knowledge so rapidly that the accumulation shocked us into the realization that our endeavors were almost completely aimless. For example, our geneticists and biochemists gave us the knowledge and techniques necessary to mold human beings to our specifications. We can now direct the evolution of mankind; it need no longer be left to chance. (Over the years Nobel prizes have been awarded for these contributions to a long line of geneticists and biochemists beginning with Morgan, Muller, Lederberg, Kornberg, Beadle, and Tatum.)

Once the genetic possibilities were available, however, we found that we were completely devoid of ideas concerning the kinds of men and women we wanted to create and the nature of the society we aspired to build. Our desire for two automobiles, a boat on a trailer, a helicopter, and a twenty-hour work week had long ago been satisfied. We had come to the point where we recognized the need for help from some outstanding scholars to try to shape new directions for mankind. Some of our ablest minds have been encouraged with fellowships and grants to follow up promising leads. The consequence is that exciting ideas are beginning to emerge and at least a dozen brilliant young philosophers are cutting across subject matter disciplines and showing signs of developing a new synthesis of knowledge.

This revival of philosophy, and the humanities in general, emerged gradually. During the middle of the last century it was clear that a spiritual malaise afflicted American life. Studies of the national character seemed to indicate that America had "run out of gas"; individuals felt dominated by the vastness of their own social institutions and by a national style of conformity also referred to as "other-directedness." Conservatism gripped the nation and the question arose whether America "had any more great business to conduct." It took the assassination of President John F. Kennedy, his brother Senator Robert F. Kennedy, and Dr. Martin Luther King to drive the nation to find a new sense of purpose, to clarify the meaning of human rights and reduce violence. The national goals were submitted to close scrutiny and individuals began to ask themselves if the zealous accumulation of creature comforts had not reached a point of diminishing returns.

College students, who so often foreshadow the emerging concerns of a generation, began to demand more from their colleges and universities than vocational preparation and a general veneer of culture. Through such organizations as the "Challenge" symposia, "Experimental Colleges," sit-ins and riots on campuses, by the various activist groups concerned with civil rights, the Vietnam war, and draft regulations, college students demanded and obtained a greater voice in administrative affairs and sparked the redesign of higher education to help them cope with the underlying problems of their day. At the same time the society surrounding the colleges needed help on its emerging problems. These forces pushed the universities toward a revival of humanistic thought, so that even our great technical institutions, sparked by the Massachusetts Institute of Technology in mid-century, sought a better balance in the education of their students through a renewed emphasis on the humanities.

We are now just beginning to take seriously Ortega y Gasset's insight first set down seventy years ago in his *Mission of the University*: "The need to create sound syntheses and systematization of knowledge, to be taught in the 'Faculty of Culture,' will call out a kind of scientific genius which hitherto has existed only as an aberration, the genius for integration." To help meet this need, then-President Barnaby Keeney in the late 50's established at Brown University an Institute for the Synthesis of Knowledge. The significance of such an institute was not at first comprehended nor were others established until some two decades later. Even the wisdom of the classics is now being re-examined in the light of machine intelligence that goes beyond the capabilities of the human brain and the biochemical discoveries that make necessary a new set of moral and ethical values.

Resources for Learning

As striking as the difference between today's colleges and those of fifty years ago in the aims of education, however, is the difference in use of learning resources. We are now using devices and techniques which were not even thought of prior to the mid-twentieth century. Curriculum has always been a subject of education debate and reform, but the actual learning resources which our students now take for granted were developed between the 1950's and 1970's. And it is these resources which enable us to fulfill the psychologist's dreams of making the best teaching available to all students and of truly adapting instruction to individual rates of learning.

Television offers an example. Its use as an educational medium in colleges developed steadily after it was introduced. But educators were typically slow to see that this revolutionary device, which in a decade had transformed the living habits of a nation by capturing the attention of the average viewer five and one-half hours a day, would inevitably have just as great an impact upon our schools and colleges. It was later, when combined with computers and a system of satellites, that the use of television soared. After a period of riots and violence, the schools and colleges finally learned that they had turned over the education of the emotions to this powerful means of communication. They then began to stress the humanities more to counteract the effects of TV programs. They even began to exert their influence on these shows and thereby brought about a striking improvement in the kind of programs offered over commercial television.

Years elapsed, however, before colleges recognized that television and computers had made the standard lecture obsolete, and the conventional laboratory demonstration inadequate and costly.

It took decades more before the quality of courses approached the dazzling technological possibilities of the medium.

One of the reasons that both television and computers made slow progress at first was the fear that outstanding lecturers would somehow displace the classroom teacher and make the campus college obsolete. In this regard the objections were essentially the same as those raised at Oxford and Cambridge in the latter part of the nineteenth century. When the "university lectures" were proposed, the Oxbridge dons predicted that the innovation would reduce the separate colleges to mere appendages. What actually happened was that the individual colleges became more important when professors were relieved of the responsibility for lecturing. Instead, they could devote themselves to probing the students' mind and spirit individually or in small groups. And the students benefited from this and the opportunity to hear, at the same time, the very best lecturers in each field.

Now, fortunately, exemplary lectures by some of the greatest scholars of the world on the basic substance of their fields are available on electronic tapes. We slowly began to record systematically the leading scholars of the world; however, we missed many of the great men who lived in the twentieth century, such as Enrico Fermi, Henri Bergson, Sigmund Freud, and even Albert Einstein and Robert Oppenheimer.

Following the experimentation with television, the most drastic instructional revolution came in the 1970's when we finally began to recognize the potential of the computers. Never before did man have available such an aid for learning. The invention of writing, the printing press with the production of books and journals, libraries, laboratories, studios, motion pictures, phonographs, telephones, tape recorders, radios, programed learning or teaching machines, and television are now merged with the computer into a single system for learning. Even with the strides made during the past half century, we are just beginning to grasp the significance of the computer. We have been forced to rethink the whole process of teaching and learning and to completely redesign our instructional centers.

Much more sophisticated learning terminals with graphic tablets, multipurpose TV type displays, etc., are now readily available to practically every college student. Each terminal includes an instrument with a keyboard that looks like an electric typewriter and a telephone. It is activated with a student dialing a number for the information or problem he wants. The response is typed or displayed immediately. The student is therefore in a position to carry on a continuous dialogue with the computer in a way that he was never able to do with a teacher. Furthermore, the computer provides accurate and detailed information which the instructor did not always have available.

Such a computerized learning system became possible with the development of time-sharing, permitting many students to use the computer at the same time with computer language in simple English. Courses in the use of the computer are now required as an essential part of general education at virtually every college and university.

Terminals are available in all faculty and administrative offices, in specially designated learning centers, and in most dormitory rooms. Indeed, they are as common in homes as TV and radio sets were thirty or more years ago. Thus for basic instruction the student living at home need not go to the university. He can proceed at his own pace. He goes to the university to see his teachers, who now serve as tutors while they supervise the student's work and judge his progress. The instructors themselves use the computers to keep up with developments in their field and for research. With long-distance electronic instruction, all classrooms have been transformed into seminar rooms for small group discussion.

The possibilities of computerized learning are limitless. For example, through simulation the student can set up a model of a real situation. He can then work out experiments on the model that were not possible in the old laboratories. He might, for illustrative purposes, simulate a major earthquake disaster and then try out various ways of dealing with it. Or he might simulate a social problem such as population growth and try out various ways of coping with it through housing transportation and communications systems. The speed of carrying out such experiments is unbelievable. As Professor Kemeny of Dartmouth pointed out some years ago, it is possible for an undergraduate student to make all the calculations in one afternoon that it took one full year working around the clock to do back at Los Alamos in 1945.

Perhaps the most effective use of computers is in the medical schools. They started early with a worldwide network to use the greatest specialists anywhere for rare diseases. The patient's symptoms and signs were coded into the computer. Within minutes from across the world came the diagnosis and prescription for treatment.

Some years ago now researchers at the University of Southern California Medical School developed a computer-controlled manikin, known as Sim One. With heart, pulse beat, blood pressure, it was sufficiently lifelike to be really representative of a human patient on an operating table. Such manikins are now used extensively for instructional purposes. Supplementing manikins are remote-controlled artificial hands, making it possible for a surgeon living in one place to operate on patients far across the world. Furthermore, it is now possible to embed sensors in human bodies permanently. These can transmit information such as body temperature, pulse rate, blood pressure, and other medically important data to computers. Through such means the medical investigator is in a much better position than ever before to keep in touch continuously with his subjects or patients and check on physiological malfunctioning. Research carried on through this means has already added measurably to man's life span.

Supplementing the computer terminals are three-dimensional color television sets over which lectures, demonstrations, and on-site studies are brought to the students.

Televised and computerized courses are used by students throughout the country. Students everywhere are privileged to listen in their homes to the great men who advanced our culture in every field of learning. They can respond immediately to the computer centers. We have made incalculable progress since the days when our youngest college students were taught almost entirely by academic novices.

After the students have mastered the basic materials, through the use of computers and taped lectures and demonstrations by outstanding teachers and scholars, they meet with senior faculty members who, having been spared the drudgery of repeating over and over the basic substance of their fields, are eager to work with students on advanced topics. Moreover, the students themselves feel that they have a firmer grasp of the subject matter, because they have studied the lectures at their own rate of comprehension, reviewing them on kinescopes and checking with the computer as often as necessary. In addition, the thorough organization and planning which has gone into each lesson has had its effect, and the result is better teaching and more thorough learning.

Television and the computer have, in short, provided us with the technology we needed to build a genuine system of education for all—one in which each student has an equal opportunity to learn, no matter where his college is located or what its resources are.

All this has helped us to make enormous strides in the teaching of the individual student. Here the most exciting developments have been in independent study, honors work, programed learning, and computerized instruction.

Independent study has had a curious history. Although we adopted the English college and the German university, we failed to import a basic ingredient of both, namely, their emphasis on independent work in higher education. Instead, we projected into the colleges and universities the elementary and secondary school notions of compulsory class attendance. Even after President Aydelotte introduced "working for honors" at Swarthmore, it took us an unconscionably long time to recognize that independent study was essential to a maturing mind.

Programed learning, to say nothing of the computer, so common today, was hardly known fifty years ago. True, Professor Sidney Pressey at Ohio State University invented the first "teaching machine" in the 1930's, a device which is now permanently on exhibit at the Smithsonian Institution. But it was not until two decades later when Professor B. F. Skinner developed a more advanced machine, and carried on his experiments at Harvard, that programed learning began to attract attention. After various experiments at Harvard, Hamilton College, and numerous secondary schools throughout the nation had clearly demonstrated that students learned as fast or faster with programed materials than with conventional texts and lectures, this scheme of instruction developed into one of the most effective resources for adjusting instruction to the individual student's rate of learning. Such results drastically changed the writing of textbooks and made possible our more sophisticated programing of computers.

The resistance to programing was different from that which had confronted television. Educators knew what television was but, by and large, refused to grasp its pedagogical implications. In the case of programed learning and computers, though, most college teachers and administrators didn't even know what the new techniques were—all that they knew was that, because of its unfortunate linkage with "teaching machines and automation," they didn't like it.

As we can now see so clearly, television and computerized instruction defined the limits of a spectrum of instructional resources. Television provided the medium for large group instruction; programed learning over the computers provided the ultimate in individualized instruction. Within this range, including other devices and procedures such as motion pictures, filmstrips, language laboratories, and independent study, a new diversity was added to the educator's repertoire. These new resources enabled us to break the ancient framework that for so long had held college education in a rigid pattern. No longer do we have to divide the school day into fixed fifty-minute periods, no longer do we measure a student's progress by the number of credit-hours he has "banked," no longer do we march all students along through the same series of lectures and classes.

Today flexibility and adjustment to individual differences are axiomatic. Each student progresses at his own rate. Much of the time he studies on his own or with fellow students—but always with instant access through the computer terminal to the complete range of learning resources: taped lectures, programed course materials, language audiotapes, multimedia (audio-visual) devices and their programed lesson units, bibliographies, and original documents on microfilm.

A professor nowadays rarely lectures to a group of thirty or forty students as his predecessors used to half a century ago. Rather, he now meets with his students individually or in small groups, after they have mastered a given block of knowledge through the use of diverse learning resources. We are no longer satisfied with partial learning but insist upon complete mastery of the basic substance in a field. In other words, all students learn the same quantum of a subject; what varies is only the time it takes them to acquire it.

Our professors now perform what no text or other learning resource can ever accomplish: they develop the mind of the individual student through intimate give-and-take based on sound knowledge and understanding. Under this system the three-year colleges have discovered their primary function in education. Instead of pretending to be microcosms of all human knowledge, they now lean heavily on the use of learning resources to provide the base of their instructional programs. But this firm foundation enables them better to motivate, inspire, and build real understanding and creativity in their students. Never before have they had such an opportunity.

At first college teachers thought that television and the computer would dehumanize teaching and learning. On the contrary, they found that these media had exactly the opposite effect. The large numbers assembled in classes under the old lecture system completely dehumanized instruction. The student felt he was only a number. Now, as he listens over television, he feels that he alone is listening and the teacher is talking only to him. Actually the television teacher has an advantage over the classroom teacher in that he looks directly into the eyes of those listening to him. When the student responds at the terminal of the computer again he feels the process is for him alone. Instruction has become truly individualized.

In recent years widespread experimentation has also been carried on through the collaboration of psychologists, biochemists, and geneticists on the effect of various drugs and electrical stimulation on learning and memory. We have long known that head injuries sometimes caused gaps in memory, that drugs such as phenobarbital and nembutal induced sleep and made it virtually impossible for the subject to learn, that pep pills could prolong the period of active learning, that the mescal bean induced a feeling of euphoria, that LSD and marijuana sent one off on a "trip."

The casual experimentation of youth with these drugs provoked more serious and controlled experimentation by scientists. Enough has been carried on to date to suggest that both learning and memory can be substantially decreased or increased and that behavior and intellectual functioning can be manipulated or modified through both biochemical and environmental treatment. There is now ample evidence to show that long-lost memories can be revived through electrical stimulation of some portions of the brain or with drugs.

The amount of experimentation on the effects of programing the environment has been greater for the simple reason that the public does not object as it does to the use of drugs. Some early demonstrations carried on by Robert Rosenthal and Lenore Jacobson showed clearly that children made greater gains on tests regardless of their scores if the teachers expected them to do better. Expectation by peers, as well, has since then been recognized as a force for learning and retention. But we are still a long way from knowing all the factors that provoke greater learning or improve memory.

But teachers and resources are still what we count on most, and cooperative arrangements among colleges and universities which reached their peak through the use of the computer provided another means of bringing the most competent faculty members and learning resources to more students. This, too, developed slowly at first. From the 1930's, when President Lotus D. Coffman at the University of Minnesota urged the Midwestern universities to share their library resources, it took about a half century before institutions of higher learning saw the folly of competing with each other by trying to build up *all* academic disciplines, which they could never succeed in doing anyway. Dr. Coffman urged uniqueness and strength rather than standardization and mediocrity. The University of Minnesota, he rightly observed, was distinguished in Scandinavian literature. Why should other universities try to be equally strong in this area? Within its W. L. Clements Library the University of Michigan possessed a rare collection of books and documents in American history. Why not send advanced students to Michigan rather than try to duplicate this resource? Some years after Coffman's death his dream was partly realized with the construction in Chicago of the Midwest Inter-Library Center.

Seeing the major advantages of pooling library resources, the Midwestern universities moved forward cooperatively in other areas. Their Committee on Institutional Cooperation gave graduate students the opportunity to move freely from one institution to another on a short-term basis to take advantage of special resources—Purdue's bionucleonic laboratory, or star scholars such as those in Egyptology at Chicago. Under the leadership of presidents Herman Wells of Indiana and Frederick Hovde of Purdue, a cooperative instructional program was further extended over a closed-circuit television system tying together the campuses at Lafayette and Bloomington and including the centers in Indianapolis, Fort Wayne, and Evansville. After the demonstration of the Midwest Program of Airborne Television Instruction (MPATI) in reaching over five million schoolchildren, and the invention of multichannel electronic tapes for broadcasting, a core of basic courses in the sciences and humanities is now given via satellite to students in all the major universities throughout the country.

The universities also recognized that by combining their purchasing power they could compete in the market place with such giant corporations as General Motors and the American Telephone and Telegraph Company. An Inter-University Authority now purchases and distributes supplies and equipment required on the various campuses. The need for such an operation was obvious when very expensive computer systems for all types of academic and nonacademic activities became essential on every campus.

The small colleges were profoundly affected by all these cooperative arrangements. Their own initial efforts included groupings such as the Claremont Colleges, the Richmond (Virginia) Center, the Connecticut Valley Colleges, involving Amherst, Mount Holyoke, Smith, and the University of Massachusetts, and the colleges and universities in the Washington, D.C., area. For a long time such simple matters as the lack of a common academic calendar prevented students from crossing campus lines in their program of courses although socially they had long done so. But during the latter part of the twentieth century the colleges found that they were still competing too much and duplicating their instruction—a costly and inefficient way of operation. Renewed efforts were made until there is hardly a college left in the country that is not a member of a cluster of institutions sharing facilities and programs. Each group is affiliated with one or more universities, an arrangement which first became dramatically visible when seven faculty members from the University of Chicago personally offered a course on "Civilizations from South Asia" to a hundred students from Swarthmore, Bryn Mawr, and Haverford colleges, with one of these faculty members flying to Philadelphia each week. This is another way by which students have available the educational resources of a widespread academic community instead of being limited to the offerings of a small institution. In the process, too, the advantages of a smaller group have been preserved.

Even more dramatic are the changes in the relationships among our libraries. As a result of research carried on not only in the United States but also in Japan, India, Belgium, Holland, France, and England we have revolutionized the techniques of storing and transmitting information. Most of our documents are now reduced to pinpoint size and stored on film in a miniaturized library. If we had not developed such procedures, some of our libraries would now be trying to store 100 million or more volumes, even with the division of academic responsibilities most have undertaken. Instead, we have established the National Research Library, which, as John Kemeny of the Dartmouth Mathematics Department predicted some years ago, has reached more than 300 million volumes in miniaturized form.

The information in these volumes is retrievable by computer systems through a multichannel cable. We can instantly transmit information from these volumes to reading units on campuses throughout the country. The space which was previously used for storing books has been freed for faculty study, reading rooms, and independent work. Also, each student now has a personal portable ultramicrofiche reader and from three to ten thousand volumes he has acquired during his college career.

Even the architecture of our campuses reflects the innovations in teaching techniques. The University of Miami in Florida with visual communications buildings, and Iowa State University and Stephens College with their comprehensive learning centers pioneered in constructing academic facilities that make the maximum use of diverse learning aids. For the lectures over television, students now quite generally listen to portable television sets which are part of a computer terminal in their own rooms. These lectures are followed by small group discussions in dormitories—patterned after the "House Plan" first tried out some years ago by

Stephens College and Wilbur House at Stanford University—and immediate responses on the computer system. The computer system operates twenty-four hours every day, and students may study whenever they desire to do so.

Higher education has also become fully internationalized. The system of satellites offering instruction on a worldwide basis has made possible an International Independent Study University which awards degrees wholly on examinations passed. Students can pursue this work anywhere and when they feel qualified can apply to take the necessary examinations that measure their achievement.

Two other trends helped establish higher education on an international basis: (1) the free flow of students from one country to another, with the growing trend for students to spend a year abroad, and (2) the growth of U.S. campuses abroad. Stanford University pioneered in the latter. Under President Wallace E. Sterling's imaginative leadership it had established centers in seven countries. In line with Stanford's tradition, it has now established the first university geological station on the moon. This station now provides the facility for regular field trips for university students not only from Stanford but from universities around the world. Soon similar stations will be set up on other planets, including Venus.

Along with the clarification of objectives, the upgrading and updating of the curriculum, the use of a variety of learning devices including the computer system, the new library system and the internationalization of higher education, we have also vastly improved the process by which students are admitted to the colleges and universities and the way in which they progress through the course of study. It is amusing now to read the hundreds of conference reports issued during the middle decades of the twentieth century dealing with the required courses in four years of liberal education. Like medieval theologians debating the number of souls which could be conveniently packed into a given corner of hell, educators then seemed to discuss endlessly the question of whether this or that course, in this or that order, should be included in the four-year program. They put subjects in, took them out, and substituted one course for another.

Little progress was made, however, until educators began to ask more fundamental questions. Why must the liberal arts curriculum fit into exactly four years? If students learn at different rates of speed, couldn't some of them achieve the goal in three years or two while others worked at it for five or six? Was the baccalaureate degree really a useful standard of the educated man? Would it not be wise to tell the student what is expected of him, what the end result of his liberal education should be—what kind of mastery he needs to earn his degree—and then let the student decide, in the light of his own personality, interests, and abilities, how he can best make use of the university's resources to achieve that mastery? In an age like ours, when work, in the old sense of a definite eight-hour-per-day job, has become obsolete, such training for individual responsibility is a real necessity.

To settle these problems, the colleges, of course, had to define more precisely the goals they were striving for in the liberal education of students. Whereas under the old system the administration could lean heavily on the accumulation of credit-hours as evidence that the student was acquiring an education, the new system required the colleges to specify what they were aiming for and to devise a more adequate evaluation of student development and the educational process.

The important point was that students began to progress with complete flexibility. The principles of early admission and admission with advanced standing, which did so much to facilitate the transition from high school to college fifty years ago, were applied as well to the transition from college to graduate work. Standard measures of achievement in each basic subject were devised. But students could meet these standards at their own rate of learning and in a variety of ways. Thus it was the criteria of achievement, rather than the students, which were standardized.

Educators fifty years ago tried to determine how all students could be given basically the same course of instruction in the same amount of time. The results were disappointing; students emerged from the standard program with very different levels of competence and mastery. Today it is unusual for any two students to take the same sequence of courses with the same balance of lecture, small-group discussion, and independent study. The "mix" is determined for each student on the basis of his needs and capacities. But at the end of the road we can ascertain with some accuracy whether the student has indeed achieved a minimum level of true liberal learning.

During the latter half of the century we also made great strides in the better use of the educational plant and facilities. Right after World War I there were feeble efforts to utilize the buildings on a year-round basis. A number of universities—notably Minnesota and Stanford—established a four-quarter system. Major progress did not come until later. With the crowding of students on the campuses there was neither time nor money enough to build on the old pattern the necessary classrooms, laboratories, and dormitories. Then the year-round campus caught on and administrators discovered that existing facilities could accommodate at least 25 percent more students. Now it would be unthinkable to permit buildings with all their learning resources and laboratories to remain idle for three summer months. The learning centers are in continuous operation twelve months a year.

Nor do we any longer tolerate such luxurious use of academic facilities as we did during the academic years of the first half of the twentieth century. Then, except for a very few metropolitan universities, we occupied our classrooms primarily in the morning and our laboratories in the afternoon. With the large federal student-aid program for veterans following World War II some universities changed their practices. Stanford University, for example, was among the first to do so. Dr. Donald B. Tresidder, who was then president, appointed a director of planning—the first position of this kind to be created in any university. An analysis of plant use during the last prewar years showed that with better use of available space the enrollment could be doubled. This was done; as a residential university, only new housing was needed. Later Stanford was among the first in the country to use computers on a university-wide basis and appoint a key central administrator to coordinate the program.

To make maximum use of land, President Tresidder planned an industrial park. And to attract to the area industries whose research interests related to a university, the university created the Stanford Research Institute. During the second half of the century this compound of a first-rate university, the Research Institute, industries with broad research interests, and government projects such as the two-mile-long linear accelerator, has set a pattern followed in most university centers of the country. Such communities are now determining the shape of things to come—they are, in fact, currently developing at a greater rate of speed than anything seen during the twentieth century.

As we look back over the progress of higher education in recent decades we may wonder when the major changes began to develop. It is difficult to fix an exact date, but I believe a turning point occurred in the mid- and late-1960's. Having been earlier spurred by Sputnik, in the middle sixties the colleges felt most keenly the upsurge in the demand for higher education and the student unrest forced changes that made education more meaningful and relevant. As educators had foreseen, the college population nearly trebled during the sixties and seventies, with the most acute increases taking place in the mid-sixties.

These factors, I think, galvanized the leading colleges and universities into action. They could see that the students were ready, willing, and able to absorb the best education that could be offered, and realized at the same time that new ways and methods of instruction would have to be found to meet this enormous upsurge in demand.

Most institutions rose quickly to the challenge, but some of the prominent universities simply announced that they could not handle more students than they had already enrolled and refused to consider ways of increasing their student bodies. This negative attitude could not last, of course. It collapsed when other institutions, more sensitive to their own responsibilities and the nation's needs, pioneered in designing improved instructional methods which could provide a first-rate education for more students. Through such relatively simple reforms as year-round operation, control over proliferating courses, better use of independent study, and computerized instruction, many colleges found they could enroll up to one third more students without any significant increase in instructional costs.

Now here we stand in the year A.D. 2000, at the dawn of another century. Clearly Ortega y Gasset was right when he said: "Yesterday's idea does not influence that of today. It influences a man who reacts with a new idea." During the past forty years colleges and universities—like society itself—have moved further and faster than in all previous history. But as Oliver Wendell Holmes once said: "The great thing in the world is not so much where we stand as in what direction we are moving." We are a long way from a system of higher education that cultivates the full potentialities of man. We are still creatures of irrational biases, vicious prejudices, and erratic temperaments. Our emotions, not our intellects, determine how we vote and, thereby, the actions of the governments of men. They make "the brotherhood of man" an illusion. The Greek ideal of a rational approach to problems still eludes us. But during the past third of a century we have advanced further on many fronts than during all previous history. Amidst these many advances—in space, under the oceans, into the heart of the atom—perhaps the greatest is that of creating the means to nurture our children's minds and hearts so that each may become all he is capable of being—regardless of where on this earth he is born, the color of his skin, or the wealth (material or intellectual) of his parents.

We have created our educational systems with the conviction that each individual is unique, with special talents and interests which when fully developed can give him the basis for a full life and the capacity to make a distinctive contribution to society. In fulfilling this ideal we have had to overcome the blind faith in dogmas such as the notion that tests are infallible as predictors of success in school and in life—a notion widely held in the first half of the twentieth century. No longer do we believe that the academic values of the educational system are alone sufficient to cope with the complexities of our society. Most important, we no longer use education to match people to a predetermined pattern. We have moved boldly toward creating an orderly world of rationally free and well informed men and women. This is our greatest achievement.

14   Final Observations and Reflections

A school or university that does not try to improve will deteriorate. In what ways should it improve? What methods should it use? How should it appraise its progress? These are difficult questions to answer.

The educational world is complex. In this brief book I have focused primarily on conditions for learning, on how those conditions can be changed to make learning more comprehensive and the process of learning continuous and meaningful. Change per se has no value other than to yield a sense of excitement in breaking away from the old. Educational innovations are worth the enormous effort they entail only if they lead to more thorough learning and understanding in less time. Because of the vast increase in knowledge in recent years and the great complexity of the world in which we live today, the need for informed citizens, disciplined in the art and techniques of learning, is greater than ever.

Think of the complexities of today's technological and scientific society: the bomb, the rapid growth of cities with their ghettos, pollution, congestion, major cultural revolutions, instantaneous communication, and to top it off, voyages to the moon. What does the citizen have to know, what must he be able to do, to cope with these complexities?

Ideals vs. Practices

There is no point in innovating or trying to make the schools and colleges better unless change contributes directly to the attainment of the goals of education. And obviously the goals of education derive from the goals of the society which it serves.

And we are not educating for today. The child who enters school now does not complete his college work until sixteen or seventeen years from now. And if he enters graduate or professional studies, twenty or more years from now. We are educating for twenty to fifty years from now when the children of today will play their productive lives in society. So, obviously, the child of today should not be educated for the adult world of today. He needs to be educated in such a way that he will achieve his full potential in the new world he will face as an adult.

The goals of society must be looked at as goals for the future. And it is here that we run into trouble when we try to use what we have thus far achieved as the basis for our educational system. The achievements conflict with and contradict our goals.

We say we want freedom and liberty.
Yet we impose more and more restraints on the individual.

We say people should strive for ideals of service.
Yet financial rewards bring the greatest prestige and power.

We say we want equal opportunity for all.
Yet we narrow the range of achievement for Negroes and other minorities.

We say we want better living conditions in our cities.
Yet we countenance slums and pollute the air with factory smoke and carburetor fumes.

We say we want a society relatively free of crime.
Yet the incidence of rape, murder, and theft increases yearly.

The list of conflicts could go on indefinitely. Does that mean the situation is hopeless? Absolutely not. Throughout history there have always been conflicts between the ideal and the actuality. The ideal generates motivation for action, but human frailties often prevent the attainment of the ideal.

Ideals, for an individual or society, are dreams of becoming; they express our highest hopes. "No man has the right to fix the boundary of the march of a nation," said Charles Stewart Parnell. "No man has a right to say to his country—thus far shalt thou go and no further." The march of civilization is a history of pushing the limits of achievement ever further.

The more public-opinion polling progresses the more concerned I become about how the results might circumscribe the limits of man's ideal. How often I've heard: "Oh, I'm all right, I'm doing just what everybody else is doing." And, of course, by "everybody" is meant the majority. In setting ideals we need not the common but the uncommon man who sees a goal beyond the present.

In his brilliant analysis of excellence, John Gardner has aptly stated the problem: "Those who are most deeply devoted to a democratic society must be precisely the ones who insist upon excellence, who insist that a free society can be a great society in the richest sense of that phrase. The idea for which this nation stands will not survive if the highest goal free men set for themselves is an amiable mediocrity. . . . Free men must set their own goals. There is no one to tell them what to do; they must do it for themselves. . . . They must cherish what Whitehead called 'the habitual vision of greatness.' "[1]

We have embodied our vision of greatness in our Declaration of Independence, in our ever-growing Bill of Rights for the nation and more recently for the United Nations. These are the guidelines that must be interpreted and reinterpreted with changing conditions. When a society is not clear about its purposes the schools and colleges are equally confused. We shift with the political winds.

[1] John Gardner, *Excellence* (New York: Harper & Row, 1961), p. 161.

As I write this I am in Cambridge, England. An election for local town offices was held the other day, a battle between Conservatives and Labourites. What did this mean for the schools? The Labourites wanted to develop comprehensive schools in Cambridge as elsewhere, giving wider opportunity for all children. The Conservatives didn't want the comprehensive school. The Tories won. Without question the development of the comprehensive school will long be delayed.

Similarly in the most recent California gubernatorial race, actor Ronald Reagan made the University of California a campaign issue. The student revolt would not have happened, he claimed, if firmer hands had been in control. What happened? He was elected governor by more than one million votes. He considered the victory a mandate and, under our form of government, so it was. Within weeks Clark Kerr, generally recognized as one of the nation's ablest university presidents, was fired.

Example after example could be given of conflicting points of view—not really worthy of being called philosophies—determining the course of the schools. There may be no difference in stated goals. Perhaps even Governor Reagan and Clark Kerr would not differ much on what they expect the university to achieve, but they certainly do differ on *how* it should achieve its objectives.

The first step toward a better educational system is *clarification of goals*.

We are very clear on certain specifics we expect of the schools:

1. Proficiency in the basic skills—reading, writing, arithmetic.

2. Study in various fields of knowledge.

3. An appreciation and enjoyment of literature, the arts, and culture generally.

4. An understanding of the basic concepts of democracy and ability to implement them.

5. An understanding of scientific developments and the scientific attitude.

6. Mastery of the tools of learning.

Through these specifics we expect the schools to produce:

1. Competent specialists in various fields.
2. Citizens with the capacity to earn a living.
3. Graduates motivated to keep on learning all their lives.

But there are other areas where there is no consensus on educational goals. For example, many people today feel that the emotional side of life—sensitivity to nature, to other human beings, and to the arts—should receive greater emphasis in schooling, since the world of tomorrow will be geared to interpersonal relationships and leisure pursuits as never before. The goals of education can never be fixed once and for all. They need to change. They must play a vital part in the lives of men. So they need to be reappraised as times and conditions change.

Our Constitution and Bill of Rights are constantly reinterpreted by the United States Supreme Court. Consider, for example, the matter of segregation in the schools. In *Plessy* v. *Ferguson,* in 1896, the court ruled segregation constitutional; in the famous 1954 case of *Brown* v. *Board of Education* a later court ruled it unconstitutional. Such reconsideration is essential in a dynamic nation. So, too, the goals of schools and colleges, which are inextricably intertwined with the goals of the nation, must be kept alive. The process which must be continuous is in effect an innovative approach to the purposes of the school.

To me the *structure* of our educational system, which has in fact remained fairly constant, is relatively unimportant except in so far as it interferes with the educational *process*. Fortunately, the innovations of recent years, such as independent study, honors courses, early admission to college, admission with advanced standing, and the nongraded elementary school, can give the structure enough flexibility so that the ablest students are no longer held back. With this beginning, if and when our structure in the years ahead yields to the central purpose of education, namely, student development, progress, and achievement, we will have arrived at an ideal. Until we do, further innovation with a variety of forms and a higher degree of flexibility is needed. Obviously, though, chaos cannot be tolerated. The effort should be to achieve a balance between order, on the one hand, and a high degree of flexibility, on the other, with student progress as the ultimate balancing criterion.

In considering the content or substance of instruction we come to the heart of the matter, which really expresses our educational goals in concrete form. All too often we express these goals in highfalutin language only to be confused, exasperated, and perhaps completely disappointed by the actual program which is supposed to put these goals into effect.

Civic education is a case in point. It always begins with a lofty statement of purposes. Seldom are these expressed in the classroom behavior one might expect. After all, if the schools are to deal with civic education, one might presume that the chief purpose is to develop good citizens. What, then, is a good citizen? How should he behave? How can you tell whether a given course has helped the student to become a good citizen? We skirt such questions. Why? Because to answer them directly might get educators and policy makers into trouble, as I have suggested earlier. The American Legion, the League of Women Voters, the City Council, the Board of Trustees, parents, taxpayers: they are the watchdogs. We simply can't satisfy all of them. So we deliberately become comfortably vague. We drift in a morass of insignificant detail. This is why goals remain lofty, substance confused, content indescribable, and personalities contentious. Under such conditions it's just better not to try. Unless there can be clarity of aims, with content and expected achievement carefully defined, the motions of the exercise are sheer wasted effort. It would be better to conserve energy for more rewarding innovations.

As suggested in this book, the content of the educational system needs to be approached from two angles: (1) the over-all design and (2) the substance of elements making up the design. In fields of specialization, I think, we are finally learning how to reform the content of education, to update it, and to discover ways it can be presented more effectively. On the development of a new rational over-all design, however, schools seem to be completely bogged down. They are dedicated to teaching and providing practice in the skills—reading, writing, numbers, handling library materials, etc. Instruction in foreign languages has improved greatly; it begins earlier and—profiting from the war experience—uses more efficient procedures. But by and large schools and colleges are still committed to the subject-by-subject approach.

Largely for the purpose of discussion, I have suggested in these pages a new over-all design for a college curriculum. To base a curriculum around such ideas as evolution, energy, relativity, liberty, and the like, which cut across subject matter lines, would require, in essence, a reorganization of knowledge. But in any case our new research reports don't fit neatly into the traditional subject matter fields of which we are so fond in college and university circles. A short time ago I talked with then-Director James Webb of the National Aeronautics and Space Administration. He startled me a bit when he said that the agency was then getting 350 to 500 research reports a week, and that *most* of them cut across subject lines. As our universities are now organized we are really not equipped to analyze such reports. With the explosion of knowledge which these reports illustrate we will be even less equipped in the future.

The design I suggest does not eliminate fields of specialization for the undergraduate. It substitutes a concentration on ideas instead of the potpourri of miscellaneous cafeteria courses that at present make up that mishmash we dignify with the term "general education" or "distribution" courses. Will the concentration on ideas work? I don't know. So far as I am aware it has never been tried except in a limited way in individual courses. To me it seems to be a logical next step. Then, too, I don't know of a better rationale for an over-all design in view of our insistence that education should nurture a mature grasp of ideas. I am simply making a plea that—through this plan or better ones—we develop a more rational and coherent design than the present mixture of unrelated and often irrelevant elements by which a student accumulates credits and finally earns a diploma which indicates less and less that the student is truly educated.

The Means to an End

And now we come to method, about which so much rubbish has been written. In many elaborate experiments the relative effectiveness of two methods of teaching has been evaluated in one terse phrase, "No significant difference," or, the favorite conclusion of investigators, "The results are inconclusive, further research is required." The reason for all these inconclusive conclusions? Given two different teachers each with his own method or one teacher instructing with two different methods, how could one possibly control all the variables in the teachers themselves, to say nothing about the students?

Several years ago, while I was with the Ford Foundation, we decided to study the qualities of superior teachers. Could these qualities be identified and described? We engaged a sensitive writer, of demonstrated ability, to travel to a number of campuses, identify the faculty members who had the reputation of being outstanding teachers, and then try to discover what makes them tick. He had no problem identifying the teachers. He then talked with students and colleagues and finally to the teacher himself in his effort to find clues to his superiority.

On one campus he identified a young assistant professor in mathematics. After talking with students, faculty, and administrators, our writer went to the faculty member himself. The dialogue ran something like this: "You know you have the reputation of being one of the best teachers on this campus."

"Yes, I do."

"Why do you think you acquired this reputation?"

"Oh, I don't know. I've thought about it a great deal. One personal characteristic may contribute to it. I just don't like doing the same thing twice in the same way. I get bored. Imagine my consternation last year when I was assigned two sections of the same course. I just could not imagine doing this. I finally decided I would teach one section the very best I could and teach the other by violating everything I had learned about effective teaching. When I taught this second section I mumbled into the blackboard, was unclear in my explanations, and purposely vague in my assignments. I was so successful in being a poor teacher some of my students actually went to the dean to complain. And what do you suppose happened? The students in the second section did *better* than those in the first."

Strange? Not at all. This story provides some clues that need analysis. First of all, as the surprising decision of this teacher to teach *badly* suggests, the genius in every field of endeavor, the individual who really excels, is qualitatively different from the mediocre practitioner, and he is different from other geniuses as well. He makes a distinctive contribution, he invents new methods, new formulae, new devices. His performance is far above that of his contemporaries. He is, in short, "one in a million." Why should we expect something different in teaching? Why should we look for common traits among superior teachers?

From the time I entered elementary school until I earned my doctorate degree I had five teachers who really were superior. I remember them all. They had vivid and distinctive personalities. They were not like my other teachers. They were not like each other. Each had a profound influence on me. Everyone, I am sure, has had similar experiences—though not many people are lucky enough to have had five outstanding teachers.

The experience just cited of the teacher who violated all that he knew about good teaching provides another clue. His intended victims were placed largely on their own. I can just hear a student saying: "I'll get this in spite of him." And so apparently he and his classmates did.

At any rate we have not solved the mystery of the gifted teacher any more than we have identified what makes a genius in any field. All we can say is "By their works you will know them."

Since I hold this view of the individuality of superior teaching, why am I advocating the extensive use of modern means of communication, which must by their very nature be uniform? There are several answers:

1. Modern communications extend the reach of the superior teacher, making it possible for him to inspire more students.

2. They make it possible to carry on instruction where teachers are not available or where good teachers are in short supply.

3. They place more responsibility on students for their learning, which means less spoon-feeding by teachers and more real learning.

4. They conserve the teacher's time so that he can have more time available for small-group discussions or individual conferences.

5. They can frequently do certain things better than the average classroom teacher, as, for example, teaching the pronunciation of a foreign language.

As I've said before, I hold no brief for *any* particular method or device. It seems to me that strong advocacy for a particular method simply means that the method best suits the advocate. Take the teaching of reading, for example. Every advocate is a missionary for *his* method. Each can garner arguments and even some proof indicating that his method is better. Is it any wonder that the layman becomes confused? Bring the various "experts" on reading together in a room, as we did several years ago in the Fund for the Advancement of Education and as James B. Conant has done. They find no common ground; the debate becomes acrimonious; they talk at cross purposes.

Or take another example. The dispute as to whether the lecture or discussion method is better has been going on in the colleges since Socrates' day. The champion of the lecture method is either a superb lecturer himself, who likes to talk without interruption, or else a mediocre teacher, who feels insecure in his knowledge and insights and does not want to be questioned for fear he will be exposed. The lecture method does, to be sure, have the advantage of introducing large numbers of students to knowledge in a field, and perhaps of exposing students to a busy expert who would not have time to meet with small groups. The ardent proponent of the discussion methods enjoys give-and-take, the probing of the students' minds, the challenge of having his beliefs or even his knowledge questioned, the new insights that emerge through discussion. The whole process is an exciting adventure because the minds of men are sometimes controllable, sometimes not.

So it is somewhat beside the point to ask which method is better. It's like asking which is better, a museum or a home. They serve different purposes. That method is good, that structure is good which best serves the purpose for which it was designed. No one method, no one structure can serve all purposes. Every school, every college and university urgently needs advocates of a variety of methods and approaches to learning. Students need to be exposed to variety to be truly educated. That's the marvelous thing about human learning. It can't be pigeonholed.

Way back in 1935 I wrote that "the gap between animal and human learning is so wide that practically no results of experimentation with animals have been useful to the teacher." In reviewing recently what has happened to learning theories and experimentation I find no change. Each occasion for learning presents a unique interplay of the individual with a teacher, other students, books, laboratories, field trips, or any other element in the environment. What ignites a spark to make one student learn may leave another student cold and unaffected. Even programed instruction entails stimuli which go far beyond animal conditioning.

That's why in our modern means of communication—especially TV and programed instruction—I see a much wider range of possibilities for learning than has been possible in the past through the restricted teacher/student/books arrangements. With the advent of the printing press and books, the church and the university lost control of learning. The learner had the opportunity to explore ideas, procedures, problems of which the teacher was not even aware. The new means of communication make the horizons of learning virtually limitless.

We've lost nothing. We still have our lectures, discussions, scientific laboratories, and libraries. We've gained a lot through the instantaneous communication radio and television afford: think of watching as a satellite zooms to the moon and then as the newest scientific equipment digs a trench on the moon's surface. Records, tapes, microfilms, Xerox machines, programed learning, the computer—all these we have, with further wonders on their way. We've barely explored existing possibilities, to say nothing of learning to use them to their fullest potential for enriching the learning process.

The problem of how to finance schools always causes turmoil. Below the college level we have moved from a time when the local community provided almost total support, through state support, and recently into federal support with an insistence on keeping effective state and local controls. Now we are beginning to enter another phase, regional laboratories supported through the U.S. Office of Education, and state compacts. As for the total amount of money spent for education, this differs radically from one state to another. Obviously the children in Mississippi are not getting education of the quality provided in New York. Should a child be deprived of the best education we can offer because he happens to be living in Mississippi? In our mobile society he might well end up in New York.

In higher education we have moved more and more to public support of education. In 1930 slightly less than half of our college students were in public institutions; today this figure has gone to approximately two thirds and is expected to reach three quarters by 1980.

An institution of higher education is no longer necessarily *all* public or *all* private. The University of Chicago, M.I.T., and Columbia, nominally private institutions, get more than half of their funds from the public treasury. The University of California—a public institution—has one of the country's largest private endowments. The use of public funds in private institutions presents some problems but government dominance is not feared as it once was. As John Nason, president of Carleton College, put it, there are no "burglars under the bed."

All in all, education has become one of the nation's biggest businesses, second only to defense in total spending. Industry is fast recognizing this, and naturally it wants some of the pie. Xerox recently bought a major portion of the Wesleyan University Press; IBM bought Science Research Associates; Time, Inc., bought Silver Burdett, a textbook publisher, and merged it into the General Learning Corporation. General Electric Company, with an additional investment, now owns half of General Learning Corporation, and RCA, CBS, Westinghouse, among others, are all betting that there's money in education. The ultimate effect of vast federal funds and the entrance of corporations into the education market are still unknown. One thing is certain: education will continue to flourish in this affluent society and emerge as a major force in the developing nations around the world.

The staffing of the schools and colleges remains one of the most urgent and perplexing problems in education. The institutions that have the money can afford not only to employ more teachers in relation to the number of students enrolled, they can attract better, more thoroughly prepared instructors. They can provide richer library resources, improved instructional materials, and in general, better learning facilities. They can also offer more scholarships to attract students with greater ability and with that advantage alone at least half the educational battle is won.

The major innovation in staffing the elementary and secondary schools has been to apply the concept of differentiated functions instead of adhering to the old notion that one person—a teacher— must do everything required in a classroom to facilitate learning.

If we are to solve the acute shortage of able teachers and attain higher levels of quality, colleges and schools must be even more ingenious in the future than in the past. The employment of mediocre teachers to maintain a constant ratio will lead only to what the late Charles Johnson, president of Fisk University, warned against: passing on mediocrity in an intimate environment.

Educational institutions have been slow, also, in modernizing facilities, which is not surprising. If the substance of education is slow to change, so is its outward form. Early in the fifties, the Fund for the Advancement of Education retained as a consultant Paul Rehmus, who was then superintendent of schools in Portland, Oregon. His assignment was to travel around the country looking into colleges and universities, school systems, and state departments of education and studying new developments in school architecture and construction. Over a period of years he probably visited more educational establishments than any other man alive. One day after he had traveled for almost three years I asked him what impressed him most. Since he was really looking at schools and colleges, I was a bit startled when he replied: "The architecture of the *churches*." It seemed that the churches, which are still thought of as conservative, were way ahead of the schools and colleges.

Since then, however, the educational institutions have moved fast (if not fast enough). A major influence in this development has been the Educational Facilities Laboratories, established in 1958 by the Ford Foundation and directed by an exceedingly able president, Harold B. Gores. EFL has seen to it that virtually every aspect of school and college facilities has been explored, worked over, redesigned, and re-engineered. New, more efficient materials have been tried out, more flexible space has been designed to accommodate the latest methods and equipment (including television and computers), to make better use of teachers' skills, to provide more opportunities for individual instruction. The principles of over-all plant planning have been re-examined. All types of building have been reconsidered—classroom, laboratory, language centers, libraries, general utility buildings, heating plants, and student housing and dining facilities. All this has been done in the interest of economy, but as Harold Gores has aptly pointed out, "The primary interest is not in 'cheaper' schools as such, but rather in making the best use of school-building dollars, in line with current construction costs."

Judging the Results

And now finally we come to what is without doubt the most important and yet the most perplexing aspect of the total educational process: *appraisal*.

What makes a good school? Who is the superior teacher? Is the student making satisfactory progress? In each area the questions could and do go on interminably. It would be convenient or comforting if we had good answers. But unfortunately we have only partial answers. Much remains guesswork.

Throughout the book I have stressed the fact that there are no fixed answers to pressing questions about human learning and growth and development. That is why I consider the innovative approach the most promising: because its essence is the effort—continuous and unrelenting—to find the best "answers" possible and then push on to find new and better ones.

In everything we do throughout the whole educational enterprise we need always to ask the question: Does this contribute to the development of the student? Does this help him form habits of learning that will be a part of his being throughout life?

When a pupil fails to learn, teachers sometimes take the attitude: "He's too dumb; you can't do anything with him." In many cases this may represent failure on the part of the teacher rather than failure by the student: failure of the teacher to find out what motivates the child, failure to set up proper conditions for learning, failure to select the right materials, lack of clarity in explanations, failure to show that learning the material at hand does have some importance, failure to associate what is to be learned with related work to reinforce learning, etc., etc.

In judging the pupil's capacity to learn we altogether too often rely on scores of intelligence or mental tests. Although these have some value, I've often thought that the biggest mistake the psychologists who developed them made was to label them intelligence or mental tests. If they had been as wise as scientists in other fields such as chemistry, physics, and biology, the psychologists would have said the tests measure ability "X," and then found out all they could about what ability "X" was. The temptation, however, was too great and they fell into the trap of using a common term to describe a new device. The chief difficulty with the common term is that everyone has his own definition of intelligence.

The tests are not useful in predicting whether a student will be successful in life. Success in life means many things and requires a variety of abilities, not necessarily including those we regard as important in school. In our materialistic society one notable criterion of success is the ability to make and accumulate money. This is apparently a very special ability to which we give no attention in school and which is not measured by any available test. Doubtful it is, too, that any test to measure this ability is likely to be devised in the foreseeable future. Yet who can say that the ability to make money does not represent a particular kind of intelligence?

Another type of ability on which we place a high value in a democratic society is the ability to get elected to a high office. This seems to be a cluster of abilities with the pattern differing among successful politicians. Again, from observation, it is clear that these traits are unrelated to success in school or on tests that may be used to estimate a student's academic ability. And yet these skills are among the most essential we require to maintain a democratic form of government.

Another cluster of abilities on which we place a high value in judging success in life are those essential in the creative arts: the theatre, the dance, motion pictures, music, painting, sculpture, industrial design, and the writing of novels, plays, and poems. We value very highly whatever talents are needed for success in these areas but they, too, are unrelated to academic competence.

Managerial ability, whether in business, government, or even university administration, remains elusive of analysis and even in its highest degree does not seem to be related to ability to do well in school or college. And yet we place very high monetary value on the ability to manage large business concerns.

We might similarly review other areas and analyze the values we place on human competence. Academic ability has its greatest value in an academic situation; as we move to other areas it has less and less value in determining "success in life," however we define it.

What does all this mean for schools and colleges, particularly when we are concerned with needed reforms? Certainly it does not dictate that we value academic ability less. It does, however, require that we place a greater value on and give more attention to the identification of abilities in other areas that are important to the development of society.

Throughout more than forty years of being closely identified with and deeply involved in educational institutions I have yet to find on faculties or among students any individual who possesses all the traits necessary for a vital dynamic society; no one I have met has been talented politically, scientifically, socially, artistically, athletically, conceptually, and academically. I have not seen—nor has the world—another Leonardo da Vinci, and even he did not excel in every way although he came close.

We do, to be sure, have straight "A" students even in universities with the highest standards, but this is a judgment on academic abilities only. The one condition that is common to all people is the unevenness of abilities and achievement when *all* capacities required for a fully developed democratic society are taken into consideration. Along with this unevenness are the different rates at which each individual progresses. Even a straight "A" student may lag far behind less academically talented students in musical ability or graphic design. We don't think of holding him back on the athletic field if he does well. Why should we hold him back with a lockstep system in academic subjects if he does well, if he learns thoroughly, if he really learns to learn? Naturally there are dangers in such a flexible system. The greatest is in the failure to require *thorough* learning. If school becomes merely a matter of going fast by skimming or skipping or cramming, much damage can be done. Innovations in recent years have suggested constructive solutions. They show that we are beginning to recognize that, with the tremendous variations in human abilities and progress, students will not fit into the same groove, even though trying to make them do so is easier for both the administration and the teachers. But, of course, the schools do not exist for the administrator or for the teacher, but for the student.

Rules frequently sterilize the human equation, which is, after all, the most important element in education. What a student really needs is someone within the system who *cares* about him, who tries to understand, who tries to motivate, who gives him confidence that he can learn, who guides and inspires and thereby spurs him on. Mark Pattison, one of the great teachers at Oxford in the mid-nineteenth century, was apparently such a man, for as John Sparrow recently said of him: "Pattison did not charm his pupils or humor them, but he made them feel that he lives for learning and for them."

Each child needs teachers like this, at given moments, at least, or at given stages. It is utopian to dream that there will ever be enough such teachers to staff our schools and colleges fully. This inevitable gap is one controlling reason for innovation and reform. We need to try harder, even though we may fail. We need to innovate with new means of communication so that the child who is not fortunate enough to have such teachers will not be denied the opportunity to learn to the maximum of his capacity, so that the teachers who possess the qualifications of greatness can be free from routine tasks to devote more time to each individual, and so that the student can really master the art of learning that continues throughout a productive and satisfying life.

Envoi: Assembling the "Unassembled Revolution"

The pages you have just read do *not* constitute a blueprint for meeting the educational challenge of our time. As I have tried to make clear, no one of the innovations mentioned nor any present combination of them constitutes *the* answer to the problems of our schools and colleges. John Gardner put it best in an interview:

I'm convinced that 20 years from now we'll look back at our school system today and ask ourselves how we could have tolerated anything as primitive as education today. I think the pieces of an educational revolution are lying around unassembled, and I think we're going to put them together in the next few years.

I would add to this only one thought: that the missing ingredient, the essential catalyst to assemble this "unassembled revolution," is not any one of the pieces. Rather, it is something which transcends the separate elements, the diverse approaches to reform.

The critical factor is the *idea* of reform itself, the notion—new in education but hardly so in our national experience—that we can do better than we are doing or have ever done, and that we can achieve this through innovation, through exploring *new* ways to achieve our objectives. The innovative spirit is the key to assembling the unassembled revolution.

Appendix:

Learning by Television: A Case Study
of Educational Technology Applied[1]

What happens when the innovative approach is brought to bear on major educational problems in a bold and controversial way? Do teachers and students grasp at the chance to try something new? Do school boards, college faculties, and educational authorities at the state and national levels react by examining the evidence? Do school systems and universities adapt their other practices to accommodate the new techniques? Do the originators and disseminators of the new ideas take sufficient care to ensure the quality of their product and the capacity of teachers to get real benefit out of it? Does the quality of learning really improve?

These are hard questions, and there are very few instances in American education where conditions have been such as to yield useful or suggestive answers. One of these rare instances has been the attempt to introduce televised instruction into American schools and colleges on a broad scale as an innovative approach to the problem of getting good instruction to more students despite a continuing shortage of qualified teachers.

[1] In this case study I have drawn heavily on a previous account of instructional television which was prepared under my supervision in 1966: *Learning by Television*, by Judith Murphy and Ronald Gross, preface by Alvin C. Eurich (New York: Fund for the Advancement of Education).

This is not a success story. After a decade and more of intensive effort and the expenditure of hundreds of millions of dollars, television has *not* made a decisive impact on schools and colleges in this country. The use of television in the classroom has demonstrated incontrovertibly that students can and do learn quite as well from television as they do from conventional instruction. However, the practical experience of school and college educators with the television medium has been quite mixed. As a result, televised instruction has not taken a central position in education. Rather, it is still a marginal enterprise.

Whether measured by the numbers of students affected, by the quality of the product, or by the advancement of learning, televised teaching is still in a rudimentary stage of development. The medium can take credit for helping understaffed schools and colleges to cope with ever-increasing enrollments. But television has not transformed education, nor has it significantly improved the learning of most students. In short, TV is still far from fulfilling its obvious promise. Television is *in* education all right, but it is still not *of* education.

Innovation in education does not often come about smoothly—through empirical research, logical analysis, sweet reason, or a count of hands. Educational change is, more often than not, hotly contested. While most educators sit out the struggle, the leaders divide into those who feel threatened by the new ways and those who complain that change does not come fast enough.

Televised instruction has been one of the most controversial innovations. Some denouncers sincerely believe that television threatens to take over the whole educational program, reducing the rich variety of the classroom to the flat surface of a tube. In an age of education, many teachers seem to fear technological unemployment. Some humanists foresee automated education, mechanized teaching, and robotized students.

Proponents, however, view television in the historical context of communications media, each of which has significantly affected the process of education. For them television is a new way of communicating: the latest in a series of advances that have enhanced man's prospect for survival by permitting him to share the knowledge and understanding of other human beings. Since education is largely a matter of communication, they argue television—like books, records, and radio before it—can be used in teaching.

In the 1950's some of the most astute educators in the country believed that television's effect on American education would be profound, that the irresistible force of the explosions in population and in knowledge would propel the education establishment into using television, if only to cope with the problems of quantity.

Professor Charles Siepmann of New York University was one who was convinced of the inevitable success of TV. In his 1958 volume, *TV and Our School Crisis,* he stated that television is "indispensable" to solving the crises of quantity and quality in the schools. In the intervening years exploding enrollment, the scarcity of good teachers, and the unceasing new demands on curriculum have reinforced the logic of his argument. But logic notwithstanding, TV has not had a profound effect on American education. The course of events has not fulfilled the revolutionary visions of TV's prophets.

Following a few college experiments in the 1940's and even earlier, TV as an instructional tool was first tried out at all levels of schooling throughout the country in the mid-1950's. At that time the general public had become aware of the acute shortages of teachers and space but was only beginning to recognize the more basic qualitative problems.

The obstacles to the adoption of television instruction were formidable. One was its cost—hard to determine but obviously high, if only for the hardware. Another was its complex technology. Another, and more critical, was the very newness of television. The medium's great success in entertainment made it suspect to many intellectuals, including teachers and educational administrators; since they disdained to receive TV programs in their own living rooms, they also excluded the "idiot box" from their classrooms.

Earlier technological tools of communication, with obvious implications for learning, have not to this day become an intrinsic part of education either. Films, radio, recordings, etc., play little more than token roles in instruction. Acclaimed in their day as TV was later, these devices have for the most part been used with little real imagination.

The fate of these other innovations seemed portentous for TV. For one thing, there was the possibility that the new medium, as the old ones, would also fail to be fully developed. For another, there was the hostility of the audio-visual establishment itself—by now a little bureaucracy on the margins of education and hardly exhilarated at the advent of a glamorous device that threatened to overshadow many of the older "new" media.

That televised instruction has achieved even its present modest success is, perhaps, a miracle. The achievement has taken massive pump priming from private foundations and government. The Ford Foundation alone has made grants exceeding $100 million to all phases of educational television. The federal government's support has added comparable amounts to equip the country's ETV facilities.

For instructional television (ITV) to get where it is today took the combined efforts of enthusiasts from various fields and disciplines; veterans of educational film and radio, communication specialists in the universities, foundation executives, workers in adult education, private citizens concerned with the quality of education, visionary school superintendents, creative professors and teachers, and fugitives from commercial television. Above all, perhaps, it took a blissful unawareness of enormous obstacles. Some early enthusiasts seemed to think that introducing television into education would be a relatively simple, though expensive and disruptive, enterprise. They were to find that this innovation would greatly tax the skill and knowledge of its practitioners.

The outlays of money and effort were expended for a variety of objectives: first, to put educational programs on commercial stations; later to stimulate in-school programs, both by broadcast and closed circuit; then to establish, equip, and staff noncommercial TV stations and to provide evening and out-of-school programs. This appendix is concerned chiefly with *in-school* television, with what is generally termed "instructional television" or "televised instruction." But ITV must be treated in the context of educational television, as so much in-school television emanates from ETV stations and is affected by the personalities and power behind them.

For many reasons, such as the nature of the medium itself, the massive campaign that launched it, and its connection to the world outside education, ITV has thus far escaped the fate of educational radio and film.

Instructional television's success as a tool for educational innovation and improvement hangs in the balance. And favorable portents seem to outweigh the unfavorable. Governmental interest and support are at a new high; federal grants have spurred belated state activity. More important, Washington is committed to the innovative approach as never before.

The physical apparatus of ITV is growing prodigiously. Televised instruction has unquestionably established important beachheads all over the country and improved instructional offerings in places as diverse as Boston, San Francisco, Denver, Chicago, and the backwoods of South Carolina and Nebraska. Its educational value has been proved in many ways: in advanced medical and dental training, in helping to teach French and Spanish to hundreds of thousands of elementary school children, in providing entire junior-college degree programs for students at home or on campus, in coping with large survey courses at many state universities, and in improving the education of prospective teachers.

On the other hand, many brave and costly experiments have petered out completely or bumbled along in low gear without inspiring others of the kind. Sometimes the basic idea proved faulty; in other cases the execution failed to generate sufficient enthusiasm; occasionally extraneous factors blocked success. "Continental Classroom," which brought high-level college courses to students throughout the nation, was dropped after a few seasons. Perhaps the most lasting contribution of the costly experiment in the previously mentioned airborne ITV, MPATI (Midwest Program on Airborne Television Instruction), was its demonstration of the possibility of school cooperation over a wide region. No state has followed the lead of Texas in creating a statewide broadcast facility to train teachers (and Texas itself let its program lapse). Despite a variety of demonstrations that television could help solve the mounting crisis in higher education, faculty resistance continues high, and ITV has made small headway in colleges and universities. Despite Continental Classroom, a nationwide program which proved television's utility in teaching extra-large classes, freeing teachers to work with small groups and individual students, most of the hundreds of schools involved have reverted to the old familiar ways and use television only in conventional instructional settings.

Unfortunately, many experiments have been evaluated with scorecard simplicity as "success" or "failure." Such judgments conceal the reasons why TV is sometimes useful, sometimes not. Even more important, they obscure the wider implications of ITV and its importance to the innovative approach.

Unfortunately, as television machinery became commonplace, it was used less as a means of innovation and more as a simple extension of practices that have been criticized for years. Teachers in the schools and colleges using television for instruction began to take it for granted; ITV, it appeared, had lost the excitement along with the fearsomeness of novelty. There is evidence of a comparable attitude among students, too.

Is ITV going to settle for mediocrity, reproducing its easy successes and continuing its marginal role? A number of its most ardent practitioners sense this danger. One of the medium's elder statesmen (even the eldest are barely fifty) is so conscious of the potential danger to ITV that he espouses "creative destruction." Like many of his colleagues, he would like to see the old molds destroyed lest the new federal and state support help to entrench the conventional product which instructional television, by and large, has so far generated. These leaders view instructional television not as an end in itself, but as one way of enhancing the education of young people—and a potentially crucial one. If they attack the establishment in their chosen field, it is because they feel their primary allegiance not to a medium but to the educational process as a whole.

Such controversies, obstacles, and resistances are inevitable in introducing any major innovation. If the innovative approach is to spread and grow stronger in American education, we need to share experiences in putting it into practice. Experiences at all levels are valuable here: from a single teacher in a classroom reporting on her introduction of a new practice or material, right up through the insights of principals, curriculum supervisors, superintendents, state education officials, and those on the national scene in the foundations, federal agencies, and professional associations.

At the beginning the Ford Foundation's Fund for the Advancement of Education made small grants to various institutions to give television a trial in actual school settings. It soon became clear, however, that such random encouragement was unnecessary: schools and colleges all over the country were dabbling in the new medium. The Fund therefore adopted a more selective policy and followed it over the course of a decade. This was to encourage and support ITV projects keyed to a basic purpose and in so doing to try out, in the greatest possible variety of situations, television's potential applications to education.

TELEVISION AS A MEANS TO IMPROVE THE QUALITY OF INSTRUCTION DESPITE THE TEACHER SHORTAGE: A great many projects of various kinds in the public schools were basically designed to demonstrate the feasibility of the so-called Stoddard plan. The plan was devised by the late Alexander J. Stoddard, long-time superintendent of schools (in such cities as Bronxville, Denver, and Los Angeles) and subsequently a consultant to the Fund. It proposed, among other innovations, to use television "as an integral part of the regular instructional program" to help meet teacher and building shortages and at the same time to improve the quality of education.

Eventually the Foundation-supported experiment, designated the National Program in the Use of Television in the Public Schools, included varied school systems throughout the United States that were assaying the advantages of using television to instruct larger than conventional classes. Common to all these projects was the hypothesis that (a) the extra-large TV classes would make it possible to enlarge the impact of the most highly qualified teachers and (b) this mass instruction would provide, as an equally important corollary, time for the classroom teacher to work with smaller-than-average groups or with individuals.

The Results

The National Program produced ambiguous results. It is noteworthy by its very size, since at its peak it involved more than 200,000 students in almost 800 schools throughout the United States, ranging from a two-teacher high school in Nebraska to schools in Detroit and Philadelphia enrolling thousands. By the same token, the program's scope and variety suggest caution in attempting to generalize its effect, especially since a prime feature of the project was to apply television to a great variety of subjects, grade levels, and school environments. The participating schools were encouraged to pursue different practices as to schedules, space arrangements, choice of student teachers, and many other matters.

Although each school's use of television differed from the others, all the projects in the National Program (except for certain small rural schools) shared one important characteristic: the introduction of the larger-than-average class, up to 175 students in elementary schools and ranging from 200 to 500 in junior and senior highs.

In general, the results showed that television could be used to teach very large classes, with corresponding savings in teacher time and classroom space, and there was at least tentative confirmation of the hypothesis that television could improve the quality of education with no increase in cost.

In attempting to integrate television into the instructional process, the National Program encountered serious difficulties, particularly in the secondary schools: most classroom teachers resisted the sharing of responsibility with the studio teacher. It became clear, too, that televised mass teaching was unworkable unless the programs were of exceptionally high quality. Thus the emphasis of the National Program shifted from the large-class objective to that of achieving quality, and of supplementing and enriching regular classroom instruction. Of the schools that participated in the National Program which are still using television, most use it now in classes of conventional size, and usually to supplement or "enrich" standard classroom fare.

TRAINING TEACHERS VIA TELEVISION: In response to America's acute teacher shortage in the 1950's, the states adopted many emergency measures to train teachers quickly, such as retraining housewives long retired from teaching. Television was a logical means to help in training new recruits. Encouraged by Foundation support, Texas became the focus of an early, large-scale experiment to test some of these new measures. Between 1956 and 1959 more than 1,000 college graduates enrolled in a program that tied together every teacher-training institution in the state, the Texas department of education, and eighteen commercial TV stations. Any recruit who enrolled for credit with one of the participating institutions qualified for a temporary teaching permit after successfully completing the one-year televised course.

The Results

Television is currently used to a limited extent to train teachers (generally for class observation purposes and for in-service training). And, of course, in-school TV programs are a prime means of educating the teachers along with their classes. But the statewide Texas experiment, for all its promise, found no followers in other states. And Texas itself dropped the program when the Foundation grant ended. Actual results of the experiment were disappointing: the pool of recruits was smaller than expected, and the per capita cost of training was high.

AIRBORNE TRANSMISSION OF ITV: A spectacular, but short-lived, variation of the network idea became a reality when, in 1961, with Foundation support, the Midwest Program on Airborne Television Instruction went into operation. Transmitting over two channels from a DC-6 circling four miles above the small town of Montpelier, Indiana, MPATI could be received over a radius of 150 to 200 miles in all directions, reaching parts of six states. MPATI put on a full day's schedule of programs, cooperatively and professionally produced.

The Results

In the summer of 1965 a long-awaited FCC ruling denied MPATI's request for six UHF channels, continued the organization's experimental use of the UHF band until 1970, and recommended conversion to the 2,500 megahertz system, also known as the Instructional Television Fixed Service (ITFS). MPATI applied for these channels and the FCC promptly granted them. Practical problems, however, proved insurmountable. The ITFS band had never been used from an airborne transmitter, and therefore the cost and performance of new equipment was unknown. Rough estimates for testing such equipment ranged from

$340,000 to $360,000. Future uncertainty forced member schools to drop out of the program, and money became more scarce than ever. MPATI was rendered economically unviable, and at the close of the 1967–68 school year it ended its transmitting function, although production still continues.

JUNIOR COLLEGE BY TELEVISION: Backed by the Board of Education and the Fund for the Advancement of Education, the Chicago City Junior College, now called the Chicago City College, undertook to determine the feasibility of broadcasting an entire two-year program over television, thus enabling students to receive a higher education and earn a degree by regular TV viewing in their own living rooms.

The Results

The TV College is an outstanding success. This early experiment proved conclusively that a student could pursue a junior college program exclusively over television—a demonstration of far greater moment today than it was in 1956 when the Chicago experiment began. Since then there has been an astonishing growth of junior and community colleges throughout the country. States and cities still without these institutions are planning to build them rapidly to provide for the millions of students pouring out of high schools who need further education but lack the ability, motivation, or money to attend a four-year institution. Television's potential use in helping to educate these students, in the face of an acute faculty shortage, is obvious. Chicago's experience has therefore aroused great interest and brought a stream of observers. A number of junior colleges are currently making use of TV and others have plans to do so. But Chicago's success in bringing education into the house has not been generally adopted.

TV ON THE CAMPUS: An early Fund grant went to Pennsylvania State University, one of the first institutions of higher education to use TV for credit courses on campus. The university was anxious to experiment with the medium in a range of uses and to make precise evaluations of the results. So over a period of four years the Fund supported elaborate studies in many areas—student response to TV under varying conditions, relative effectiveness of television, and direct instruction in different subjects, comparative costs, etc.

The Results

Penn State continues to make extensive use of television for on-campus instruction, with the project entirely self-supporting since 1960. TV enrollment reached a peak of just over 20,000 in 1962; since then it has leveled off to about 13,000. The decrease is attributable primarily to a university decision to make optional certain previously required courses that had inflated the TV enrollment figures in the early 1960's. Penn State has taught a wide range of subjects over television, and now offers twenty-eight courses, from archaeology to zoology. It has embarked on a policy of taping a number of carefully planned courses for use on its branch campuses—some eight of which have video-tape playback facilities—with additional installations planned for the near future.

In recent years the types of uses of television have increased. Among these are the use of television for facilitating laboratory work in biological science courses and for recording and immediate playback of student performances in such fields as speech, demonstration teaching, and gymnastics. The university is also experimenting with the use of two-way television in upper division and graduate courses, between the main campus and one of its branches.

Unfortunately, Penn State's experience and its exhaustive evaluation of ITV's effectiveness, feasibility, and appropriate uses have influenced relatively few colleges and universities to make comparable use of the medium, even in Pennsylvania. By now, to be sure, various big state and municipal universities have enrolled large numbers of underclassmen in televised courses, but in general faculty resistance to television continues strong. Many promising applications of television to higher education—some, as in Texas and Oregon, linking institutions together in cooperative ventures —have ceased or are continuing in low gear. In 1963 a definitive survey of the uses of new media in higher education came to this conclusion, as stated by Professor Lewis B. Mayhew of Stanford University: "With few exceptions, such as at Pennsylvania State University or the Chicago city junior colleges, college teaching seems to go on as always. . . . After the experiments have been completed and reports written, the matter too frequently is dropped or is reinterpreted so as to leave undisturbed the slow waltz of lecturing, testing, and grading which is the conduct of education."

These, then, were some of the areas of inquiry to which the Fund and Ford Foundation grants were devoted. Meanwhile other promising ventures got under way with little or no outside support. An outstanding self-starter was South Carolina's statewide system of televised instruction over closed circuit inaugurated in 1960, with connections into fifteen high schools in nine cities, and designed for eventual coverage of every elementary and secondary school in the state.

There were also a number of experiments that were only slightly augmented by Foundation grants. The closed-circuit program for the elementary schools of Anaheim, California, is a good example. After two years of careful study and preparation, Anaheim in 1959 initiated a program of televised lessons for fourth and fifth graders, later extending it to the two grades below. James Brier, director of the ITV project, reported that "Anaheim's school board, believing that television could help improve education, convinced the town to start full throttle with financing, studios, and everything." The district committed $300,000 for the first year, and $40,000 each for the next two. The Foundation granted $25,000 the first year, $40,000 the second year, and $29,000 the third year.

Televised instruction has demonstrated but not achieved its considerable potential for improving instruction. What went wrong? Many of the schools and colleges that early adopted television are still using it, and there has been a steady accretion of new users. But even in considering sheer volume it is apparent that something, or a number of things, went wrong with ITV. Much more serious is the scant evidence that many of the schools and colleges that use television have thereby substantially improved the quality of education. It is significant that, by and large, the really innovating schools are doing little with it.

Why has American education been so ready to reject this apparently logical solution to many of its problems—as it has rejected others in the past and is still doing? And when it *has* adopted ITV, why has it used the medium primarily for supplemental, optional, or marginal purposes? The answers to these questions throw light on the challenge and also on the problems of using the innovative approach.

American education's operating decisions are usually made according to immediate local demands and resources. If excess enrollment threatens, the local educational organization is apt to adopt makeshift measures to meet the crisis. It may put on double sessions or eliminate kindergartens or commandeer a church basement for overflow classes—short-term and regressive measures, to be sure, but they have the advantage of economy and familiarity. The innovative approach is avoided as too controversial.

Peter Schrag, journalist and educational administrator, made the point well in *Voices in the Classroom:*

> There is no American school system, only a multitude of different systems, each with its own concerns, its own problems, its own needs and its own internal kind of perfection. Each is affected by a complex interaction of national and local attitudes and pressures, community conditions, university scholarship, and

legislative requirements. Many of them are similar, and few may be almost interchangeable, but each of them is in some respect unique. . . .

While the schools are often responsive to national demands and attitudes, and while they are affected by state laws specifying who may or may not teach, by regional accrediting associations, professional organizations, and by legislative curriculum requirements, they are also the creatures of local conditions and local demands. The new programs and ideas, the formulas, the new books are wares in a vast new educational supermarket from which particular schools can make choices, but there is no model school, no model system applicable to all situations.[2]

The heterogeneous American educational "system" helps to explain why the ITV record—and that of other innovative approaches—varies so radically from place to place. What is of importance is not an abstraction called "instructional television," but a boy in a rural school who learns enough chemistry via televised courses to enter premedical training at the state college; or a student in a Boston parochial school who takes a vicarious trip to the Vatican over television; or second graders in Indiana, whose teacher never took a college science course, awakening to the delights of botany through a series of lessons broadcast into their classroom; or a housewife in Chicago who takes a full junior college course without ever leaving her home; or a freshman at the University of Houston who receives most of his basic courses over TV at home and who otherwise might have been denied college because applications for enrollment outran facilities.

Even in these instances the stress is on quantity. Has television made a substantial contribution toward meeting the real needs of education? In the light of the current educational crisis compounded by soaring individual and social demands, on the one hand, and shortages of staff and facilities, on the other, the answer is probably "No." ITV's accomplishment is even more dubious when one considers America's enormous resources, the undisputed

[2] Peter Schrag, *Voices in the Classroom: Public Schools and Public Attitudes* (Boston: Beacon Press, 1965), pp. 1–4.

potential of the television medium, and the actual resources that have already been poured into it. Jack McBride, an outstanding ETV expert, made a sobering observation not long ago: "If something happened tomorrow to wipe out all instructional TV," he said, "American schools and colleges would hardly know it was gone. I say this as an ardent, and undiscouraged, believer in the efficacy and importance and ultimate full use of TV in education. But TV is still far from the point of playing an integral role in education. We're still peripheral."

Time itself may vindicate ITV. Enrollment pressures and the attendant shortages that could be ignored when they were merely national statistics or projections will undoubtedly make school and college administrators ready for technological solutions when the statistics come to life in their own institutions.

Ten or fifteen years are a very short time for any innovation, especially in education. Even Marshall McLuhan (who sees electronics rescuing misguided literates from the evils of Gutenberg) views the modest accomplishments of instructional television to date as normal growing pains. There is no doubt that television has already contributed substantially to the knowledge and skills, even to the insights and intellectual growth, of countless students from kindergarten to medical school—if only as a replacement for a missing, or inadequate, teacher. But such considerations cannot be used to explain away TV's failure to really change educational practice. The need to upgrade instruction is more urgent than ever and any new tool designed to fill that need must prove its worth quickly.

We now come to the difficult question of quality. What is the actual quality of the televised instruction currently available in the United States? And how well is it used in the nation's classrooms to actually promote learning? The answers to these two questions largely explain ITV's limited influence on our schools and colleges, and they suggest useful lessons for proponents of other innovative approaches.

On balance, ITV is still deficient in quality. To be sure, programing has been immensely improved since its beginnings. ITV producers have learned a good deal more about education and how to apply their professional talents to classroom needs. Teachers and other educators have learned to respect and, in some measure, to exploit the medium itself. There is no question that there are many good courses and even more individual programs of merit.

But it is generally conceded that other countries—Britain, Japan, France, Italy—have outdistanced the United States in the quality of their educational television, including instructional programs. Broadcasting facilities are owned and operated by the government in these countries and most ETV is produced in centers for national or regional distribution.

Many critics, domestic as well as foreign, believe that America's ITV product cannot compete with its counterparts overseas so long as American production remains local and decentralized. It is hardly fair to apply an absolute standard of values to the American product without regard to the context of the programs. As a sympathetic foreign critic said recently, observing the adverse reaction of a visiting group of educational broadcasters: "I agree the American programs should be better—and they *would* be better if they commanded national resources. But I realize, too, how superior the ITV programs we just reviewed may be to the conventional instruction available in the average little schoolhouse."

In judging a televised series of daily algebra lessons designed to take over the entire task of teaching ninth graders in rural schools spread wide over the state of South Carolina, it is neither fair nor useful to apply the same criteria by which one judges a once-a-week music appreciation program produced for sixth graders by WGBH with all of that station's expertise and the musical riches of Boston. Nor to compare the algebra series with the first-rate geography series produced, to supplement classroom teaching, by Denver's KRMA with an array of outside resources and ingenious studio techniques.

The "talking face" has come in for a considerable amount of

blame in the continuing attempts, by insiders and outsiders both, to pinpoint the deficiencies of America's ITV. The attribution is natural, since so much ITV is, in effect, the teacher on camera. The traditional classroom technique has been automatically transferred to the screen—a familiar practice when introducing new techniques. Interestingly enough, some British critics, for all their BBC conditioning, see nothing wrong with the talking face per se; it all depends on what is done with it. And John Schwarzwalder, manager of KTCA-TV, Minneapolis–St. Paul, has extolled "the mobile, intelligent, infinitely flexible human face as the best audio-visual or 'production' device ever invented, or which ever will be invented." Indeed, the whole matter of production values and their correlation to instructional values and effectiveness is one of the unresolved questions of ITV. Schwarzwalder believes that "production, as such, does not increase learning. Indeed, it is doubtful that it has anything much to do with learning." The point is provocative and highly arguable. An answering critic suggested that Schwarzwalder was referring to measurable curricular learning, but not to deeper and less measurable kinds. Overemphasis on production values can lead to mere gimmickry but, on the other hand, sensitive techniques may encourage better classroom use of ITV.

Most of the investigation of television's quality as an instructional medium has been concentrated on measuring objective results. The results are overwhelmingly affirmative: students learn through TV. There has been no comprehensive analysis since the well-known study in 1962 by Wilbur Schramm, director of Stanford's Institute for Communication Research, which the same author's more recent compilations have reaffirmed. At that time Mr. Schramm concluded:

> There can no longer be any doubt that students learn efficiently from instructional television. The fact has been demonstrated now in hundreds of schools, by thousands of students, in every part of the United States and in several other countries. . . . Instructional television is at least as effective as ordinary classroom

instruction, when the results are measured by the usual final examinations or by standardized tests. . . . [And] employing the usual tests that schools use to measure the progress of their students, we can say with considerable confidence that in 65 per cent of a very large number of comparisons between televised and classroom teaching, there is no significant difference. In 21 per cent, students learned significantly *more*, in 14 per cent, they learned significantly *less*, from television.[3]

Besides this over-all conclusion, which has been cited again and again by TV's proponents in education, Schramm reported certain other positive findings, as well as some that tended to cancel each other out or at best left particular areas of inquiry in doubt. The studies showed important correlations between subject matter and grade level (for instance, televised instruction in mathematics is more effective in the elementary grades than in high school); they indicated that class size appeared to make little difference in learning via instructional television; and they revealed that students and teachers were most favorably disposed toward television in the lowest grades, becoming less well disposed in high school and college.

Since Mr. Schramm's survey many researchers have produced many papers and monographs on TV in education. A recent listing of doctoral dissertations on television and radio includes more than 200 entries for educational broadcasting, most of them written in the past decade and a half. In 1964 Wilbur Schramm's Institute for Communication Research, under a U.S. Office of Education contract, compiled some 350 abstracts of research on instructional television and film, representing a substantial sampling of the work done between 1950 and 1964.

The largest category by far in all these studies deals with comparisons between the effectiveness of televised instruction and that of face-to-face, or conventional, classroom instruction. These

[3] Wilbur Schramm, "What We Know About Learning from Instructional Television," *Educational Television: The Next Ten Years* (Stanford: Institute for Communication Research, 1962).

studies preponderantly document "no significant differences" in the measured results of the two modes of instruction.

While careful and imaginative studies have made substantial contributions to the understanding of the uses of TV in education, recent research in ITV does not add much to earlier findings. Nor does it provide the specific information needed to answer such important questions as those listed in 1962 by Mr. Schramm: How can television be best used, and for what? How can televised instruction deal with different levels of ability? How can television be best combined with other experiences to enhance a child's learning of a given subject or idea?

The following case histories of two famous ITV projects suggest how such questions can be answered in practice. One is set in the grade schools and operates by closed circuit, the other makes use of broadcast television for higher education.

The closed-circuit system centered in Hagerstown in Washington County, Maryland, has produced positive evidence of television's value to the learning of students at all grade levels of the public schools. The experiment began in 1956, subsidized by the Electronics Industries Association and the Fund for the Advancement of Education. The project as such ended in 1961, but television had proved itself so valuable that the county continued and even expanded its use as an integral part of the instructional program. Today the completed system links forty-five schools to the Hagerstown studios, which can send out six lessons simultaneously by cable to more than 800 TV sets throughout the county. Fifty-six courses are now televised. The county's final report on the project noted: "Television has been accepted as an important educational resource. . . . School staffs feel that instruction has been strengthened, pupil educational opportunity broadened, and achievement improved. All this has been accomplished by regular school personnel with a minimum of outside technical assistance."

Superintendent William Brish and his staff attribute other gains to television: "The use of instructional television has stimulated teachers, supervisors, and administrators to examine more closely the teaching-learning process and to pursue curriculum development with a new interest." For instance, televised courses have been highly effective in training or retraining teachers on the job, and they have encouraged "a new approach to teaching—by teams."

TV has changed and upgraded the county's curriculum patterns. A notable example is science. Before TV there was only a small amount of science instruction in Washington County's elementary schools, and the high schools taught the standard one-year courses in physics, biology, and chemistry. Now television has made possible a science program extending from first grade through high school. Substantial science instruction in the lower grades has laid the groundwork for two-year sequences in the high schools.

Other curriculum improvements spurred by the use of television make it possible for elementary school pupils to receive instruction in the specialized fields of art, music, and French, and for secondary school students to continue the study of a foreign language started in elementary school and to study advanced mathematics. The county's experience shows that television is helpful in relieving teacher and classroom shortages, but more than that it has provided instruction in special areas, such as music and art, for which it would have been impossible to find qualified teachers to cover all the schools. Without TV, according to Assistant Superintendent T. Wilson Cahall, the county would have needed thirty-four music teachers. And the county has found that the use of television, at the same time it was improving the educational program, was producing savings that cover TV's annual operating costs. The Washington County report had this to say about the savings:

> In terms of duplicating in conventional classrooms what is now offered on television, the county's savings are substantial. Without television, the county would require more than one hundred additional teachers and a budget increase of almost $1,000,000 to duplicate the courses that have been added to the instructional program. This is more than three times the annual operating cost

of the television network. For example, without television, it would cost more than $250,000 annually to provide art and music specialists for the elementary schools.

The Washington County project has proved itself in ways that the school people value more highly than an expanded curriculum or reduced costs. The county's careful evaluation of television's effects on learning indicate that, unlike most of the studies showing that pupils learn as well with television as without it, Washington County's pupils "often achieve better—sometimes much better—in television classes than in conventional classrooms." Outstanding results emerged, for instance, in arithmetic instruction and in music and art. In arithmetic the county had long wanted to do something to improve student achievement, which was generally low by national norms. Television proved to be the answer. Beginning in 1956 with intensive experiments in the fifth grade, the county school system found remarkable improvement in nine months: fifth graders had made almost two years' progress in arithmetic, from five months below grade level to four months above it. By the spring of 1961, 42 percent of the county's sixth graders tested two years above grade level. The success of this pilot experiment prompted the introduction of televised arithmetic lessons in Grades 1 through 8, with comparably substantial gains.

Progress in music and art is, of course, harder to measure. But, in general, tests showed that television pupils in the elementary schools performed more successfully than their counterparts in conventional classrooms. And teachers agreed that, in both subjects, pupils receiving the televised lessons improved in both performance and appreciation.

Another highly successful experiment is Chicago's TV College. Like the Washington County project, it began with a Ford Foundation subsidy and has continued on its own since the end of the original grant. It is now in its twelfth year.

Unlike Hagerstown, Chicago's program utilizes broadcast television, renting space and facilities from the community ETV station, WTTW Channel 11.

TV College, a part of Chicago's free junior college system, was initiated to bring credit courses leading to a degree to at-home viewers, which is still its primary concern. But the college has expanded into many new areas: teacher training, in cooperation with local teachers colleges; direct instruction on campus; teaching gifted high school students.

It has modified and improved its television procedures in a number of ways, notably in response to the demonstrated need to augment TV lessons with direct student-teacher exchange via scheduled telephone conferences, open meetings, and the use of self-scoring programed materials for reinforcement of learning. College authorities discovered fairly early that the performance of teen-age students taking TV courses on campus fell consistently below that of more mature students taking courses at home. Campus viewers also lost interest rapidly and withdrew in sizable numbers from the TV classes. Experimenting with various means to overcome this disparity, TV College settled on the successful device of giving campus students of college age and average ability at least one hour's extra instruction a week to supplement the twice-a-week telecasts, in a class conducted by an experienced teacher who integrated his instruction with the televised lessons and related materials. The results were excellent: in a year or two campus TV students matched the at-home viewers and soon outdistanced the achievement of students taking only conventional classroom work.

The importance of augmenting straight TV instruction with personal interaction and follow-up can be illustrated with the course in mathematics given by Jerome Sachs, president of Northeastern Illinois State College (formerly Chicago Teachers College North) and a top-notch teacher. The first time Sachs' course was televised, only about a quarter of the viewing students persisted to the end of the semester. Then the college ran the course again, augmented by regularly scheduled student conferences with President Sachs over two-way telephone and by more interim tests. This time the course retained close to 60 percent of its original enrollment.

TV College has always enrolled thousands of noncredit students—in the early years two or three times as many as students enrolled for credit. Noncredit enrollment fluctuates according to the kinds of courses televised in a school year, rising when vocational or cultural subjects of wide appeal are offered. Credit enrollment, which averaged around 5,000 a year during TV College's first four years, jumped to over 10,000 in 1964–65, mainly because of the increased emphasis on teacher training, services for handicapped students, and advanced-placement courses for high school students. In 1966–67 Chicago had about 150 students working for the associate in arts degree via television alone and close to 1,000 working toward the degree by combining TV with on-campus courses. A common pattern is for students to take one semester's work via television, then to spend three semesters on campus. There are also many students during any semester who do both—take TV courses at home and regular courses on campus.

TV College in the school year 1966–67 presented nine courses during each semester of the school year, four of them live and five taped reruns from past years. Every lesson was repeated at night, which is when two thirds of the TV students attend "class." Six video-taped courses were presented over the eight-week summer term, but with each lesson played only once. A new wrinkle is to put all programs on audio tape: students who miss both telecasts can listen to the tape at the campus in the Loop.

Dean James Zigerell, like his predecessor Hymen Chausow, currently academic vice-chancellor of the Chicago City College, emphasizes the fact that accrediting agencies, professional associations, colleges, and universities accept credit earned at TV College. He is also an enthusiastic exponent of the economy of ITV as demonstrated by the Chicago experience. By TV College's fifth year the unit cost of TV instruction per student, which at the start had been double the cost of conventional instruction, matched on-campus costs. Since then the unit cost of teaching by television has dropped well below the on-campus cost. A TV enrollment of 650 to 700 full-time equivalent students represents the break-even point, with all costs charged off to the students enrolled for credit. The present enrollment more than covers all basic costs, with noncredit students getting a free ride. TV College can now handle additional students with minor additional costs, making possible further service to gifted high school students, the handicapped, and various other special groups.

Dean Zigerell is especially proud of TV College's unique ability to bring higher education to students who otherwise might miss it entirely. In its twelve years TV College has awarded approximately 200 associate in arts degrees for work completed *exclusively* via television. Zigerell and Chausow especially emphasize the opportunity TV College brings to housebound housewives, recalling that one of the first graduates was a 34-year-old woman with ten children ("she had three of them while taking her TV courses").

The TV College hopes to strike out into new territory in the future, to include such areas as nursing and other professional education, special classes for the Chicago Police Department, and training programs in data processing and electronics. In 1968 two courses were offered as part of an adult education program—courses that are not part of the college's roster of regular credit courses. In addition, since 1965, colleges outside the Chicago junior college system have leased video-taped courses through the Great Plains Instructional Television Library of Lincoln, Nebraska, the organization with which TV College listed thirty-one recorded tele-courses after securing the permission of teachers involved.

TV College also plans to focus more, in the words of its 1964 report, "On television as a catalyst for instructional and curricular development," especially in conjunction with programed learning. The college is seeking to recruit and train college teachers and production people with fresh new ideas. Most of TV College's production to date has followed the familiar pattern of merely projecting the lecturing professor on the television screen. It is encouraging, therefore, that the 1964 report concludes by stressing the need to explore "the teaching force of the visual and non-verbal dimensions, as opposed to the almost exclusively verbal emphases of conventional instruction."

In a 1967 article Dean Zigerell summed up TV College's hopes for the future as follows: "Waiting to be drawn upon are the skills of liberally educated production personnel and the special know-how of learning psychologists willing to experiment with television as a learning tool in itself, rather than as a distribution system."[4]

In summary, the schools of Washington County, Maryland, and the Chicago City College both have proved to their own satisfaction and to the extent permitted by available measures that television has regularly matched and often surpassed the effectiveness of conventional classroom teaching.

Harold Wigren, who is associate director of the Division of Educational Technology of the National Education Association, probably sees more classroom television than anyone else in the country. Combining an audio-visual background with an undaunted belief in televised instruction, he finds encouraging signs in Boston, Seattle, Los Angeles, Washington, D.C., Pittsburgh, Houston, and Miami, where devoted and perceptive practitioners are trying to harness the medium's highest potential to the revolutionary ideas now current in American education.

Wigren sees a real revolution taking place in school curriculum and methods. "The emphasis on the structure of history and mathematics and physics, the use of methods of inquiry and discovery as against exposition by the teacher, new approaches to fostering creativity and many-sided human talents beyond sheer academic prowess are transforming American classrooms," he pointed out. "ITV needs to exemplify the same creativeness and imagination." He then went on to explain in one interview:

4 "Chicago's TV College," AAUP Bulletin, Spring, 1967, p. 54.

There are many healthy signs that we have at long last turned the corner and are moving into programing which is much more challenging and provocative than was the "talking face." I have been greatly heartened by the programs I have seen in these cities recently. The current efforts in Dade County (Miami) to validate instructional television programing should certainly be encouraged because these represent a step in the right direction. I also feel that Eastern Educational Network is making a valiant effort in the area of humanities to add to the very creative programing they already have under way. I am encouraged, too, by the grass roots character of current ITV programing to supplement regional programing. Any number of cities with 2500 megahertz installations, for example, need to be watched carefully. Among these are Fresno and Pasadena, California, and Rochester, New York. Entirely new concepts in programing are being experimented with in Framingham, Massachusetts, and in Osseo, Minnesota, as well as in Beverly Hills, California.

In other words, I think that instructional television is currently on the move, and I see much more excitement in this field at present than I have seen for quite a long time.

ITV, like any innovation, is only as good as the use to which it is put by the classroom teacher. Lucille Miller, principal of an elementary school in Washington County, Maryland, observed: "The highest quality televised lesson in the world, if misused in the classroom, is worse than nothing." A Boston ITV man believes that scarcely one classroom teacher in a hundred understands television and knows how to use it.

In ITV projects all over the country there is serious concern about how to capture the interest and cooperation of the classroom teacher and her superiors—a key problem in introducing any innovative practice. One Michigan producer reported: "You can transmit ITV to your heart's content all school day long, but if the school principal is indifferent, or the classroom teacher hostile or bored or ignorant of how best to use television, you might just as well address your program—regardless of its merit—to the monitor in your own studio."

Despite the proliferation of teachers' guides, manuals, and workshops, of questionnaires and other feedback devices, it is the consensus of ITV people that not nearly enough has been done to integrate television into the classroom, either into the average teacher's day-to-day program or, in combination with other instructional aids, into the total curriculum and educational purpose of the school or college.

For ITV or any new practice to succeed it must have the allegiance and cooperation not only of classroom teachers and professors but also of superintendents, principals, and department heads. As Lee Franks of the Wisconsin TV project has said: "Your typical classroom teacher cares much more about what her principal says and wants than she cares about what signal she gets from WXXX."

TV's record to date in improving education—like that of many another innovative approach—might have been better if greater attention and resources had gone, first, into programing that incorporated new ideas in curriculum and methods, and then into preparing the ground for actual classroom use. Television's failure on these two counts is related to another basic problem: the critical shortage of manpower to get the job done right. By and large ITV has been in the hands of educators concerned primarily with subject matter and of communication specialists concerned primarily with the production quality of ITV programs. Rare is the practitioner who, by some combination of training or experience or natural talent, really functions as an educational communicator. The supply may increase as time and the colleges nurture more of these specialists.

ITV is now at the crossroads. In recent years it has received sizable assistance from both federal and state governments. Washington began to take up the financial slack about the time that private support was tapering off. The first indication of federal interest in educational television came with the National Defense Education Act of 1958, which provided funds of close to $42 million for research and demonstration projects designed to find effective ways of adapting television and other communication devices to education.

The Educational Television Facilities Act of 1962, an extension of the Communications Act of 1934, authorized matching federal grants to the states, up to a maximum of $1 million, for constructing and improving ETV stations. The act, which authorized a total of $32 million over a five-year period, was extended and liberalized by Congress in 1967: state ceilings were almost doubled, restrictions were removed on the amount of money available for specific types of equipment and educational radio was included and given the same benefits as television.

In general the federal government has shied away from direct support of ETV or ITV *production*. There are various explanations for this reluctance. The parochialism that has hobbled ITV's growth has been noted before; and it was not surprising that Congress reflected the insistence of most schools and colleges on local production for local use. Even more to the point is the American distaste for anything that smacks of centralized control or direction of educational content. Some argue that, in any event, federal assistance to programing might have been premature in the fifties or early sixties, since it has taken about a dozen years to amass the requisite hardware and create a climate favorable to sharing production, regionally or nationally.

The 1967 amendments to the Communications Act were historic for several reasons. In addition to providing for improved facilities, Congress established, amid controversy and opposition, a Corporation for Public Broadcasting specifically authorized to assist "in establishing innovative educational programs." Though the corporation had only seed money as it got organized early in 1968 and still had to face the hurdle of long-term financing, its creation was considered of momentous significance to the future of television. The corporation's first order of business is programs; by providing money for high-quality programing to educational stations and networks and to production groups, it will in effect subsidize a noncommercial TV service to vie with the commercial product.

There are other new sources of federal support for ETV and ITV which have still not been fully spelled out. One is the various antipoverty measures, where television could be a prime vehicle for the war on illiteracy, disease, and the handicaps of slum children. Another new prospect for federal ITV support appeared in the Higher Education Act and the Elementary and Secondary Education Act of 1965. Title III of the latter appropriated $100 million for supplementary educational centers and services, which are designed "to enrich the programs of local elementary and secondary schools and to offer a diverse range of educational experience to children of varying talents and needs." An Office of Education official with many years of service has observed that "no piece of legislation has ever caught the imagination of educators like Title III." With such unprecedented funds available for financing innovation, there is the prospect that public schools will form consortiums to try out all kinds of educational ideas and arrangements never before attempted, including ITV. One section of Title III specifically authorizes funds for "developing, producing, and transmitting radio and television programs for classroom and other educational use." All together it has been estimated that various sections of the act provide up to $400 million for educational television and radio. The Higher Education Act provides less generously for TV, authorizing $2.5 million in 1966 and an annual $10 million in the two succeeding years for the purchase or repair of television equipment.

The states have responded to federal legislation by actions of their own. The majority of them have appointed ETV authorities of one kind or another, in some cases by naming independent new bodies, in others by investing existing bodies, such as the state department of education, with new responsibilities. Most activity at the state level has been directed at television hardware, with emphasis on interconnections. However, Pennsylvania, Massachusetts, and several Southern states have for some time taken an active role in the production of ITV (as in the example noted earlier) and by 1966 other states were beginning to appropriate money to help local school systems with actual production of instructional programs. Texas and California, for example, both passed bills in 1965 to provide matching funds to school districts for the purchase of instructional television services from ETV stations.

By 1968 ETV activities in many states had reached a new high. In some states educational television was still at a rudimentary stage of development, but it was the rare state that had no ITV and no plans for it. An encouraging number had legislation passed or pending to expand ETV and, in many instances, to build statewide networks. Activity continues especially enthusiastic in the South, which had seized on television early as a powerful tool for upgrading the region's low educational standards and reaching its large number of illiterates. Alabama, Georgia, North Carolina, and South Carolina are expanding their already extensive ETV coverage.

The South's most spectacular plans are the ones that Mississippi has in the works. Until very recently ETV was virtually nonexistent in that state, with a plan devised some years ago apparently shelved. Now, as part of an ambitious campaign to boost the state's economy and to bring in industry, Mississippi is creating an elaborate research-and-development complex that includes an ETV center.

The Mississippi Educational TV network is to broadcast its signals in full color. The target date for broadcasting is some time early in 1969. Materials specialists, curriculum experts, and classroom teachers are redesigning courses of study to make them appropriate for broadcasting on TV. The first efforts of the studio will be broadcast over two channels, Channel 29 UHF and Channel 2 VHF. Channel 2 will be in Jackson and Channel 29 will be near State College, Mississippi.

States in other parts of the country also are making significant progress. In Maine a full-scale statewide ETV network went into operation in the fall of 1965, combining a variety of organizational arrangements, with one station owned by a combine of private colleges and three others by the state university. In New York State, under a ten-year development program announced by Governor Rockefeller in 1964, the State University of New York will operate a statewide ETV network (called the New York Network). In its first phase, which began in October of 1967, the network linked by two-way microwave the state's five independent ETV stations and also the libraries of the university's three medical schools. Eventually, a two-way interconnection will make the programing resources of SUNY's four university centers available to the other fifty-odd units of the university as well as to the public at large. Delaware, in September, 1965, inaugurated its closed-circuit network linking all 163 public schools in the state, as well as the University of Delaware and Delaware State College, with a production center in Dover. Other states have extensive plans ready and reasonable expectations of getting the funds needed to put them into effect soon.

Meanwhile the technological apparatus has continued to expand, improve, and become more versatile. The number of ETV stations on the air reached a total of more than 150 early in 1968 and were expected to number at least 200 by 1970. Closed-circuit systems have also increased apace and are expected to double in number by 1970. Among the relevant technical advances are the following: improvement in the UHF (ultrahigh frequency) signal and reception; establishment of the Instructional Television Fixed Service, to utilize channels from 2,500 through 2,690 megahertz for ITV; the great spurt in community antenna television (CATV), which as a by-product extends the coverage of many ETV stations; the availability of increasingly inexpensive video-tape recorders, which can free schools and colleges from the strait jacket of the single-channel broadcast day. Today the old rivalry between broadcast TV and closed circuit has abated; states and institutions are in the process of using the two modes to complement each other. But more important to education than full utilization of television's own capabilities is the use of television with other media in the instructional process itself. A recent study reveals the growing trend toward planning closed-circuit facilities in schools and colleges as part of integrated audio-visual systems, in which television, teaching machines, programed texts, language laboratories, and other tools are combined into single automated teaching systems.

Such systems will be able to command a versatile array of components, among them video discs (television pictures via phonograph records), G.E.'s slow-scan TV, and single-concept films made possible by the inexpensive 8mm cartridge projector. There are already such ingenious variations as Westinghouse's "do-it-yourself" closed-circuit television system designed, at the behest of several Catholic schools, to allow a single teacher unaided to produce a program at will. On the horizon are all manner of new possibilities in what the *New York Times* has called "the relentless march of TV technology." Some with the greatest potential benefits for ETV and ITV are development in the storage and retrieval of television programs. One revolutionary device already perfected and which CBS plans to have on the market by July 1970 is EVR—Electronic Video Recording—the brainchild of Peter Goldmark (who also fathered color TV and the long-playing record). In essence EVR, at very low cost, transfers picture and sound to a tiny cartridge of miniature film which can be replayed at will into a TV set. The special film, very much like any home-movie film in size and appearance, stores an almost unbelievable amount of information: a 7-inch reel holds a half-hour show in color—or all the pages of the Encyclopaedia Britannica. Goldmark calls EVR "a new medium, a new dimension, not just another tool in the audio-visual kit." In his view, which many experts share, EVR can not only free the individual set owner from complete dependence on programer and broadcaster but can immensely advance the use of TV as an individual medium in schools.

The miniaturization exploited by EVR at one end of the spectrum and globe-encircling satellites at the other—these are some of the technological breakthroughs with profound implications for education. Hardheaded educators and communications experts are discussing the prospect of a satellite for educational intercommunication throughout the United States and even satellites shared with other countries for the worldwide exchange of instruction. (Now under public scrutiny are various proposals to provide free satellite interconnection for ETV and ITV, notably that of the Ford Foundation, which in 1966—in McGeorge Bundy's first major announcement as Foundation president—submitted to the FCC a detailed plan for a nationwide system of synchronous satellites to distribute TV programs.) Satellites and lasers in combination open up boundless new possibilities—a laser beam can transmit a thousand different television signals simultaneously.

Another development of incalculable importance for ITV and ETV and other innovations is the entry into education of some of the largest and most imaginative corporations in American industry. Often the prelude is the coordination of a major electronics corporation with a publishing enterprise; for example, Sylvania Electric Products and the Reader's Digest announced, early in 1966, the formation of a joint venture to investigate the potential of electronic systems in education. Previously, RCA had acquired Random House, a New York publishing firm; IBM bought Science Research Associates and signed a licensing agreement with Dun & Bradstreet; Xerox had purchased American Education Publications, Inc., Wesleyan University Press, and Basic Systems, Inc.; and General Electric joined up with Time Inc., to form the General Learning Corporation.

Surveying these developments, Francis Keppel put forward the view, in The Necessary Revolution in American Education,[5] that the new role of private enterprise in educational research, development, and distribution of new materials was "comparable in importance to the expanding role of the federal government in education." Mr. Keppel subsequently resigned as Assistant Secretary

[5] Harper & Row, 1966.

of Health, Education, and Welfare to become board chairman of the General Learning Corporation.

The effect of these enterprises on instructional television is still to be seen. "These firms may get their feet wet by playing around on the fringes of education, for example in enrichment, as many educational broadcasters do, since this is the easiest," commented Lew Rhodes of the NAEB Instructional Television project in an interview.

But there's no reason to expect them to be content with that, when the challenge lies in direct instruction. I think in a few years these firms will be right in the mainstream of education, just as textbook publishers are now. They're efficient, they can use mass-market leverage to fund their research, production, and selling operations, and they can afford to hire the best people without the restrictions which hamstring educational producers.

However, after the initial ballyhoo accompanying the creation of these new organizations, most of them have had to stop at the first plateau while their top management ponders one basic dilemma which faces all who would use tools or systematic procedures in the educational process. This is, do they devote their energies to making more efficient and effective the *process* of education—which is learner oriented; or the *institutions* of education—which are teacher and administrator oriented? As the sociologist Kenneth Clark has stated, do we use these tools merely to "automate dehumanization?"

In simpler terms, do these new companies sell the "answers" to the "questions" that are currently being asked, or to the ones that *should* be asked? In the latter case, it would require them to first devote a portion of their resources to "sell" the new "questions" in order to then have a market for their "answers."

This problem of creating a market for what their companies can best produce, i.e., systematically designed, learner-based materials and environments, is further hampered by the knowledge that, in the commercial world, the company which provides the seed money to break ground with a new idea is frequently the only one to end up not making a profit with it.

As presently conceived, I am sure that television has a minor role to play in the thinking of these companies. What they may fail to realize, however, is that electronic communication is one of the few ways that they have to tie together the disparate elements of educational systems in order to achieve the objectively organized environments that will make systematically produced materials meaningful. This means that they have to see the use of electronic media as more than just singular display devices—as facilitators of cooperation, participation, and new synergistic efforts.

In the past few years there have been other significant nongovernmental developments that betoken growing concern over the future of ETV (and inevitably, though less directly, ITV). One was the formation in mid-1967 of the National Citizens Committee for Public Television, under the chairmanship of Thomas P. F. Hoving, the head of the Metropolitan Museum of Art. The objective of this committee is to stimulate general support for noncommercial TV and its 120 members represent a wide range of U.S. citizens, including writers, actors, scientists, businessmen, educators. The group held its first plenary session early in 1968 and has been a vocal and noteworthy force in the field ever since.

The Hoving committee, the Corporation for Public Broadcasting, and a good deal of the current upsurge of concern with the future of noncommercial television stem both directly and indirectly from the report of the Carnegie Commission on Educational Television. This eagerly awaited report was issued in January, 1967, after more than a year's extensive work by the prestigious commission, which was headed by M.I.T.'s James R. Killian, Jr., and which included James B. Conant, Lee DuBridge of Cal Tech, Edwin Land of the Polaroid Corporation, pianist Rudolf Serkin, and other eminent figures from many fields. The commission's report made an eloquent plea for solid support, financial and otherwise, of public television "which includes all that is of human interest and human importance which is not at the moment appropriate or available for support by advertising, and which is not arranged for formal instruction." Though the commission focused on services to the community in general, the spirit of the report and its recommendations seem bound to influence instruction through the in-school broadcasts of ETV stations. The Carnegie Commission's central recommendation has now been put into effect: the establishment of the Corporation for Public Broadcasting.

These, then, are some of the major developments in the mid-sixties affecting educational television in its broadest definition. As for ITV specifically, there is a feeling throughout the country that it is marking time, that the medium is at a critical turning point. In Boston, Hartford Gunn and his staff at WGBH brush aside "21 Inch Classroom's" enviable reputation as perhaps the nation's outstanding series of instructional programs. "Far too much ITV transmits no more than a fuzzy image of a teacher teaching in a traditional way, using the traditional and impoverished resources of the classroom," Gunn stated. "There is too little experimentation, and no rewards for it either. School people who try to use their imagination and bring the world into the classroom by TV have no way of tapping the resources they need. And the educational broadcasters don't know who these innovating people are."

In San Francisco, R. Lawrence Smith of KQED observed that ITV now confronts a fateful temptation: "It has managed to achieve a certain acceptance in the schools, and I don't doubt it could continue to maunder along at its present level indefinitely, grinding out routine stuff that the schools will keep on using, not realizing how very routine it is." He has no use for such complacency. "Unless there is a marked improvement very soon in the quality of televised instruction, I think we'd all better get out of the business and abdicate to the film people, who do a much better job."

James Loper, vice-president and general manager of Los Angeles' new KCET, and a representative of the new breed of trained educational communicators, stated: "The average KCET school program costs $1,000—peanuts! To get real quality, we should double or triple that amount—that is, if we really want to experiment with the process of teaching and try out new formulas. It's about time we got beyond televised instruction that makes 'no significant difference.' Precisely what we need are programs that *will* make a significant difference."

Ralph Steele of the Oregon State System of Higher Education, who as director of the Joint Council on Educational Television played a leading role in launching ETV in the early fifties, also warned of complacency. In a June, 1965, address to an NDEA institute on educational media he said:

> It is possible—I think it is probable—that the newer and initially unconventional methods of instruction have begun an untimely slip into routinely accepted patterns of conventional use.
>
> In the early days of educational television, for example, the research studies compared results of teaching by television with conventional teaching. I wonder today if there has not grown up a body of information about the uses of television too quickly solidified by dependence on limited practice and tending to hold innovation to the levels of the recent past.

However, major developments have encouraged Frederick Breitenfeld, Jr., executive director of the Maryland Center for Public Broadcasting, to comment: "The focus seems to be shifting from television to *education*. . . . As the novelty of television wears off in our daily lives, educational television becomes, as it should, a part of education, and not simply a form of television."

A picture of education in the year 2065 was painted not long ago by an educator skeptical of ITV, William Cartwright, head of the Department of Education at Duke University:

> For a generation after 1950, school systems—even entire states and regions—tried to teach whole courses by television. Ultimately this costly experiment failed. It seemed promising for some time, and temporarily it improved instruction in many places, even though it damaged it in others. The improvement came because the television teachers often were better prepared than most classroom teachers and could call on better and more varied services. But as the general level of teaching improved and

the public came to provide the facilities needed for good teaching, the disadvantages of the system led to its downfall. The major factor involved was that it proved impossible to apply what the educational scientists learned about the values of individualized instruction in a class in which all of the members were forced by a television set to move at the same pace. Another factor was the near revolt on the part of competent teachers and prospective teachers who said that there was no purpose in spending time, energy and money in preparation for teaching if they were not to be allowed to teach. In the fields involving controversy, the social studies and humanities, society came to realize the great danger inherent in a situation where any agency, public or private, can decide what should be taught to all persons.

Nevertheless, we have profited much from the great TV experiment. Almost all classrooms are equipped with television apparatus, even though it seldom carries live programs. As a result of the spectacular developments in technology, teachers can readily select, from vast repositories of films and tapes, programs or parts of programs that fit in with their own plans and use them when they are appropriate.[6]

And Mr. Smith of KQED, who unlike Mr. Cartwright is one of ITV's most outspoken champions, sees the quite imminent future this way:

A silently flashing board . . . your number comes up . . . you pick up your videotape from the library cart, step over to one of the soundproof cubicles in your classroom, deftly thread the tape onto the playback spool, push the "start" button . . . and there's your lesson on sea anemones on the TV monitor. Just routine. Nothing to it. Everybody does it. With the help of the teacher, Mrs. Thompson.

She knows all about you—your strengths and weaknesses in each subject—and somehow always seems to have the right tape for you just when you're ready for it. Same for everybody. In all subjects. Oh, you don't spend all day watching tapes; there's lots of regular class discussion time; muscle tune-up activities, too.

Time goes fast. You're interested. . . .

Remember 1965 when you could hardly find an ITV program

[6] William H. Cartwright, "The Teacher in 2065," *Teachers College Record*, Vol. 66, No. 4 (January, 1965).

worth *local* acclaim—not to mention regional or national? Remember the apathy of the teaching profession—especially school administrators and principals—when ITV was mentioned? Remember the stumbling of the teachers trying to invade the field of the professional broadcaster? Didn't they often look inept in the cold light of the classroom receivers? . . .

As the vision for television emerged from the fogs of early pioneering, it became clear that only by organizing for production and distribution on regional and national levels could ITV be expected to reach its potential. . . .

And what marvels these [production] centers have wrought! Compact, transistorized electronic units for production, combined with the computer technology for measurement and research have spawned a vigorous new species of videotapes, kinescopes (both 16mm. and 8mm. sound), LP recordings, audiotapes, filmstrips, photographs, attractively printed teacher's manuals, and a host of other related instruction materials.[7]

More and more it appears that if television is to fulfill its potential for enhancing the educational process it will have to be used flexibly and imaginatively to encourage individual learning and it will have to take its place in an instructional system where the classroom teacher plays a new and critically important role as the director of learning. Tom Clemens of the U.S. Office of Education pointed this out in his comment that the kind of television that is needed will "enhance children's learning and their understanding of the world and themselves, contributing its own special attributes to the processes of education. American education has to reorient itself to focus on *learning*, on what's actually happening to this kid or that kid. To do so, we'll have to stop using teachers like self-propelled tape recorders dishing out information, and we'll have to stop using instructional television as though it were radio—only you can see the announcer."

Such reorientation in the role of ITV means a shift in the emphasis on TV as an instrument of mass instruction. It is that, of course, and can, like film, bring into the classroom the widest

7 "TV as a Private Tutor: A Look Ahead to 1975," *National Association of Educational Broadcasters Journal*, September–October, 1965.

possible view of reality. A documentary on civil rights, the international programs beamed from Telstar, Robert Frost reading his own poems, the unforgettable scenes of President Kennedy's funeral or Pope Paul VI's visit to the United States, the debate on Vietnam—it doesn't matter whether a student views these by himself or with five or six of his fellows or in a group of 100 or 500. But with instructional programs pinpointed in purpose, and with TV integrated into the classroom and made flexible, ITV could be used for individual as well as mass instruction, and for highly focused purposes in between.

Subsidies from various sources have helped to launch ITV and to make it a recognized instructional tool. Further support is now needed from government, business, and foundations to help ITV to move more rapidly into the mainstream of education.

Most ITV observers agree that the only way to overcome limitations of time, talent, and money and still achieve first-class production of instructional programs is by pooling resources. Many believe that the solution lies in regional centers serving several or even many states. Only a broadly based operation, they feel, can marshal enough money and talent to produce really superior programs.

The following is a listing, selected from informed opinion in the field, of promising educational developments in television that need financial support:

IMPROVEMENT OF EDUCATION IN THE PUBLIC SCHOOLS THROUGH CO-OPERATIVE PRODUCTION OF SUPERIOR TELEVISED INSTRUCTION: A broadly based ITV production center, or centers, could be established beginning perhaps with one state and then expanding across state lines to perform regional services. The pilot project could build on the production facilities of one ETV station—Boston's WGBH, for instance, or Pittsburgh's WQED, or San Francisco's KQED—whose staff has had considerable experience in producing good in-school programs. The center could produce taped TV programs, classroom guides, and integrated instructional materials and might be tied in with the supplementary centers and services provided for in the 1965 federal school legislation. The pivotal part of the project would be to establish solid school support for the center and to integrate the TV lessons and related materials into the curriculums. The center could exploit the opportunity to experiment with television and other media; it could be, in effect, a laboratory for ideas, unhampered by the practical obstacles that keep the average ITV enterprise from attempting the new and untried.

IMPROVEMENT OF THE TRAINING OF TEACHERS: A pilot project, related to the project suggested above, could be initiated to tie a joint school and university teacher-training program into the work of the production center. A trainee's clinical experience then would include a period of internship at the center as well as a teaching internship in the cooperating school system. The university could also work out, in conjunction with the production center, summer training and retraining programs for teachers in various fields, including the best use of the new media.

HELPING TO MEET THE EXPLODING DEMAND FOR POST–HIGH SCHOOL EDUCATION FOR STUDENTS WHO ARE NOT GOING TO ATTEND A FOUR-YEAR COLLEGE: A cooperative venture could be set up to exploit the experience (and perhaps the product) of the Chicago TV College. It could include crash courses to upgrade high school teachers and industrial experts to provide the faculty for the two-year institutions.

RAISING THE QUALITY OF COLLEGE AND UNIVERSITY INSTRUCTION DURING THIS PERIOD OF EXPLODING ENROLLMENTS AND SCARCITY OF FULLY QUALIFIED FACULTY: College courses of high quality could be developed like those produced for "Continental Classroom" through intensive collaboration with college teachers in each subject and workshops to ensure the best possible use of the televised lessons on the campus.

A variety of single lectures could be produced and taped by eminent and gifted scholars, which could serve, as in the English universities, to stimulate independent study. By dividing the costs among several universities it should be possible to draw on the greatest names in the scholarly world: the Toynbees and the Bronowskis, for example.

Through cooperative arrangements among colleges and universities, instructional units—single programs rather than entire courses—could be produced. One major obstacle to the interchange of entire courses has been the classic reluctance of the scholars of one university to accept *in toto* the work done by scholars in other institutions. One solution might lie in the suggestion of Dean Jackson W. Riddle of the Ohio State University "to produce and deposit in videotape libraries units of instruction of varying degrees of complexity. . . . For example, if Professor X at University A, who is a renowned scholar in the area of photosynthesis, would develop instructional materials on this topic and if Professor Y at University B would develop similar materials on the DNA molecule (and so on), each of these individual units could be made available on loan for the construction of a course or courses, as desired."

Complete courses or single lectures could be produced, specifically designed to upgrade instruction in the smaller colleges that are at the greatest disadvantage in recruiting faculty, in particular the predominantly Negro institutions. A model for this kind of enterprise might be the previously mentioned Moses Hadas lectures of 1963, supported by a grant from the Fund for the Advancement of Education, which brought superior instruction in the classics to four of these institutions via a two-way telephone communication system. A pilot project could utilize one-way video, two-way audio connections.

HELPING TO KEEP PROFESSIONAL PEOPLE ABREAST OF KNOWLEDGE IN THEIR FIELD: A collaborative project to produce and disseminate top-flight programs in the various professional fields could be initiated. This project might start with medicine, proceed to law, engineering, etc. Each project could begin by reviewing and then airing widely the best tapes available, to take advantage nationally of the excellent television courses produced thus far.

TRAINING IMAGINATIVE LEADERS FOR THE ITV FIELD: A new breed of educational leader must be trained to unite the science of communication with educational insight. A model program at a major university, in cooperation with a strong ITV production center, could serve as a prototype for adaptation throughout the country. The program could include internships at the production center.

UPGRADING ESTABLISHED ITV LEADERS: A modest program of grants to ITV leaders, or to the ETV stations or school systems they work for, could be set up to supply adequate manpower to these chronically understaffed operations; to relieve talented and experienced practitioners from the grinding day-to-day pressures of producing programs, raising funds, and endless other duties; and to give these veterans time to think.

ENCOURAGING PROFESSIONAL INTEREST AND ACTIVITY IN SIGNIFICANT RESEARCH: Grants could be made to selected professional groups concerned with television and other instructional media, for the purpose of supporting promising research, experiment, and evaluation in areas directly related to the improvement of instruction.

INCREASING THE UNDERSTANDING OF TELEVISION TECHNOLOGY AS IT CAN BE APPLIED TO IMPROVE EDUCATION: A nonprofit agency (somewhat along the lines of the Ford Foundation–supported Educational Facilities Laboratories) could be organized to explore and publicize the best in instructional hardware, including TV equipment. One pilot project might work out ways to encourage the mass production of small, cheap TV receivers: A manufacturer for instance, could be assured of a huge market for sets in some developing country where the government was sponsoring a project to use television for education.

PROVIDING ADMINISTRATORS WITH A PRACTICAL WAY TO GAUGE ITV COSTS: A study could be made to relate the costs of televised instruction to specific educational objectives, such as frequency and number of lessons, relation of televised courses to other media and to curriculum as a whole, etc., and to compare the costs of various media.

At this writing the national Commission on Instructional Technology, authorized under the Corporation for Public Television legislation, has been appointed by the U.S. Commissioner of Education. It is conducting a comprehensive study of the use of new media in American education. The members of the commission are:

Dr. Sterling McMurrin (chairman), Dean of the Graduate School, University of Utah

Dr. David Bell, Vice President, International Division, The Ford Foundation

Dr. Roald Campbell, Dean of the Graduate School of Education, University of Chicago

Dr. C. Ray Carpenter, Professor of Psychology, The Pennsylvania State University

Dr. Nell Eurich, Dean of the Faculty, Vassar College

Dr. Harold B. Gores, President, Educational Facilities Laboratories, Inc.

Honorable A. Leon Higginbotham, Jr., Judge, Eastern District of Pennsylvania

Mr. Kermit Morrissey, President, Community College of Allegheny County

Dr. Kenneth Oberholtzer, former Superintendent of Schools, Denver, Colorado

The primary goal of ITV in the future must be to raise quality and improve classroom utilization. Here, as elsewhere in education today, mere expansion of present practices is not enough. The way forward is necessarily a new way—the innovative way. To create the new some of the old must be constructively destroyed.

Instructional television now stands at the most significant crossroads in its history. Recent developments—governmental, technological, educational—have set the stage for advance to a new level of usefulness and excellence. Opportunities have opened to apply television to new educational challenges, to intertwine television fruitfully with other new media, and to undertake new experiments with augmented research funds.

Indeed, there is evidence that undue concentration on the medium as such has limited television's usefulness. Television has usually been introduced into schools and classes without changing anything else, just as movies were used in the assembly programs of an earlier day. Few educators have used the new technology to help bring about a basic change in instruction and there has been little relating of television to other new media and technologies.

As applied to education thus far, television has largely put current modes of teaching on the screen. The result has been widespread disenchantment as the mediocre level of much instruction has been exposed to professional and public scrutiny for the first time. The need for imagination, ingenuity, and the innovative approach in the whole process of education has been forcefully demonstrated.

As one who has been deeply involved with much of the experimentation from the early 1950's to the present time, I am concerned about the future of American education and the possibilities of applying what we have learned in the struggle to give ITV a fair trial. We are now ready for the next stage, which calls for a thorough, dynamic effort to improve the quality of instruction, not just over television but throughout our entire educational system, with television as one of the many instruments that can be used to give each child, wherever he may live, the opportunity to become all he is capable of being.

Selective Bibliography: An Educational Innovator's Basic Bookshelf

The Process of Reform

CONANT, JAMES B. *Shaping Educational Policy*. New York: McGraw-Hill Book Co., 1964.

GARDNER, JOHN W. *Self-Renewal: The Individual and the Innovative Society*. New York: Harper & Row, 1964.

GROSS, RONALD, and MURPHY, JUDITH (eds.). *The Revolution in the Schools*. New York: Harcourt, Brace & World, 1964.

HOWE, HAROLD II. *Education . . . Everybody's Business: Remarks on Four Aspects of the Contemporary Educational Scene*. Washington, D.C.: U.S. Government Printing Office, 1967.

KEPPEL, FRANCIS. *The Necessary Revolution in American Education*. New York: Harper & Row, 1966.

MORPHET, EDGAR L., and RYAN, CHARLES O. (eds.). *Planning and Effecting Needed Changes in Education*. Denver, Colo.: Designing Education for the Future, June, 1967.

National Education Association Project on the Instructional Program of the Public Schools, *Schools for the Sixties*. New York: McGraw-Hill Book Co., 1963.

The Dynamics of Change in Individuals and Educational Systems

BLOOM, BENJAMIN S. *Stability and Change in Human Characteristics*. New York: John Wiley & Sons, 1964.

BRICKELL, HENRY M. *Organizing New York State for Educational Change*. Albany, N.Y.: State Education Department, 1961.

CARLSON, RICHARD O. *Adoption of Education Innovations.* Eugene: The Center for the Advanced Study of Educational Administration, University of Oregon, 1965.

LEWIN, KURT. *Dynamic Theory of Personality.* New York: McGraw-Hill Book Co., 1935.

LIPPITT, RONALD, WATSON, JEANNE, and WESTLEY, BRUCE. *The Dynamics of Planned Change.* New York: Harcourt, Brace & World, 1958.

MILES, MATTHEW B. (ed.). *Innovation in Education.* New York: Bureau of Publications, Teachers College, Columbia University, 1964.

WILLIAMS, ROGER J. *You Are Extraordinary.* New York: Random House, 1967.

Curriculum: Innovations in What and How to Teach

BRUNER, JEROME S. *The Process of Education.* Cambridge, Mass.: Harvard University Press, 1960.

GOODLAD, JOHN I. *The Changing School Curriculum.* New York: Fund for the Advancement of Education (Ford Foundation), 1966.

HEATH, ROBERT W. (ed.). *New Curricula.* New York: Harper & Row, 1964.

Education's Technological Revolution

BUSHNELL, D., and ALLEN, D. W. *The Computer in American Education.* New York: John Wiley & Sons, 1967.

FULLER, R. BUCKMINSTER. *Education Automation.* Carbondale, Ill.: Southern Illinois University Press, 1962.

Fund for the Advancement of Education. *Four Case Studies of Programed Instruction.* New York: Fund for the Advancement of Education (Ford Foundation), 1964.

GOODLAD, JOHN I., O'TOOLE, JOHN F. JR., and TYLER, LOUISE L. *Computers and Information Services in Education.* New York: Harcourt, Brace & World, 1966.

HOCKING, ELTON. *Language Laboratory and Language Learning.* Washington, D.C.: Department of Audio-visual Instruction, National Education Association (no date).

MURPHY, JUDITH, and GROSS, RONALD. *Learning by Television.* New York: Fund for the Advancement of Education (Ford Foundation), 1966.

Trow, William Clark. *Teacher and Technology: New Designs for Learning.* New York: Appleton-Century-Crofts, Inc., 1963.

The Reorganization of Teaching in the Schools

Brown, B. Frank. *The Nongraded High School.* Englewood Cliffs, N.J.: Prentice-Hall, 1965.

Goodlad, John I., and Anderson, Robert. *The Nongraded Elementary School.* New York: Harcourt, Brace & World, 1963.

Morse, Arthur D. *Schools of Tomorrow, Today.* New York: Doubleday & Co., 1960.

Shaplin, Judson T., and Olds, Henry F. Jr. (eds.). *Team Teaching.* New York: Harper & Row, 1964.

Trump, J. Lloyd, and Baynham, Dorsey. *Focus on Change: Guide to Better Schools.* Chicago: Rand McNally and Co., 1961.

Innovations in Higher Education

Barzun, Jacques. *The American University.* New York: Harper & Row, 1968.

Baskin, Samuel (ed.). *Higher Education: Some Newer Developments.* New York: McGraw-Hill Book Co., 1965.

Brown, James W., and Thornton, James W. Jr. (eds.). *New Media in Higher Education.* Washington, D.C.: National Education Association, 1963.

Eurich, Alvin C. (ed.). *Campus 1980: The Shape of the Future in American Higher Education.* New York: Delacorte Press, 1968.

Goodman, Paul. *The Community of Scholars.* New York: Random House, 1962.

Hatch, Winslow R. (ed.). *New Dimensions in Higher Education* (series of pamphlets). Washington, D.C.: U.S. Office of Education, Government Printing Office, 1960—

Sanford, Nevitt (ed.). *The American College.* New York: John Wiley & Sons, 1962.